Key issues for primary schools

D0549750

What are the main issues currently facing those involved in primary education?

How can you keep up with the changes affecting primary schools?

'A succinct, up-to-date summary of the main official requirements.'
Professor Colin Richards, former HMI for Primary Education

This book gives a series of briefings on the main issues in primary education and the implications for schools and is presented in a convenient A–Z format.
   The essential information provided includes coverage of:

- special educational needs
- attendance, truancy and exclusion
- bullying and behavioural problems
- management and administration
- safety and security

There is also a review of up-to-date DfEE requirements and suggestions for further action and further reading. The addresses of useful contacts help to make it a reference book no primary school should be without.

Michael Farrell is an education inspector for the London Borough of Hillingdon. He trained as a teacher and psychologist and has been a head teacher and a lecturer at the Institute of Education.

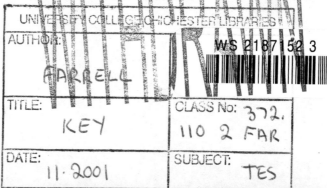

Key issues for primary schools

Michael Farrell

London and New York

This book is dedicated to my dear daughter Sarah, aged 9, my primary school consultant.

First published 1999
by Routledge
11 New Fetter Lane, London EC4P 4EE

Simultaneously published in the USA and Canada
by Routledge
29 West 35th Street, New York, NY 10001

Typeset in Times by Routledge
Printed and bound in Great Britain by Clays Ltd, St Ives PLC

British Library Cataloguing in Publication Data
A catalogue record for this book is available from the British
Library

Library of Congress Cataloging in Publication Data
A catalogue record for this book has been requested

ISBN 0–415–18262–X

Contents

Foreword

Key Issues for Primary Schools provides a series of briefings on a range of contemporary topics facing those professionally involved in primary education. It ranges widely and eclectically – in alphabetical terms from 'admissions' to 'very able pupils', in management terms from 'appraisal' to 'value-added measures', in pastoral terms from 'attendance' to 'support for children' and in assessment terms from 'baseline assessment' to 'target setting'. Readers are given a succinct, up to date summary of the main official requirements, a review of relevant professional issues and a series of suggestions for action for each of the forty-nine topics considered. Each too has its own memorable quotation or anecdote to attract the reader's interest and promote thought. Some have addresses, fax or e-mail numbers for further information and useful contacts.

The book lists its entries alphabetically and thus its contents page forms an index. Comparing this with the index in the Plowden Report of 1967 is salutary. Very many of the issues listed and analysed here simply were not identified as issues thirty years ago: appraisal, benchmarking, efficiency, inspection, marketing, media management, project management, school security – the list is extensive. Very many reflect a degree of control, regulation, and compliance to the demands of central agencies far removed, rightly or wrongly, from the *laissez-faire* approaches of the past. Very many demand knowledge and understanding removed (some would say 'far' removed!) from the primary classroom.

Yet all are part of the *extended*, though paradoxically constrained, *professionalism* now demanded of those who work in the interests of primary school children. All are important and all demand a reflective professional response. This book makes a valuable contribution to analysing, clarifying, coding and assisting that redefined primary professionalism. It is interesting but impossible to speculate how its index of key issues will differ from that of a parallel book (if such a medium still exists) thirty years on!

Colin Richards
Professor, University College of St Martin and
former H.M. Staff Inspector for Primary Education

Acknowledgements

I am most grateful to the following people who read sections of the book and made many helpful suggestions.

Head teachers and teachers

Mrs Pat Lock, head teacher, Christ Church Church of England Infants' School, New Malden, Surrey; Mr Ian Baker, head teacher, Long Buckby Junior School, Long Buckby; Mr Philip Hawkins, Head teacher, Clipston Endowed Primary School, Leicestershire; Mrs Christine Linnitt, Head teacher, Crick Primary School, Crick; Mr Steven Lord, Head teacher, East Haddon Church of England Primary School, East Haddon; Mr Jon Parsons, Head teacher, Great Creaton Primary School, Creaton; Mr Tony Henretty, Head teacher, Guilsborough Church of England Primary School, Guilsborough; Mrs Lois Johnson, Head teacher, Long Buckby Infant School, Long Buckby; Mrs Beverley Gascoin, Head teacher, Spratton Church of England Primary School, Spratton; Mrs Sandra Hoskins, Head teacher, Welford Sibbertoft and Sulby Endowed School, Welford; Mrs Diane Roberts, Head teacher, West Haddon Endowed Primary School, West Haddon; Mr David Boucher, Head teacher, Yelvertoft Primary School, Yelvertoft; Ms Wendy Harknett, Miss Helen Williams, Early Years Co-ordinator and Mrs Val Newman, Special Educational Needs Co-ordinator St Helen's Primary School, Huntingdon; Mr David Narracott, teacher, Kingswood House Preparatory School, Epsom.

From the Department for Education and Employment

Ms Debra Gilder, Head of Under Fives Policy Development Team, Under Fives Division; Mr Giles Hedley, Teachers Appraisal and Training Team; Ms Alison Jeffrey, Standards and Effectiveness Unit; Mr Darryl Lester, Standards and Effectiveness Unit; Ms Barbara Miller, Discipline and Attendance Division; Ms Beverley Samuel, School Government Team; Ms

Dawn Taylor, Team Leader, School Security and Behaviour Support Team; Mr Ian Thompson, School Attendance Team; Ms Sarah Wainer, Admissions Team; Mr Peter Wilkinson, Class Sizes Team.

From the Qualifications and Curriculum Authority

Ms Alix Beleschenko, Principal Manager (Primary Curriculum); Mr Andy Cleasby, Subject Officer for the Under Fives; Mr Tim Coulson, Principal Manager, School Improvement and Support; Mr David Hawker, Head of Curriculum and Assessment; Mr Peter Jackson, Principal Officer, School Improvement.

From other organisations

Dr Eric Blaire, Education Inspector, London Borough of Hillingdon; Ms Cath Bracher-Giles, Bully Advisor, Kidscape; Ms Sue Crieghton, National Society for the Prevention of Cruelty to Children; Ms Eileen Devonshire, Assistant Chief Executive, British Educational Suppliers Association; Dr Felicity Fletcher-Campbell, National Foundation for Educational Research; Mr Simon Goodenough, National Governors Council; Mr Malcolm Griffin, on behalf of Merlin Publications; Mr Colin Jarvis, Professional Officer, The National Association for Able Children in Education; Mr Kevin Jeffery, Assistant Director, National Literacy Strategy; Ms Gill Lenderyou, Senior Development Officer, Sex Education Forum; Ms Margaret Lynch, Education Inspector, London Borough of Hillingdon; Ms Anne Madden, Education and Training Department, Equal Opportunities Commission; Mrs Margaret Morrisey OBE, National Confederation of Parent Teacher Associations; Ms Irene Ordidge, The British Educational Communications and Technology Agency; Ms Sue Plant, Chair of the National Standing Committee of Advisors, Inspectors and Consultants of Personal and Social Education; Ms Linda Rhead, Senior Inspector, London Borough of Richmond Upon Thames; Mr Hugh Self, National Association for Language Development in the Curriculum; Ms Anita Straker, Director, National Numeracy Project; Dr Mariane Talbot, Brasenose College, Oxford; Mr Tim Toulmin, Press Complaints Commission; Ms Angela Walsh, Professional Officer, Continuing Professional Development and Research Team, Teacher Training Agency.

The whole text was read by Mr John Dewhurst, Education Inspector (Primary), London Borough of Hillingdon, to whom I am particularly grateful.

I am thankful to all the colleagues who read and commented on earlier drafts of the text. Their assistance does not indicate that the people or organisations endorse or necessarily agree with anything in the text. Nor does the inclusion of an address at the end of a section indicate that members of that organisation agree with or endorse anything in the preceding section. The address is a potential source of further information and does not indicate that any documents listed as references or as further reading can be obtained from the address. Where references are given to a publication which was prepared by an organisation, the name of the organisation as it was at the time of the publication is given. For example, the present Department for Education and Employment has had several previous titles so a publication made when the Department was, say, the Department of Education is cited with that earlier Department name.

The information and views expressed in *Key Issues for Primary Schools* are my personal views and do not represent those of any organisation. Any shortcomings of the book are, of course, entirely my own.

Introduction

Readers of this book

This book is intended for a wide range of people professionally concerned with education: head teachers, teachers, governors, Office for Standards in Education inspectors, local education authority inspectors, advisors, officers and support staff, educationalists in universities and colleges of higher education, students in training doing Bachelor of Education (BEd.) or Post Graduate Certificate in Education (PGCE) courses, teachers on professional development courses (including management courses) and post graduate Master of Education (MEd.) courses, and civil servants involved in education.

The focus is on primary schools in the United Kingdom whether community, foundation, aided or independent schools. The book gives briefings on the main issues in primary education and the implications for schools. 'I want advice to tell me where sharks are in the water' one head teacher graphically stated, and the book gives this guidance in a compact way.

Format of the book

The book comprises entries on key issues presented in alphabetical order. The title of each section has been chosen so that the first word of the title gives a clear indication of the content of the section. Consequently, the alphabetical listing of sections also acts as an index, enabling readers to find quickly topics of immediate or particular interest.

Uses of the book

Key Issue for Primary Schools gives a series of briefings on a wide range of topics. Because the book is aimed at a professional readership it is able to assume a level of knowledge that enables it to cover issues in some depth in a relatively short space. The book sets out to offer practical help while stimulating debate on the issues covered. Many of the entries will inform staff in schools as they prepare and develop policies, guidelines and practice.

Key points in the text are identified by bullet marks and lists. Towards the end of each entry is a list of suggestions about what a school should be doing. A small number of references are given, normally two or three, although occasionally more if the subject demands it. Addresses, telephone numbers, faxes, and e-mails are given as appropriate for further information or for useful contacts.

Written in a clear accessible style and free of jargon the book presents and explores relevant issues and trends. The usefulness to readers has been assured by widely trialling the list of topics and the drafts of the book on potential readers.

Suggestions

I have tried to cover areas in this book that potential readers would find most helpful. I would be pleased to hear from any readers with suggestions for amendments and additions so that future editions will continue to be as informative as possible. Please write to me: Dr Michael Farrell, Education Inspector, London Borough of Hillingdon Education Services, Civic Centre 4E/O7, Uxbridge, Middlesex UB8 1UW.

Admissions

Towards greater transparency and equity

Groucho Marx did not want to join any club which would accept somebody like him as a member. If admission arrangements to clubs can be opaque, those to schools are often not exactly transparent. Where parents can afford it, they may seek admission for their child to an independent school by contacting the school to establish its admission arrangements. Independent schools have, in theory, complete control over admissions but schools tend to be chosen by parents so that the ethos, support and curriculum of the school match the parents' perception of what their child needs. Leaving the issue of preparatory schools aside, the government wants parents to be able to send their children to their preferred school, wherever possible, whether it is a community, voluntary or foundation school (Department for Education and Employment, 1997).

An Audit Commission survey (1996) estimated that one parent in five was unsuccessful in gaining a place for their child in their preferred choice of school. At the same time there were some 800,000 unfilled school places in England. This in part reflects the fact that parents tend to express a preference for their children to attend successful schools and are loath for them to attend unsuccessful ones. Among the information which parents use to assess the suitability of a school is its proximity to home, its standards of achievement and Office for Standards in Education (OFSTED) reports. When a school is under-subscribed, it makes some aspects of school life more difficult. For example, parents may feel that they can take their children on long holidays abroad in term time with impunity despite intimations from the head teacher that they cannot be guaranteed a place at the school after a long absence. Where parents are sure that the school will have spare capacity, such intimations will tend not to worry them. The attendance levels and therefore the standards of achievement are consequently affected, which may lead to lower standards in national tests. This in turn may further deter more conscientious parents, who would be more supportive of the school's attendance policy, from seeking a place there.

At the other end of the scale, where a school is over-subscribed, parents should feel that they are getting a fair opportunity for their child to attend the school of their first choice. Clear criteria for deciding applications help. There should be nothing about the school's application procedure which could give a parent just cause for complaining that some covert selection procedure was taking place.

Church schools have a legitimate reason for interviewing parents to assess their religious commitment. Where interviews take place and a child is not accepted it is particularly important that the procedures are demonstrated to be fair and open, to reassure parents that no judgement is being made about anything other than religious commitment.

The admissions process can create problems unless procedures are clear and widely understood by all participants, including the head teacher and parents.

Parental choice has become interpreted in some quarters as being unrestricted, so it is difficult for some parents to accept that preferring a school does not guarantee the child getting a place in it. There is no requirement for any admission authority to use a waiting list. Where such lists are used, the school's published arrangements should make clear how these children will be ranked.

Where parents express a first and second choice of school they may have the impression that should their first choice be unsuccessful, their second choice of school will be more likely to meet with favour. But where the places in their second choice school have all been filled by children whose parents made the school their first choice there may be a double dose of disappointment. Such parents come up against the reality that expressing a preference for a school does not mean that the preference will be met.

Until the School Standards and Framework Bill (1998) becomes law, local education authorities are the admission authorities for county and controlled schools. Governing bodies have the equivalent role for grant maintained, voluntary aided and special agreement schools.

The government expressed a wish in the *Excellence in Schools* White Paper (Department for Education and Employment, 1997) to see forums established to develop local admission procedures. These could include, among others, head teachers and governors of community, aided and foundation schools. The forums would help develop useful information for parents to aid their choice of schools and would work towards a common timetable for school applications in their area.

The process and the structure would be as follows. The Secretary of State would issue a Code of Practice giving guidance on admission functions. All admission authorities would be able to determine policies giving regard to the Code and would discuss these at an early stage with other admission authorities in the area.

If there was disagreement on a school's admission arrangements, there would be access to an independent adjudicator. Where parents have been refused a place at a school, they may appeal to an independent appeals panel. The government proposed that appeals by an individual parent would be heard by an independent appeals panel which would not contain any members of the admission authority or members of the school governing body.

The government's plans would rule out any new partial selection of pupils by academic ability and the adjudicator would have the power to end this practice where it already existed. It is intended to continue to allow a school with a specialism to give priority to a child if the child had the relevant aptitude, so long as the effect of this was not to select pupils according to general academic ability. Those involved in deciding the arrangements for admissions for September 1998 were expected to have regard to government policies.

Regarding selective (grammar) secondary schools, the decision whether to continue to select pupils on the basis of high ability would be made by parents.

There is a difficult balance to strike, given the realities of choice and lack of choice. First, parents who can afford it have the choice of schools in the independent sector. Such schools will have smaller classes than state schools and may select according to ability, providing an environment of high achievement. For parents who depend on the state system, this first level of choice is not available.

Where grammar schools exist and where parents wish them to remain, this will take out from the local community the more academically able pupils, leaving the remaining schools to share the rest.

The extent to which LEAs are able to devise and enforce equitable admissions with aided and foundation schools, in comparison with community schools, remains to be seen. Where aided and former grant maintained schools have already developed selective admissions they will presumably be resistant to any erosion of their control.

Such resistance may make itself felt not in the obvious reluctance to admit pupils but in unwillingness to retain pupils whom the school feels it has been forced to take, for example, pupils with behavioural difficulties. Such pupils could be admitted only to be excluded quite soon, or guided to another school by the persuasion of voluntary transfer.

If there was a system of tracking excluded pupils which related the exclusion to the original reluctance of a school to accept the pupil, it is unlikely that this would be effective. An exclusion could be seen equally as a vindication of the school's reluctance to take the pupil originally, or a working of the system by the excluding school. It would be difficult to determine which was the true picture.

Yet steps could be taken to clarify admissions systems particularly for parents. The school could:

- recognise that expressing a school preference for most parents already excludes the choice of an independent school or a selective state school
- be honest with parents that expressing a preference in the remaining schools does not guarantee a place in the preferred school
- encourage the LEA to advise parents that a school may not 'persuade' the parent to seek a voluntary transfer
- be as clear as possible in what is left of admission arrangements, including waiting lists.

References

Audit Commission (1996) *Trading Places*, London, Audit Commission.
Department for Education and Employment (1997) *Excellence in Schools*, London, DfEE.

Address

The Admissions Team, Admissions and Information for Parents Division 2A L1, Department for Education and Employment, Sanctuary Buildings, Great Smith Street, Westminster, London SW1P 3BT, tel: 0171 925 5568, fax: 0171 925 5179.

Appraisal

An integrated system

Few people could be quicker at appraisal than W. S. Gilbert of light opera fame. Standing in a theatre resplendent in a red waistcoat with brass buttons Gilbert was approached by a man feigning to mistake him for a door attendant as an insult to his rather showy apparel. But when the fellow demanded of Gilbert, 'Call me a cab!' Gilbert appraised the situation immediately and retorted, 'Sir, you are a cab, but certainly not a handsome one'.

In a more mundane way, the appraisal of teacher performance is a concern of the Miscellaneous Matters of Education Act 1986. This Act empowered the Secretary of State to require local education authorities, school governors and others to ensure that arrangements are made for regular teacher appraisal.

A plan for national teacher appraisal, implemented by the Secretary of State in 1990, was intended to ensure that all teachers were appraised by the mid-1990s. From the mid-1990s, the Department for Education and Employment, the Office for Standards in Education, and the Teacher Training Agency all indicated their recognition of the importance of appraisal.

The White Paper *Excellence in Schools* (Department for Education and Employment, 1997) made it clear that the appraisal of school staff is to be linked to the raising of standards. As part of their support for high quality teaching government is committed to act when head teachers and teachers are not performing satisfactorily. Performance has to reach a standard which government and parents 'have a right to expect'. The vagueness of this notion requires clarification.

A performance appraisal system is required which is fair and robust and which recognises success and acts on failure. *Excellence in Schools* argued that the previous system of appraisal gave insufficient emphasis to standards and performance in teaching.

The perceived disadvantages of the appraisal systems were as follows:

• targets often do not concentrate on improving teacher effectiveness in the classroom

- targets are often not specific or measurable
- poor performance can be overlooked or ignored
- the process may be bureaucratic and lack accountability
- the process tends not to be regarded by local education authorities (LEAs) or schools as vital to securing and raising pupil performance.

Government therefore proposed to review the arrangements and undertook to make necessary changes. The implications of the government's view of the appraisal system is that any new arrangements would need to involve:

- specific, measurable targets focusing on improving teacher effectiveness in the classroom
- a system which identifies poor performance
- a process which reduces bureaucracy and is more accountable
- a process which LEAs and schools recognise as central to raising pupil performance.

Excellence in Schools states that teachers who are successful will find effective appraisal useful in identifying their strengths and development needs. Less effective teachers will need help to identify their weaknesses and to have targets for improved performance. Government believes that effective appraisal arrangements must involve classroom observation, an assessment of the results achieved by pupils taught by the teacher, and an annual performance review related to targets for improved pupil performance.

A difficulty can be foreseen in the case of groups of children who are taught say a certain subject by more than one teacher, where there are job shares and where for any other reason it is difficult to assign the performance of pupils to the teaching of a particular teacher.

Regarding head teachers, the Office for Standards in Education (OFSTED) has raised concerns about the quality of headship in a minority of schools. To help ensure the quality of head teachers, government will seek to improve arrangements for head teacher appraisal to ensure that it is:

- robust and effective
- clearly focused on the key skills of good leadership.

An important issue is that of who appraises whom. For example, is it appropriate that a chairperson of governors who may not be an education professional appraises a head teacher? Also, schools where resources are tight will have to look very carefully to find non-contact time to release staff to observe colleagues as part of appraisal.

Whatever the arrangements for appraisal, it is important that they give an early indication of development needs and targets for improvement. An appraisal system which acts early to identify strength and weaknesses is likely to be more effective than one which is slow and cumbersome. For head teachers and others to have confidence in appraisal and to find the time and undergo the stress that it can entail, it will have to be very clear that there are benefits to the school.

Prompt identification of development needs and targets for improvement will tend to save money which otherwise may need to be invested in retraining to correct embedded poor practice. It will mean prompt action to save children from the consequences of poor teaching. It will encourage good teachers that their work is being recognised and will save them the burden of carrying incompetent colleagues. Also, it could save untold stress on teachers who know they are failing but who soldier on because their difficulties may be ignored or papered over. The central role of the head teacher means that the appraisal of head teachers must be no less strong than that of teachers.

Before the new Labour government's *Excellence in Schools* White Paper and during the period of office of the Conservative government which preceded it, the Teacher Training Agency (1996) indicated its recognition of the importance of appraisal. It gave as one of its priorities for 1996/97 the aim of reviewing teacher and head teacher appraisal with OFSTED after consulting with the profession.

Clear criteria for success and failure are needed so that the performance of teachers and head teachers is assessed on an agreed basis. The work carried out by the Teacher Training Agency on national standards for teachers, subject leaders, head teachers and special education co-ordinators could contribute to the standards which will be sought when appraisal takes place.

While OFSTED inspectors can comment on appraisal, the OFSTED guidance makes it clear that inspectors should not seek access to confidential staff appraisal information (Office for Standards in Education, 1995, p. 19).

All aspects of appraisal need to be recorded clearly so that there is no misunderstanding later on. The more transparent the process, the more it is likely to be accepted by staff. The positive aspects of any appraisal process need to be given sufficient emphasis in order to give the scheme balance. Where an appraisal system is linked to reward as well as prompt action against failure, it is more likely to earn the support of staff.

Possible developments were indicated in a speech by Estelle Morris, Parliamentary Under-Secretary of State for School Standards. The speech, 'Appraisal: Effective Teachers, Effective Schools' was given to the Seventh British Appraisal Conference on 26 January 1998. Appraisal was seen as part of the raising standards agenda and one aim is to keep any system administratively simple. The proposals for appraisal include pupil performance targets for individual teachers and head teachers, indicating the importance of having an integration between school target setting and the school's appraisal process. LEAs in their Education Development Plans, when considering action to improve the quality of teaching, should include teacher appraisal.

Core elements of appraisal are seen as an annual appraisal cycle linking in with other planning cycles. For head teachers, one objective at least would be connected to the achievement of school targets for pupil performance. The LEA would arrange and conduct head teacher appraisal together with a nominated representative from the governing body. Regarding teachers, at least one objective would relate to pupil performance and would be linked to the attainment of school targets. Also, the appraisal would take in evidence of performance, including classroom observation. The head teacher would be responsible for seeing that teachers are appraised by their line managers. There are no proposals to introduce an explicit link between appraisal and issues of pay and competence. But it is open to head teachers and LEAs to take account of appraisal information in relation to these.

A Handbook on teacher and head teacher appraisal will be developed by a consortia of schools, an LEA or others for 1999. It will aim to give practical guidance on implementing appraisal arrangements and will not have statutory force. The handbook should demonstrate the flexibility of the new arrangements, which should encompass a variety of approaches conversant with the requirements of different types of school.

To improve appraisal the school should:

- integrate school target setting with the appraisal process
- seek ways of relating pupil performance to at least one appraisal objective
- reduce the administrative burden in such ways as ensuring that the appraisal cycle is informed by other school planning cycles.

References

Department for Education and Employment (1997) *Excellence in Schools*, London, DfEE.

Office for Standards in Education (1995) *The OFSTED Handbook: Guidance on the Inspection of Nursery and Primary Schools*, London, HMSO.

—— (1997) *Inspection and Re-inspection of Schools from September 1997: New Requirements and Guidance on their Implementation* (August 1997), London, OFSTED.

Teacher Training Agency (1996) *Corporate Plan 1996: Promoting Excellence in Teaching*, London, TTA.

Address

Teachers Appraisal and Training Team, Department for Education and Employment, Sanctuary Buildings, Great Smith Street, Westminster, London SW1P 3BT,
tel: 0171 925 5162, fax: 0171 925 6073.

Assessment complexities

'Fashion is a form of ugliness so intolerable that we have to alter it every six months', stated Oscar Wilde. If this is so then assessment cannot be the most attractive feature on the educational landscape.

Assessment arrangements for national school tests and tasks and teacher assessment seem to be forever changing and becoming more complex and interdependent. This is partly the result of assessment being developed for more subjects of the curriculum and existing assessment arrangements being refined.

The importance of the assessment of pupil attainment is unquestioned and its relationship with benchmarking and target setting and with value added measures can only increase its profile. Yet some teachers still lack confidence that their own assessments of pupil attainment are as valid as tests and tasks. There is also unease that teacher assessments may not be consistent nationally.

Each summer, all children aged 7, 11 and 14 take national tests in English and mathematics. All 11-year-olds and 14-year-olds also take national tests in science. The tests indicate how well a child is doing in different subjects on a particular day.

At 7 years old, a child is tested in mathematics and in English (reading, spelling and writing, including handwriting). In reading, most children are tested on their ability to read aloud and on their comprehension. The tests are all short and in total probably occupy about three hours spread over several days in the Spring and Summer terms. Children judged capable of achieving level 4 or above should be enabled to undertake the relevant Key Stage 2 tests.

The scores on one assessment may have implications for others. For example, in English, a reading task awards levels 1 and 2. It provides grades A to C at level 2. It must be used with all children who are judged to be working towards or within level 1 or within level 2. The reading comprehension test for level 2 provides grades A to C at this level. This test must be used with all children who achieve level 2 in the reading task. Children who attain grade A at level 2 in both the level 2 reading comprehension test and the reading task must be taken on to level 3 reading comprehension test. Children who do not achieve level 2 on the reading comprehension test have only their task result recorded and reported.

The reading comprehension test for level 3 must be used with all children:

- who are judged to be working within levels 3 or 4 or above in reading; and
- who have attained level 2A through both the reading task and the level 2 reading comprehension test.

Schools should make every effort to complete the levels 1 and 2 reading task and the level 2 reading comprehension test with all those children who do not achieve sufficient marks in the reading comprehension test for level 3 to be awarded.

Similarly, the administration of the spelling test is dependent on other assessments. The spelling test for levels 1 to 3 must be given to children whose teacher assessment in writing is level 2 or above, or who achieve level 2 or 3 in the writing task.

In mathematics, there is a task for mathematics level 1 which must be used with children judged to be working towards or within level 1 in mathematics as a whole. There is a test for mathematics at levels 2 and 3, which must be used with all children judged to be working within level 2 or above in mathematics as a whole. It provides grades A to C at level 2.

At Key Stage 1, some children will achieve very highly at level 3 across the range of Key Stage 1 tasks and tests in either English, mathematics or both. These children may be assessed at level 4 or above through the Key Stage 2 tests. Children who are given a teacher assessment level of 4 or above should usually attempt the Key Stage 2 tests.

Assessment at level 4 or above in English is made through Key Stage 2 tests at levels 3 to 5 in reading, writing, spelling and handwriting. Assessment of level 4 or above in mathematics is made through the administration of Key Stage 2 tests at levels 3 to 5. In the case of science, Key Stage 1 assessment arrangements consist of teacher assessment alone. It is possible to record an assessment at level 4 or above but Key Stage 1 children are not entered for Key Stage 2 tests in science.

Interim assessments for end of Year 4 were introduced in 1997. Support material was developed by the then School Curriculum and Assessment Authority (SCAA) to support teachers in assessing children in core subjects during Key Stage 2 especially at the end of year four by May 1997. Standardised tests were available to schools in reading, writing, spelling, numeracy and mental arithmetic. In Autumn 1997, assessment units were available in English, mathematics and science comprising a range of assessment materials for teachers to use with children. From 1998, optional progress tests produced by the Qualifications and Curriculum Authority (QCA) were available for Years 3 and 5 as well as for Year 4.

At 11 years old, the child is tested on English (reading, writing, spelling and hand writing) mathematics (with and without a calculator) and science. Most 11-year-olds spend about 5 or 5½ hours on the tests which are similar in form to short examinations.

In 1997, a national pilot took place for a mental arithmetic test. Statutory assessment of children working at levels 1 and 2 were by teacher assessment alone and classroom based tasks for these children were optional.

At the end of Key Stage 2, teacher assessment involves assessing a level for each attainment target in English, mathematics and science. An overall subject level in English, mathematics and science is calculated by averaging the teacher assessment target levels according to prescribed weightings.

In 1998, the following arrangements existed. In English, tests comprised a reading test (levels 3 to 5), a writing test (levels 3 to 5), a spelling and hand-writing test (levels 3 to 5) and an English extension test (level 6). In mathematics, the tests comprised Tests A and B (levels 3 to 5), a mental arithmetic test (levels 3 to 5) and a mathematics extension test C (level 6). In science, the tests comprised Test A and B (levels 3 to 5) and Science Extension Test C (level 6).

Teacher assessments are reported alongside the national test and task results. Teacher assessment judges the child's performance in the whole subject over time. Carried out as part of the teaching and learning in the classroom, it can cover the full range and scope of the programmes of study. It can also take account of evidence of achievement in a range of contexts, including that gained through discussion and observation. Both tests and teacher assessment are meant to be equally important.

For teacher assessment in English, mathematics and science, teachers decide at which level children are on the National Curriculum scale at the ages of 7, 11 and 14. In this scale, most 7-year-olds are expected to reach level 2. Most 11-year-olds are expected to reach level 4. This expectation is not of course peculiar to teacher assessment.

Teachers assess the child in each part of the subject. In English, this is in reading, writing (including handwriting), speaking and listening. Teachers are required to summarise their teacher assessment at the end of the key stage in the form of:

• a level for each attainment target in English, mathematics and science
• an overall subject level for mathematics and science.

The basis for judging these levels of attainment are the level descriptions in the National Curriculum. A few 11-year-olds are still working at levels 1 and 2. Formal written tests are not appropriate for these children so they are only given a teacher assessment level.

Over and above the complexities of National Curriculum assessment, arrangements were introduced in 1998 to help ensure that tests were kept in secure conditions until they were administered to pupils. A number of special arrangements for pupils with special educational needs were also made.

It is to be hoped that national tests and task procedures will be gradually stabilised and simplified. They may then form a secure and integral part of the school's battery of assessment information to be used to inform class-room organisation, teaching approaches and other aspects of teaching and learning. In this way their value will be enhanced and their important role in conveying to parents and others the overall standards of the school will be retained.

Preparatory schools have common entrance examinations or scholarship examinations at the end of Year 8. Many schools start the syllabi for this in Year 6 or 7, depending on the subject concerned. Many schools also have internal examinations at the primary level from Year 3 and may also take national tests.

Schools should:

- allow sufficient time for assessment co-ordinators and subject co-ordinators to assimilate the overall changes and complexities and the subject specific changes each year
- make full use of the Qualifications and Curriculum Authority seminars, telephone enquiry service and publications
- make full use of LEA training and advice on all aspects of assessment
- ensure that assessment results are carefully analysed by gender, social background and other relevant features to inform provision and improve standards
- ensure that a careful item by item analysis is made of returned scripts to focus subsequent teaching on very specific areas of weakness.

References

Qualifications and Curriculum Authority and Department for Education and Employment (1997) *Key Stage 1 Assessment and Reporting Arrangements 1998*, London, QCA.
Qualifications and Curriculum Authority (1997) *Key Stage 2 Assessment Arrangements 1998*, London, QCA.

Addresses

QCA Key Stage 1 Team Qualifications and Curriculum Authority, 29 Bolton Street, London W1Y 7PD, tel: 0171 243 9330, fax: 0171 221 5221.

QCA Key Stage 2 Team Statutory Assessment Team, address as above, tel: 0171 243 9351, fax: 0171 221 5221.

QCA Publications, P. O. Box 235, Hayes, Middlesex UB3 1HF, tel: 0181 867 3233, fax: 0181 867 3233.

Attendance

Improving pupil attendance

In the idyllic world of Tom Sawyer, playing hookey was a harmless habit providing opportunities for adventure and for finding out what real life was all about. Outside the realms of fiction poor attendance represents a corrosive influence on standards which schools and others have to tackle vigorously.

Absence from school lowers standards of achievement. It affects the education of the absentee, has an impact on the wider community and wastes precious resources. It is important to be clear about the scale and nature of problematic attendance.

Department of Education and Science *Circular 11/91* gives guidance on *The Education (Pupils' Attendance Records) Regulations 1991* and on other matters. The Regulations provide that all schools which have day pupils are required to maintain attendance registers. These registers must show pupils either as present, engaged in an approved educational activity away from the school site, or absent. Where a pupil is marked as absent, the register must show whether the absence was authorised by the school or unauthorised. Schools may keep computerised attendance and admission records. Maintained school prospectuses and annual reports must include specified information on rates of unauthorised absence.

The school also has to inform the local education authority (LEA) of children who are not attending regularly or who have been absent for two weeks without adequate explanation.

Parents have duties relating to their child's attendance under the Education Act 1996. They must ensure that their child receives efficient, full time education appropriate to the child's needs or aptitudes and appropriate to any special educational needs the child may have. The education is to be by attendance at school or by other means.

An LEA's duty to enforce attendance is defined under the Education Act 1996 and the Children Act 1989. This mainly concerns children whom the school identifies as being absent without authorisation. The LEA has a right to inspect the registers of the schools which they maintain.

Any school working to improve its attendance record must first ensure that it is not including in its unauthorised absence figures instances of authorised absences. The school must therefore be conversant with the reasons for authorised absence. These include absences when:

- a pupil is prevented from attending by sickness or any unavoidable cause
- the day is exclusively set apart for religious observance by the religious body to which the parents belong
- suitable transport has not been provided and the school is not within walking distance.

Other reasons for authorised absence include participation in an approved public performance.

A school might reasonably grant leave in other circumstances such as absence following the death of a close member of the pupil's family. Schools have a discretionary power to grant limited leave for holidays during term time. Such permission is granted in accordance with the governing body's policy. Only in exceptional circumstances may the total amount of leave granted exceed (in total) more than ten school days in any one school year. Parents do not have an automatic right to withdraw pupils from school for a holiday and in law they have to apply for permission in advance.

In order to distinguish between the different types of absences schools may wish to use the symbols as suggested by DES Circular 11/91. For example:

B   receiving part time and/or temporary education at an off-site unit other than at the school where registered
C   other circumstances (to be specified)
E   excluded (short term and permanent, still pending confirmation by governors/LEA)
H   annual family holiday (with permission)
I   attending interview
M   medical/dental (this applies only to whole sessions and not to children who arrive late or leave early for a hospital or doctor's appointment)
R   day of religious observance
S   study leave.

From January 1998, approved educational activities conducted away from the school site no longer count as approved absence. Approved educational activities cover specified types of supervised activity, for example, work experience, educational trips and visits (including overseas trips and exchanges, sporting activities and link courses involving colleges).

To distinguish between educational visits and authorised absence, schools may wish to use the following symbols:

P   approved sporting activity
V   educational visit
W   work experience
Z   link courses.

The relevant legislative change for this was the Education (Pupil Registration) (Amendment) Regulations 1997.

Assuming that a school is accurately recording absences, percentages for unauthorised and for authorised absences may be compared with the local and national equivalents.

Particular populations of pupils may have differing attendance rates. For example, in 1994–95 the national average attendance rate for travelling pupils in primary schools was 41.3 per cent, compared with an attendance rate of around 94 per cent for primary school pupils generally. Such low figures should not of course encourage schools to slacken their realistic expectations that traveller children should attend school regularly. However, they can help put into perspective seemingly low school figures achieved after much effort.

Establishing the pattern of absences can be a useful aid in directing effort where it is likely to be most effective. Are significant numbers of pupils taking extended holidays during term time? Are a few families having a disproportionate effect on absenteeism? Are certain days of the week more prone to absences than others? Why?

In primary school a key to pupil attendance is the attitude of the child's parents or carers. The school should have a clear written attendance policy and procedures on attendance, and these should be conveyed unequivocally to parents. The policy should include the procedure for registration, strategies for encouraging attendance, how unauthorised absences are dealt with and how partnership between the school, parents and others works to improve attendance. It is vital that, the school having ensured that attendance is recorded accurately, parents are involved. Parents should be absolutely clear about what constitutes an unauthorised absence. They should be contacted when their child is absent without authorisation. This quickly alerts parents to situations where the child is missing from school without their knowledge.

Where parents are allowing absences, thus condoning them, the school has the opportunity to emphasise that casual absences are unacceptable. A letter to parents pointing out the importance of attendance can be effective. The school can advise parents who take authorised holidays in term time to avoid the month in which national tests are administered.

The message that the school takes attendance seriously can also be conveyed in the school prospectus, the annual report to parents and general letters home, as well as in specific letters picking up on particular absences. The school should seize every opportunity to get this message across.

The school should ensure that its policies and practices support improving attendance. For example, an effective anti-bullying policy can reduce absences related to bullying. Attendance should improve where education is made more relevant to pupils' needs in general and better tailored to the needs of particular groups of pupils including disaffected pupils. As attendance is an aspect of school standards, good attendance should be recognised and rewarded, along with other aspects of achievement, perhaps by termly or annual prizes.

Governors and LEAs should convey their support of efforts to improve attendance. The role of the educational welfare service is important in enforcing attendance. Some education welfare services have developed staged procedures on dealing with absenteeism, and it is important that schools discuss and implement such guidance. In some areas carefully planned truancy sweeps have been made by police working closely with the education welfare service and schools. Legal sanctions can ultimately be enforced on parents who do not secure their child's education.

The Electronic Attendance Registration Scheme is used by teachers to monitor pupils throughout the day. The project has been developed by giving parents electronic pagers to encourage them to be more responsible for their children's behaviour. On a less sophisticated but still effective level, spot checks may be made of attendance and punctuality.

Punctuality is an aspect of attendance involving prompt arrival at school and at subsequent lessons. Procedures for children moving from outside play areas to the classroom need to be examined if they take longer than a few minutes. If lessons are scheduled to start at a particular time, then the time that it takes for children to move from the playground to class and be ready for work needs to be allowed for when signalling the end of play.

Consequently, if a lesson starts at 10.45 a.m., the signal for the end of play may need to be given two or three minutes before so that pupils have time to enter school and be settled in class. While this may seem pedantic, it is worth remembering that the cumulative effect of starting four lessons (the first lesson of the day, the lesson after morning break, the lesson after lunch and the lesson after afternoon break) five minutes later than scheduled is one hour and forty minutes per week.

Staff themselves set the standards for attendance and punctuality and should be beyond reproach in this respect.

The school should:

- precisely record authorised and unauthorised absences
- compare its own absence rate to national and local figures
- analyse patterns in absences and use the information to inform strategies to improve attendance
- ensure that it has a clear policy and procedures
- take all reasonable opportunities to convey that attendance is important

- reward good attendance
- work closely with parents and educational welfare officers and others.

References

Department of Education and Science (1991a) *Circular 11/91: The Education (Pupils Attendance Records) Regulations 1991*, London, DES.

—— (1991b) *The Education (Pupils Attendance Records) Regulations 1991, Statutory Instrument 1582*, London, DES.

Department for Education (1994) *School Attendance Policy and Practice in Categorisation of Attendance* (May), London, DfE.

Department for Education and Employment (1995) *The Education (Pupil Registration) Regulations 1995, Statutory Instrument 2089*, London, DfEE.

—— (1997) *The Education (Pupil Registration) (Amendment) Regulations 1997, Statutory Instrument 2624*, London, DfEE.

Address

School Attendance Team, Discipline and Attendance Division, Department for Education and Employment, Sanctuary Buildings, Great Smith Street, London SW1P 3B, tel: 0171 925 5719, fax: 0171 925 6986.

Baseline assessment

Strengths and limitations

Words can be as misleading as they can be precise. One is reminded of William Whitelaw, the loyal lieutenant of the Thatcher administration, accusing certain colleagues of, 'Going around stirring up apathy'. It looked for a time as though baseline assessment might disappear under a sea of confusion about nomenclature. Initial assessment, starting points, on-entry assessment, entry assessment and entry profile were among the alternatives suggested before the term baseline assessment prevailed.

Centrally, baseline assessment aims to provide information about a child's knowledge, skills, understanding and attitudes which will help the teacher plan learning to meet the needs of the child. It may be used to help teachers familiarise themselves with individual pupils and the class and to form a link with parents. But it is important that the teacher also has time to familiarise herself or himself with the class as a whole. Baseline assessment can give information to help curriculum planning and can aid identifying pupils with special educational needs, and more able pupils. Also, it can be used as part of a value added measurement focusing on pupils' progress later in their education.

In January 1996, the then Secretary of State for Education, Gillian Shepherd asked the then School Curriculum and Assessment Authority (SCAA) to carry out a survey of current practice in baseline assessment. SCAA was asked to prepare proposals for formal consultation for Autumn 1996.

The resulting proposals (School Curriculum and Assessment Authority, September 1996), recognised the work that had already been developed locally. Over half of English local education authorities (LEAs) already had baseline assessment schemes in place. SCAA recommended therefore that in order to retain good local practice but to encourage areas where there was no scheme, there should be a National Framework. Within this, the schemes that met certain key principles could be accredited and continue to operate. For a scheme to be accredited, there must be at least 30 schools which have expressed an interest in using it in order to ensure that the data which is produced is sufficiently robust.

The National Framework requires that schools which did not have a scheme should implement one. All schemes have to provide formative and diagnostic information and also measure the child's attainment so that subsequent progress can be recognised and monitored. Parents and carers are to be involved as fully as possible.

The baseline assessment should take place within seven weeks of the child starting school. All schemes should cover early literacy, numeracy and personal and social development and the National Framework should encourage schemes to encompass all of the 'Desirable Outcomes' (Department for Education and Employment, 1996).

It was proposed that SCAA would provide assessment materials allowing schools to evaluate their pupils' progress in relation to the national situation. SCAA would sample children's results in each of the three school terms each year, to be able to give schools data related to their own entry arrangements. All schools would be expected to have schemes in place by September 1998 which were consistent with the National Framework. SCAA would accredit local schemes and would publish a list of accredited schemes each year.

Three models were put forward by SCAA regarding assessments from baseline to Key Stage 1: descriptive recording sheets, criteria using desirable outcomes and a checklist of skills such as literacy and numeracy. The outcomes of the consultation were that draft criteria for accrediting baseline assessment schemes were put out for consultation and these led to the National Framework containing the final criteria for accreditation (School Curriculum and Assessment Authority, 1997a).

Baseline Assessment Scales were subsequently published (School Curriculum and Assessment Authority, 1997b). These cover reading, writing, speaking and listening, mathematics, and personal and social development. Each scale was developed with sets of four items. The first item was designed to be achieved by more than 80 per cent of children in the reception age range. The second was to be achieved by between 40 per cent and 80 per cent of children. The third item represented the Desirable Outcomes standard and would be achieved by between 20 per cent and 60 per cent of children. The fourth item usually represented level one of the National Curriculum and would be achieved by less than 20 per cent of children. The scales are the assessment materials which are used to produce national data. A number of schemes have been accredited which incorporate the scales as their core assessment materials.

To take an example, 'reading' has three subsections: A, B and C. Subsection A is 'reading for meaning and enjoyment'. In this subsection are four items. One of these items requires the child to recognise his or her own name. For each item there is guidance for the assessor as to what to do and what to look for and what to record on the child's individual record sheet.

While being manageable for teachers, assessment should relate to classroom practice and should involve parents. In practice, teachers will have to work hard to ensure that baseline assessment does not initially over-ride good classroom practice. For some teachers, it will mean changing the way they organise their classes. The role of classroom assistants will be affected and training will be necessary to meet the new demands.

The relationship of SEN to baseline assessment is unclear. The Baseline Assessment Scales warn that low attainment does not necessarily imply that the child has special educational needs. If apparent difficulties persist, the publication advises, then further assessment will be required. The principle is that where baseline assessment suggests that a child may have special educational needs then closer monitoring and subsequent careful assessment would be necessary.

SCAA published a trialling version of scales for children with special educational needs in September 1997 (School Curriculum and Assessment Authority, 1997c). This appears to be a possible form of the closer monitoring and the further assessment that was implied in the Baseline Scales. It could also be used for children who are already identified as having special educational needs. For example, the scale could be used with 4-year-olds in special schools.

Whether it would be appropriate for such 'special' scales, which are for optional use, to be subsumed into the 'ordinary' scales is not clear. It might make the ordinary scales too daunting and cumbersome. Also, it would seem to be reasonable to use the special scales after the ordinary scales or if it appears to the teacher that the child would not reach any of the items on the ordinary scales.

As SCAA was subsumed into the Qualifications and Curriculum Authority (QCA) in October 1997, all the duties relating to SCAA and baseline assessment were passed to the new body. The school year 1997–98 was the pilot year for baseline assessment during which most schools trialled a baseline assessment scheme. In May 1998 all schools received a baseline assessment information pack from QCA.

The school should remember to keep closely in touch with what the scheme is sampling. It is easy when one is converting observations into numbers on a scale to be seduced into believing that the numbers have a more precise meaning than the observations which generate them. The limitations of observations should encourage the school to use baseline assessment as only one part of a wide ranging evaluation of children's learning.

Particular care needs to be taken to ensure that baseline assessment does not lead to early labelling of a child and, however subtly, affecting the attitudes of teachers and others towards the child and the subsequent provision for him or her. It is important to remember that assessment is taking place when children may not yet feel secure in their new environment. They may not have yet developed working relationships with those observing them nor settled into relationships with other children.

The Association of Assessment Inspectors and Advisers (1997) proposed a helpful series of principles which they referred to as several 'key purposes'. In line with these proposals, schools should ensure that their scheme:

- is formative so as to support teaching and learning for individual pupils
- establishes what children know, understand, and can do as they enter compulsory education
- has clear learning objectives so that teachers are able to match the curriculum to children's needs
- assists in the identification of special educational needs and the needs of more able children;
- aids communications between such parties as parents, teachers and support assistants by creating a framework
- improves continuity and progression between home, pre-school provision and school
- supports high validity assessment
- provides a structure for developing consistency and reliability.

Also, as appropriate, the scheme should :

- support the introduction of children to the National Curriculum Programmes of Study.

References

Association of Assessment Inspectors and Advisers (1997) *Baseline Assessment*, London, AAIA.
Department for Education and Employment (1996) *Nursery Education: Desirable Outcomes for Children's Learning on Entering Compulsory Education*, London, DfEE.
School Curriculum and Assessment Authority (1996) *Baseline Assessment: Draft Proposals September 1996*, London, SCAA.
—— (1997a) *The National Framework for Baseline Assessment*, London, SCAA.
—— (1997b) *Baseline Assessment Scales*, London, SCAA.
—— (1997c) *Baseline Assessment Scales for Children with Special Educational Needs: Teachers' Guide*, London, SCAA.

Addresses

Under Fives Team, Qualifications and Curriculum Authority (QCA), 29 Bolton Street, London W1Y 7PD, tel: 0171 243 9493, fax: 0171 221 5221, e-mail: info@qca.org.uk.

Behaviour and its improvement

Bad behaviour may be tolerable when it is witty. An example is the behaviour of the Oxbridge don who said of a colleague, 'Such time as he can spare from the adornment of his person, he devotes to the neglect of his duties'. Of course, in schools the question of discouraging unacceptable behaviour and encouraging appropriate conduct is a more serious matter.

The educational standards of attitudes, behaviour and personal development are considered together in a section of the *OFSTED Handbook: Guidance on the Inspection of Nursery and Primary Schools* (Office for Standards in Education, 1995).

According to this guidance, the attitudes, behaviour and personal development of pupils are interrelated and are promoted by teaching; the curriculum and assessment; and provision for spiritual, moral, social and cultural (SMSC) development. Indeed, SMSC development represents four aspects of personal development in which schools play an important role.

Attitudes to learning relate to the extent to which pupils show an interest in their work and the degree to which they are able to maintain concentration and build up their capacity for personal study.

Behaviour includes the extent to which pupils behave well in and around the school. Courtesy, trustworthiness and respect for property are important. The incidence of exclusions is in one sense an indicator of behaviour. It is also a measure of the values and ethos of a school and the skills of staff in managing difficult behaviour. The formation by pupils of constructive relationships with other pupils and with teachers and other adults are other important aspects. The degree to which pupils can work collaboratively when required is also important.

Personal development involves pupils showing respect for the feelings, values and beliefs of others; and their initiative and willingness to take responsibility.

Not only are attitudes, behaviour and personal development interrelated but the core of these features is behaviour. Pupils' attitudes are inferred from their behaviour. If pupils are thought to have a negative attitude towards a subject of the curriculum, this would be inferred from the way they behave in lessons where that subject is the main focus. It could also be inferred from what they say about the subject, because talk is of course another form of behaviour.

Similarly, personal development is defined by behaviour or by changes in behaviour over time if we are to concentrate on the developmental aspect. If personal development concerns pupils' respect for the feelings, values and beliefs of others, and their initiative and willingness to take responsibility, all this is shown in their behaviour.

Given the importance of pupils' behaviour to their learning, much attention is paid to encouraging good behaviour and discouraging poor conduct. Poor behaviour inhibits both the learning of the child exhibiting the behaviour and that of others. This in turn adversely affects achievement and progress and also increases stress levels of staff. A systematic approach to behaviour is essential to the smooth running of a school. The following points arise when considering raising standards of achievement in behaviour.

In reviewing the whole school behaviour policy the levels of achievement in behaviour can be considered and targets for improvement set. Baseline measurements of behaviour may be decided, and audits of whole school, class and individual teachers and pupils may be taken. Patterns of behaviour may emerge which could suggest ways of raising standards of behaviour. For example, certain times of the day may lend themselves more to poor behaviour than others. Leading on from this the school could set challenging but achievable targets based on what would be reasonably expected in a similar school.

This suggests strategies for reaching the targets, for the whole school, the class and the individual. This would involve rewards, including praise, achievement certificates, and sanctions such as punishment and the withdrawal of anticipated rewards. The school may develop a code of conduct. 'Modelling' of appropriate behaviour is important as a strategy whether it is adult modelling behaviour for a child, or a child modelling the behaviour for another child.

Staff training in behaviour management is vital. Self esteem plays an important part in pupil behaviour and this needs to be encouraged through such means as the ethos of the school. Other strategies include 'time out' and behaviour contracts. In the classroom there need to be reward and punishment programmes and, to raise self esteem, 'circle time', an approach which seeks to develop individual potential and enable emotional and social development within a supportive structured group setting.

Whatever strategies are developed, monitoring and evaluating the effect of approaches is essential in order to see what is working and what is not. All this becomes part of a school's process of self evaluation and improvement.

The values of mutual respect, self discipline and social responsibility underpin good behaviour. Consequently, such behaviour as co-operation should be rewarded in the same way that success in competition is rewarded. The school ethos can value both competitiveness and co-operation. Class rules should reflect the whole school ethos.

Curriculum contributions to raising behavioural standards include personal and social education (PSE) and the knowledge, skills and attitudes which are part of it. The same care needs to be given to this area of the curriculum as to others. For example, PSE should have a programme of study developed by the school, schemes of work, class planning, assessment opportunities and resources.

Motivating and managing pupils and general classroom management make a major contribution to improving behaviour and the sharing of good practice in this area is important. Related to this is support among colleagues, particularly for supply teachers and new teachers.

Staff roles and responsibilities must be clear and understood by all. Particular issues arise in playground management partly because. the management may not be by teachers but by School Midday Supervisory Assistants (SMSAs) The role of pupils is important. A school council is one structure which reflects the value placed on the views of pupils. Above all, pupils should be encouraged to take responsibility for their school.

Parents' attitudes contribute to establishing a positive school culture where work is valued. Sometimes, the parents with whom the school most needs to work are the most difficult to engage. The school may need specific strategies to overcome this difficulty. It can help if parents who may not support the school are surrounded by those who do. This can mitigate some of the negative effects of unsupportive parents and can provide such parents and their children with role models of parents who do co-operate with the school.

Local education authority (LEA) support services can make an effective contribution to improving behaviour if the services and the school are clear from the outset about their respective roles.

Where poor behaviour constitutes a special educational need, particular strategies are available under the *Code of Practice on the Identification and Assessment of Special Educational Needs* (1994). A comprehensive behaviour management approach may be used, including: strategies, identification assessment and observation approaches, evaluation and provision, reporting and monitoring systems, and staff training and guidance. Individual education plans should set clear behavioural targets and have strategies for reaching them.

Assertive discipline is one behaviour management technique mentioned in the White Paper *Excellence in Schools* (1997). This approach sets clear rules, gives continuous positive feedback when pupils are sticking to these rules, and offers a hierarchy of sanctions which are applied sequentially when the rules are broken.

Under the Education Act 1997, LEAs must issue a statement setting out the arrangements made or proposed to be made regarding the education of children with behaviour difficulties. The statement includes information on the arrangements for the provision of advice and resources to schools in the LEA area (community and foundation). The arrangements should cover:

- meeting requests from schools for support and assistance connected with promoting good pupil behaviour and discipline
- assisting schools to deal with the general behaviour difficulties of individual pupils.

These provisions came into effect from April 1998 and LEAs had to have their statements and plans in place by the end of 1998.

Behaviour support plans are intended to reduce the number of pupils excluded from schools. LEAs had to produce the support plans and targets for reducing the number of exclusions by April 1998. There is an important role for educational psychologists and others in this. The plan details the support schools are offered in managing behaviour and what the LEA will do about excluded pupils.

To improve pupil behaviour, the school should:

- audit behaviour
- set targets for improvement
- develop common-sense strategies to meet the targets
- monitor and evaluate the strategies according to the extent to which they are contributing to reaching the targets
- actively teach social and personal education with conviction
- draw on the support of pupils, parents and professionals as far as possible.

References

Department for Education (1994) *Code of Practice on the Identification and Assessment of Special Educational Needs*, London, DfE.

Department for Education and Employment (1997) *Excellence in Schools*, London, DfEE.

Further reading

Department for Education and Science and Welsh Office (1989) *Discipline in Schools: Report of the Committee of Enquiry Chaired by the Lord Elton (The Elton Report)*, London, HMSO.

Department for Education (1994) *Circular 8/94 Pupil Behaviour and Discipline*, London, DfE.

—— (1996) *Improving Schools: Teamwork for School Improvement*, London, DFE.

Address

Discipline and Transport Team, Discipline and Attendance Division, Department for Education and Employment, Sanctuary Buildings, Great Smith Street, Westminster, London SW1P 3BT, tel: 0171 925 6312, fax: 0171 925 6986.

Benchmarking

A machete not a scalpel

Comparisons are not always generous. The pugnacious politician Denis Healey compared being attacked by a gently civil politician, Geoffrey Howe, to 'being savaged by a dead sheep'. But benchmarking may involve flattering as well as unflattering comparisons between schools.

Benchmarking is the process of comparing the standards of performance achieved by members of a group sharing similar characteristics, so that individuals can see how well they are doing compared with the rest. The benchmark is the performance achieved by the more successful members of the group. For schools, benchmarks provide comparative information about how they are performing in relation to others which they can use in setting targets for improvement.

The approach is to encourage all schools to reach the standards of the best whilst recognising that progress towards this aim may be incremental. Once the best performing schools are identified, it is possible to identify best practice and to disseminate this to similar schools who are not performing as well.

National school performance data includes Office for Standards in Education (OFSTED) reports and National Curriculum assessments and examinations. Schools and local education authorities (LEAs) use this to identify how particular schools are performing. Value added work carried out by the former School Curriculum and Assessment Authority (subsumed into the Qualifications and Curriculum Authority in October 1997) also contributes to this raft of information.

The Conservative government asked the School Curriculum and Assessment Authority (SCAA) to seek the views of schools, LEAs and others on the government's target setting proposals and on the nature of the benchmark information to support the target setting process. The relationship between target setting and benchmarking is that schools require information about the performance of other schools that share similar characteristics to their own, to support the target setting process. This is, of course, the benchmark information which is used to enable schools to compare themselves with others.

During the course of the consultation period, the SCAA was merged with the National Council for Vocational Qualifications to form the Qualifications and Curriculum Authority (QCA) which advised the Secretary of State on the outcomes of the consultation so that regulations could be in place early in 1998.

When setting targets, schools need to take account of their own circumstances, based on an analysis of their assessment and examination results compared to the performance of pupils in similar schools. National benchmark information enables schools to make like-with-like comparisons. This is intended to help schools set appropriate targets for improvement, bearing in mind what more successful schools like them are already achieving.

The characteristics which are chosen to identify similar schools are important. They include prior attainment, which is the best predictor of a pupil's subsequent performance. The Value Added National Project carried out by SCAA found that at least 50 per cent of the difference in performance at any key stage is accounted for by differences in attainment at the end of the previous key stage. Once the national value added system is in place, pupils' prior attainment will be used to form benchmark groups. Then the QCA will be able to benchmark schools according to the percentage of pupils reaching a certain level (prior attainment profiles).

In 1998, the National Curriculum data did not go back far enough to include all the children in the system, so pupils' prior attainment data (that is benchmarks based on pupil level information) could not be produced. Consequently, school level factors were used, taken from information supplied by schools on the School Census (Form 7). The school level factor which most strongly correlates to school performance is the proportion of pupils in the school known to be eligible for free school meals. In primary schools (but not in secondary schools) this correlation appears to be strengthened when the proportion of pupils for whom English is an additional language is taken into account.

Eligibility for free school meals is a relatively weak proxy indicator for general social disadvantage. However, it correlates strongly with performance. QCA have used the School Census data relating to 'the number of pupils who are known to be eligible for a free school meal'. This comprises all the pupils who had a free school meal and the number of pupils who were entitled to, but did not take, a free school meal on census day.

The greater the number of pupils from the lower socio-economic groups indicated by the take up of free school meals, the lower the performance. However, the relationship does not indicate a necessary causal link. The fact that a pupil is from a lower socio-economic level does not inevitably dictate that his or her performance will be low. There are variations in achievement between schools with a similar proportion of pupils taking free school meals.

It may be more demanding to teach children who have to cope with the difficulties of social disadvantage, but the experiences of such children should be the same as those of children elsewhere so far as is possible. Some schools with relatively high levels of socio-economic disadvantage achieve performances among the best in the country. The benchmark information illustrates this range of performance. Lower performing schools in the same group therefore need to ask how this is achieved and to see what can be done by their teachers to raise achievement at their own school.

The factor of pupils for whom English is an additional language (EAL) impacts particularly on the early years of a pupil's education. Pupils beginning to cope with English for the first time, perhaps returning to homes where it is not spoken, have particular difficulties. Despite this, research over many years has shown that a large number of these pupils demonstrate a strong commitment to their studies and make up ground quickly. At Key Stage 1, however, a high proportion of pupils with EAL is likely to be associated with lower overall school results.

When SCAA determined the groupings of pupils, it kept under consideration various points. Schools within the groups should be similar enough in their characteristics to be compared like-with-like. The number of groups should be small and manageable. Each group should contain enough schools for comparisons to be meaningful.

Flow charts guide schools to the section of the tables which give the best like-with-like comparisons with the school in question. Intervals between groups in the flow chart were chosen so that the performance of one group is sufficiently different from that of another group to be separated justifiably. When following the flow diagrams to the particular table the school should first apply the percentages that it supplied to the DfEE on Form 7. Where a school is at the extreme of a band, it may be appropriate for the head teacher to consider the information contained in the adjacent table.

To guide a school to the appropriate table the first step is a decision concerning the percentage of pupils in the school who have EAL. If this is above 50 per cent then the school goes directly to a table which allows comparisons with similar schools. Once the percentage of pupils is greater than 50 per cent it was found that further divisions according to the percentage eligible for free school meals made too little difference to justify separate tables.

If the percentage of children in the school with EAL is below 50 per cent there is a further choice of tables depending on the percentage of pupils in the school who take free school meals.

When a school has identified its group the tables show the range of performance in the group in terms of 'quartile tables'. These are tables in which the school at the exact mid point of the performance in the group is at the median. A school at the 25th percentile is 25 per cent of the way up the performance table and is said to be in the lower quartile. It is in the lowest 25 per cent of schools in the group. A school at the 75th quartile is 75 per cent of the way up the table and is said to be in the upper quartile. It is in the highest 25 per cent of schools in the group.

Schools in quartiles other than the upper quartile would be expected to set themselves targets to aspire to that upper quartile. Schools already in the upper quartile could aim for a level of achievement indicated by, say, the top 5 per cent of schools in the group, that is schools at the 95th percentile point in the group.

National benchmark information is now published annually. QCA compiles booklets of benchmark tables for each key stage and the information is also available on the Internet and on computer disc. The tables are laid out with spaces to enable a school to plot its own results as compared with like schools.

Benchmark tables present information for English, mathematics and science for each group of schools. At Key Stage 1 this is the proportion of pupils achieving level 2 and above; for Key Stage 2, the proportion of pupils achieving level 4 and above.

Performance and Assessment profiles (PANDAS) of individual schools are published by OFSTED. These enable head teachers and governors to compare their inspection results and examination scores with those of other schools. QCA have produced a national benchmarking analysis which groups the school's results with those of others on a like-with-like basis (according to the proportion of free school meals) and this information forms part of the school PANDA.

QCA are continually seeking to improve the usefulness of the benchmark publications. There is some emerging evidence that EAL may not provide the additional strength to free school meals correlation that was first thought. As prior attainment data becomes available (in 1998 for Key Stage 3 to Key Stage 4) school level benchmark information will be produced based on 'prior attainment profiles'.

The school should bear in mind the following important points about benchmarking:

- it will be improved when national value added data on prior achievement is included
- it cannot dictate the targets which a school should set, but it provides information to help in setting targets
- it is a broad guide and not a precise scientific tool.

References

Department for Education (1996) *Raising Standards for All: Report on the DfE Conference on Systematic School Self Improvement* (20 November 1996, Westminster Central Hall, London), London, DfE.

School Curriculum and Assessment Authority (1997) *Target Setting and Benchmarking in Schools – Consultation Paper* September 1997, London, SCAA.

Address

School Improvement and Support Team, Qualifications and Curriculum Authority (QCA), 29 Bolton Street, London W1Y 7PD, tel: 0171 243 9343, fax: 0171 243 9434, e-mail: entia@qca.org.uk.

Bullying
Not in our school

Lord Chesterfield thought that an injury is much sooner forgotten than an insult. Edward Moore in 'The Foundling' linked the two when he wrote, 'This is adding insult to injury'. Bullying may involve injury resulting from physical violence, but may also involve insults and intimidation.

Bullying is associated with both psychological and physical intimidation. It may involve excluding a child from a group, and physical violence or threats of violence. Uncovering bullying is made more difficult by the victim's fear of telling about the bully, peer pressure not to tell, and sometimes the bully's hold on other pupils.

Some studies have included name calling within the definition of bullying. The charity Kidscape includes sarcasm and spreading rumours in its view of bullying. Such wide definitions can be unhelpful. First, they begin to stray away from what most people would regard as bullying, which is not to deny, of course, that a behaviour such as name calling or sarcasm can cause deep unhappiness. Second, it is not always made clear why a particular definition is being adopted. For example, is name calling grouped with physical violence because they have a similar cause or can be dealt with in schools by similar strategies? Third, over-concern with comparatively less serious acts may divert attention and consequently thorough investigation and intervention from more serious behaviours.

It is important that children and adults in the school strive to develop a common language for bullying. Children may, for example, use the word bullying for some behaviour which an adult might not interpret in the same way. For example, an over-enthusiastic tackle in a contact sport. Conversely, children might not associate name calling and ostracism with bullying. Until a shared understanding is developed, adults and children may not be communicating effectively about bullying and its effects.

The Elton Report (Department for Education and Science and Welsh Office, 1989) resulted from the setting up of a government committee of enquiry into discipline in schools. Among its recommendations was that head teachers and staff should be alert to signs of bullying and racial harassment, deal with this behaviour firmly, and take action. This action should be based on rules which are backed by sanctions and systems which protect and support those who are bullied.

Government Circular 8/94 (Department for Education, 1994) concerns pupil behaviour and discipline and builds on the Elton Report. It distinguishes bullying from other forms of unacceptable behaviour. The Circular regards bullying as distinctively involving the dominating of one pupil by another or a group of others. Such bullying is premeditated and is not usually a single isolated incident but follows a pattern. The consequences of bullying are: unhappiness, reduced academic progress, truancy and, in extreme cases, even suicide.

The importance of staff acting against bullying, and being seen to act, is recognised. For children who are being bullied, seeing the bullying of other children being successfully dealt with may give them the confidence to come forward and break the cycle of bullying which, as part of its hold on the bullied pupil, intimidates the child from telling. Circular 8/94 advises that school behaviour policies and rules of conduct should make explicit reference to bullying. Like other policies, these should be regularly reviewed by governors, staff, pupils and parents.

While the Circular suggests that school prospectuses and other documents should make it clear to pupils and parents that bullying is not tolerated, it is important that schools should go further. All the relevant documents of the school should be checked when they come up for review to see if it would be appropriate to include a mention of bullying and anti-bullying measures.

As the Circular states, there should be clear ways in which pupils who are bullied or know of others who are being bullied can bring this to the attention of staff. This would be done in confidence so that incidents would be investigated and acted upon as necessary.

It appears that bullying exists in most schools. It follows from this that every school should consider the issue, even if it thinks there is no bullying, in case there is undetected bullying. The school has to be careful that its actions are not misinterpreted by parents and others. The steps that it takes should not lead parents to infer that there is a greater problem than in other schools but that the school is keen to make sure that all children are as safe and secure in the school as is practicable.

Any approach to bullying needs to lay the groundwork carefully. Staff, pupils and parents should be closely involved from the start so as to avoid alarm and to present the move as a positive one. External support may be called on as appropriate. For example, close working relationships with the educational welfare service may reveal that a pupil's absence is related to incidents of bullying.

A whole-school policy should be developed as a result of wide ranging discussions and the policy should be widely publicised, discussed and clarified as necessary. A policy on bullying should not proscribe the use of common sense when responding to incidents. Staff should know the school guidelines and work consistently within them, but should not feel constrained from interpreting a particular situation and responding to it. A balance should be sought between intervening too little and stepping in too early or too vigorously, so stifling the normal process of disagreement and reconciliation that goes on all the time in schools and in society in general.

Appropriate values and attitudes have to be encouraged as well as directly tackling the behaviour of bullying. General letters to parents, the school prospectus and many other communications with parents and others can reinforce the message that the school does not tolerate bullying.

In OFSTED inspections, inspectors look for any evidence of 'inappropriate behaviour, including harassment or bullying, by or towards particular groups of pupils'. The school itself should be aware of any such evidence. The nature of the group exhibiting or receiving the bullying may indicate ways of dealing with the problem. It may for instance indicate racial or gender antagonism.

Inspectors also judge the degree to which the school 'has effective measures to promote discipline and good behaviour and eliminate oppressive behaviour including all forms of harassment and bullying' (Office for Standards in Education, 1995). This indicates that the school should not just directly tackle bullying. It must also nurture positive discipline and good behaviour to create an ethos in which bullying is regarded as completely unacceptable.

Action to prevent and deal with bullying is normally part of the school's behaviour and discipline policy and may feature in teaching programmes. Teaching programmes may look at the causes of bullying and its consequences and will help create a climate in which bullying can be discussed and, with trust, brought more into the open.

Inspectors assess how well the school recognises and records incidents, how well it deals with them and what the school does to prevent the behaviour happening again. The school will need to agree what constitutes bullying and decide how to record it and what action to take. The school should monitor the policy to ensure that it is effective.

The charity Kidscape offers help to the parents of bullied children and to the children themselves. It organises a telephone help line for parents concerned about bullying in school. Kidscape provides a publications list and holds a national conference for parents, teachers and other professionals. Kidscape also conducts in-school training courses for teachers.

Schools should:

- lay the groundwork for consultation carefully
- develop a clear and widely agreed policy and ensure that other policies reflect the school's approach to bullying

- ensure that procedures to deal with bullying are clear and understood by everyone concerned, particularly children
- pursue positive approaches which develop the school ethos and build good relationships and consideration for others so that these enhance the effectiveness of more direct ways of dealing with bullying.

(See also 'Behaviour and its improvement', p. 24.)

References

Department for Education and Science and Welsh Office (1989) *Discipline in Schools: Report of the Committee of Enquiry Chaired by Lord Elton* (The Elton Report), London, HMSO.

Department for Education (1994) *Circular 8/94: Pupil Behaviour and Discipline*, London, DfE.

Office for Standards in Education (1995) *The OFSTED Handbook: Guidance on the Inspection of Nursery and Primary Schools*, London, HMSO.

Further reading

Byrne, B. (1994) *Coping with Bullying in Schools*, London, Cassell.

Address

Kidscape, 152 Buckingham Palace Road, London , SW1W 9TR, tel: 0171 730 3300, fax: 0171 730 7081, e-mail: kidscape@dial.pipex.com.

Child protection

Awareness and procedures

Expectations of security in childhood vary from anticipating little to hoping for much. Joe Orton's cynicism lies behind his observation that 'It is all any reasonable child can expect if the dad is present at the conception'. The morality of protecting childhood faith informs Blake's thought that, 'He who shall teach the child to doubt/The rotting grave shall ne'er get out'. Children who are injured, neglected or abused learn to doubt and to fear, and protection is essential for them. Child protection is a vital and difficult whole-school issue.

Child abuse is legally defined as the abuse of a child under the age of 18 through physical or emotional injury, neglect or sexual abuse. More specifically, physical abuse involves the child being physically hurt either by such means as hitting or burning or the administration of poisonous substances or inappropriate drugs or alcohol. Evidence of physical injury without adequate explanation may be a sign of physical abuse. Emotional abuse involves the child consistently experiencing a lack of love and affection or being continually threatened. Signs such as sadness, excessive crying, apathy, aggression, lack of confidence and low self esteem may point to emotional abuse. Neglect arises where carers fail to provide the child with basic needs such as food and medical care, or when they simply leave the child alone. Neglected children may appear withdrawn or miserable, may be over-aggressive, or may have eating or nutritional problems or be dirty and smelly. Sexual abuse arises when adults exploit children to meet their own sexual needs. This includes sexual intercourse, fondling and exposing the child to pornographic material. Sexually abused children may become depressed and withdrawn, may be aggressive, or may have eating problems and relationships with adults which shut out others. They may exhibit sexual behaviour which is inappropriate for their age (National Society for the Prevention of Cruelty to Children (NSPCC), 1989).

Child abuse is usually perpetrated by a person within the family home and is more likely to occur in disadvantaged families where one or both parents were themselves abused as children. Local authorities have a duty to investigate any suggestion of child abuse. When legal measures are deemed necessary to protect the child, orders are available for child assessment, emergency protection, care, and supervision. (For a more detailed summary of these orders and a summary of the Children Act 1989, see Farrell, 1998.)

A child assessment Order may be applied for under the Children Act 1989. A local authority or an authorised person can apply for this order when:

- there are reasonable grounds for suspicion that a child is suffering (or is likely to suffer) significant harm
- there are insufficient grounds to apply for an Emergency Protection Order, a Care Order or a Supervision Order
- those caring for the child are unwilling to co-operate.

The court has to be satisfied that it is necessary to assess the child's health, treatment or development to establish whether suspicions of harm or potential harm are justified.

Any person, including a teacher, may apply for an emergency protection order. An Emergency Protection Order is made by a court under the Children Act 1989 if the court is satisfied that there are reasonable grounds for believing that a child is likely to suffer significant harm unless (s)he is moved urgently to suitable accommodation. The order lasts for eight days and may be extended once for up to seven further days.

A Care Order may be made under the Children Act 1989 placing a child under the care of the local authority. A local authority or the NSPCC may bring care proceedings through a Family Proceedings Court. While a Care Order is current, a local authority has rights and duties in relation to the child which includes the duty to decide where the child is placed. The court must be satisfied that: the child is suffering harm (or is likely to suffer harm) from the care currently being given (or likely to be given), or the child is out of parental control.

A Supervision Order may be given by a court under the Children Act 1989 under the same grounds that a Care Order is made. The child is placed under the supervision of the local social services authority or of a probation officer. A Supervision Order may be made as a result of criminal proceedings and may last for up to three years. There are also education supervision orders.

DFE Circular 4/88 gave guidance on child protection procedures within the education service and was part of an interagency approach later revised by the Children Act 1989. More up-to-date guidance can be found in the publication *Working Together Under the Children Act 1989: a Guide to Arrangements for Interagency Co-operation for the Protection of Children from Abuse* (Department for Education, Home Office, Department for Health, 1991).

Good practice for schools includes complying with the guidance in those documents. This involves having a designated member of staff with responsibility under procedures laid down by the Area Child Protection Committee (ACPC) and the local education authority (LEA) for co-ordinating action in the school and liaison with other agencies.

Following local ACPC procedures, the school should promptly refer suspected cases of child abuse to the local social services department or to the police. These are the agencies which investigate in cases of child protection.

The school should liaise with all other agencies involved in child protection. This is achieved by monitoring the progress of children placed on the child protection register, by providing reports to social services departments and case conferences, and by ensuring the school is represented at child protection case conferences.

Contributing to the prevention of child abuse, the school should teach pupils to be aware of the dangers of abuse, and help them to protect themselves and develop responsible attitudes to adult life and parenthood.

The school staff should participate in training which:

- develops understanding of the signs and symptoms of child abuse
- makes participants familiar with the ACPC and LEA procedures for dealing with individual cases
- informs participants about the roles and responsibilities of other agencies with which the school liaises
- offers advice on using the curriculum to develop preventative approaches to child protection.

It is essential that sufficient discussion of the issues around child protection takes place in school so that all staff develop a clear view of their responsibilities. Awareness of the signs of child abuse needs to be well established so that neither are potential signs missed nor innocent factors misinterpreted. The systems in place try to ensure that suspicions are investigated by those with experience of cases of child abuse so that balanced and safe judgements are made so far as is possible in this difficult area.

The booklet *Protecting Children: A guide for Teachers on Child Abuse* (National Society for the Prevention of Cruelty to Children, 1989) offers practical advice. Among the areas covered is working together under the Children Act 1989; the identification of child abuse; responding to the child; listening and talking to abused children; reporting concerns; listening and talking to parents; the investigation; getting support; curricular and extra-curricular provision that can help bridge the area between protection and prevention; and whole-school behaviour policies.

The NSPCC (address below) works in England, Wales and Northern Ireland as a specialist child protection agency. It has a network of more than 100 centres, teams and projects and the National Child Protection Helpline.

Through these the NSPCC provides services to children at risk of significant harm, and their families. It operates a National Child Protection Helpline which offers counselling and advice. The NSPCC has a network of child protection teams and projects protecting children from abuse and working with children who have been abused. This is a freephone number which operates 24 hours a day.

The school should:

- ensure that all staff are conversant with the different forms of child abuse and the possible signs
- ensure that staff are aware of the legal structure around child abuse
- comply with the guidance given in government documents such as *Working Together Under the Children Act 1989: a Guide to Arrangements for Interagency Co-operation for the Protection of Children from Abuse* (Department for Education, Home Office, Department for Health, 1991)
- be familiar with local guidance and procedures for dealing with individual cases
- consider curriculum-based preventative approaches to child abuse.

References

Farrell, M. (1998) *The Special Education Handbook*, London, David Fulton.

Department for Education, Home Office, Department for Health (1991) *Working Together Under the Children Act 1989: a Guide to Arrangements for Interagency Co-operation for the Protection of Children from Abuse*, London, HMSO.

National Society for the Prevention of Cruelty to Children (1989) *Protecting Children: A guide for Teachers on Child Abuse*, London, NSPCC.

Addresses

National Society for the Prevention of Cruelty to Children (NSPCC), National Centre, 42 Curtain Road, London EC2A 3NH, tel: 0171 825 2500, fax: 0171 825 2525.

NSPCC Helpline (freephone), tel: 0800 800 500.

Classroom management
Developing interrelated skills

Otto Klemperer, conducting a modern piece of music about which he did not have a high opinion, noticed a member of the audience walk out in the middle of the performance. Klemperer was heard to mutter, 'Thank God somebody understands it'. The member of the audience, he might have supposed, had gazed through apparent complexity and seen nothing.

Yet with classroom management the complexity is genuine. It includes using time and resources well; fitting teaching techniques and organisation to the requirements of the curriculum and the needs of the pupils; and making effective use of assessment to inform subsequent planning.

The simultaneous management of many demands is at the heart of successful teaching. The successful teacher is aware of the numerous threads that feed into good classroom management and recognises and responds to the times when those threads begin to unravel. Such a teacher's expertise will continue to develop. This recognition and response is part of what it means to be a 'reflective practitioner'. But a great and essential part of reflecting is recognising which are the important features to reflect upon (and often to immediately act upon) in the busy classroom.

A report of case studies of six teachers (Office for Standards in Education, 1991) outlining features which contributed to well-managed classes, included the following:

1 *Classroom context*: neatly stored resources are easily accessible to teacher and pupils. Equipment is cared for and pupils accept responsibility for getting and replacing resources. Parts of the classroom are earmarked and resourced for specific subject studies. Displays enhance and stimulate current work or record and show off completed work. Different furniture arrangements reflect the requirements of subject matter or pupils' learning needs. Class routines and procedures are understood and followed. Relationships are good and behavioural expectations are high. Posture, eye contact and voice modulation is used by teachers to keep control and encourage learning. Pupils have good attitudes to work and are motivated to complete work to an acceptable

standard within a specified time. Pupils are sometimes able to make choices about the work to be carried out within boundaries set by the teacher. The teachers are skilled at managing the work of other adults in the classroom whose roles and tasks are clear and complement the teacher's work. Sometimes groups are formed to give pupils experience of leadership and responsibility by helping less skilled or less knowledgeable pupils.

2   *Organisational strategies*: teachers use various groupings, deciding the size and formation of teaching groups according to subject matter and/or the learning needs of pupils. Certain subjects, usually mathematics, science and some aspects of English, are taught in ability groups. Other subjects are more often taught in mixed ability groups. In all subjects, pupils have opportunities to participate in collaborative group work. When other adults or pupils are used (in the teaching of particular groups of pupils or individuals) they are well briefed and supported by the class teacher. Where teachers focus on one group for an extended period, other pupils are given more self-supporting tasks. The organisation and management of the classroom and the preparation of teaching materials link directly to the learning. The deployment of audio-visual equipment and material supports teaching and its use is managed effectively and efficiently.

3   *Teaching techniques*: teaching styles suit the purpose of the subject and the learning needs of the pupils. Planning includes the duration of different aspects of the teaching. There is a good balance between instruction; explanation; discussion; different kinds of questioning; listening to answers; task setting; organising; and assessing. Teachers encourage pupils' learning through direct and indirect teaching, pupils receiving instruction but also working on investigative and exploratory tasks. A variety of tasks is set, some with one correct answer and others with several possible solutions. Particular teaching points are illustrated and reinforced by demonstrations by teacher or pupils. Teaching points are made before, during and at the end of lessons. Pupil groupings, time, resources, space and adult assistance are well managed and are used to promote the learning of specific knowledge or skills and to keep pupils on task. Instructions convey expectations to pupils. Pupils are required to work at a good pace with an understanding of the quality and quantity of work required of them in a particular time scale. Teachers monitor the work in the classroom knowing when and when not to intervene.

4   *Assessment, diagnosis and task setting*: assessment is regarded as central and integral to teaching and learning. Much assessment is informal and based on discussion and observation. This is supplemented by the recording of observations and other evidence such as test results. Information on the pupils' attainment informs planning to help ensure

that the work is suitably challenging. Teacher planning reflects the need to gather and use accurate assessment information. Specific groups of pupils or individuals are sometimes targeted for assessment. Assessment information is used to identify pupils needing additional or specialised assistance. Teachers give evaluative feedback to pupils on current and completed work. They have strategies to encourage pupils to evaluate the tasks they are given, to evaluate the way in which they carry them out, and to assess their own work. Teachers have suitable expectations founded on the skilled assessment of pupils' previous performance.

Many of the points identified in these case studies are recognisable in the section of the OFSTED Framework for the Inspection of Schools relating to the quality of teaching. Inspectors' judgements are made on: the security of the teachers' knowledge of the subject they are teaching; their high expectations of pupils; effective planning; the extent to which teachers manage pupils well and achieve high standards of discipline; effective use of time and other resources; assessing pupils' work and using assessments to inform teaching; and using homework effectively.

Turning to other perspectives on classroom organisation, the way in which time is used is important. 'Evaporated time' has been found to account for some 10 per cent of teaching time which is itself only a proportion of the time a teacher is in school (Campbell and Neill, 1992). Evaporated time is spent on the classroom management tasks which are needed to lay the ground for teaching and learning, and include getting equipment, tidying and moving to different locations. While such tasks are necessary, the careful planning of the lesson and planned best use of available space and resources can help keep it to a minimum. For example, it may save time to 'rotate' the resources rather than children in some lessons.

Classroom layout in relation to the best use of resources has been seen in terms of three broad options: a series of working areas; having resources and materials round the outside of the classroom; and having them in the middle of the classroom (Clegg and Billington, 1994). The first option might include within the classroom a writing area, a science area and an art area. Such an arrangement could have the positive effect of helping children associate particular resources with certain activities and could help to engender a sense of purpose. On the other hand designated areas may, through their very convenience, discourage curricular links being made. This approach also presupposes an 'integrated day' form of organisation, which currently is not widely approved. Having resources around the periphery of the classroom with the children working in the middle tends to encourage more movement around the classroom than the alternative approach of having resources in the centre. In reality many teachers use a combination of the three approaches. Having a clear understanding of the potential benefits of each arrangement should help the teacher more carefully mix the three approaches to the best effect.

Carefully maintained organisational records are an important part of classroom management. These include attendance registers, records of those attending for school dinners and dinner money payments, records of payments for school trips and voluntary activities, records of the membership of classroom groupings and those relating to resources such as maintenance schedules (Pollard, 1997). While such record keeping may be a chore, some, such as attendance registers, are legally required and a little ingenuity can help ensure that they do not get in the way of learning activities.

The school should:

- support teachers in developing high levels of classroom management skills
- encourage the systematic development of these skills in the areas of classroom context, organisational strategies, teaching techniques, and assessment diagnosis and assessment, the use of time and organisational record keeping.

References

Campbell, J. and Neill, S. R. St. J. (1992) *Teacher Time and Curriculum Manageability at Key Stage 1*, London, Assistant Masters and Mistresses Association.

Clegg, D. and Billington, S. (1994) *The Effective Primary Classroom: Management and Organisation of Teaching and Learning*, London, David Fulton.

Office for Standards in Education (1991) *Well Managed Classes in Primary Schools: Case Studies of Six Teachers*, London, OFSTED.

—— (1995) *The OFSTED Handbook: Guidance on the Inspection of Nursery and Primary Schools*, London, HMSO.

Pollard, A. (1997) *Reflective Teaching in the Primary School: A Handbook for the Classroom, Third Edition*, London, Cassell.

Further reading

Wragg, E. C. (1993) *Class Management*, London, Routledge.

Curriculum changes

According to the theologian Richard Hooker 'Change cannot be made without inconvenience, even from worse to better'. In the area of curriculum change, there has certainly been inconvenience. But it is not entirely certain that the changes offer the consolation of having been from worse to better.

The Education Act 1988 (The Education Reform Act) specified that the curriculum for a maintained school should be balanced and broadly based. It should promote the spiritual, moral, cultural, mental and physical development of pupils at the school, and of society. The curriculum according to the Act should also prepare pupils for the opportunities, responsibilities and experiences of adult life.

The National Curriculum was intended to provide a common entitlement, particularly at primary level. This measure has brought certain benefits, such as consistency for pupils who have to move from school to school and the potential for continuity and progression between primary and secondary phases.

The introduction of the National Curriculum, it is now widely accepted, was rushed and the result was what has been called 'a dream at conception: a nightmare at delivery' (Campbell, 1993). From the outset, there were concerns that there was insufficient room in the curriculum to fit in all the subjects and aspects that ideally the school would like. Overloaded and fragmented, the curriculum was eventually slimmed down following the recommendations of the Dearing Report (Dearing, 1993).

As performance 'league' tables concentrate on English, mathematics and science and attract annual media attention both locally and nationally, there is pressure to concentrate on these areas. Also, it is felt that if pupils at least get the core subjects (English, mathematics, science) then this will enable them to benefit from a broader curriculum later. More recently, information and communications technology has increased in importance and is seen by some as a fourth core subject.

One difficulty with this concentration on the core subjects is that it overlooks the massive contribution of other subjects to the core subjects. For example, history contributes to speaking and listening by focusing on concepts and words associated with time, such as past, present, now, then, long time, short time, ancient, modern and so on. Not only does it introduce such words but it provides a context in which they are used and refined through discussion.

Geography introduces approaches to measuring which relate to mathematics and science. For example, instruments are used to measure temperature and rainfall. Geographical vocabulary is developed. In art, visual elements of pattern, space, form and shape are taught which relate to mathematical knowledge and vocabulary.

A subject within a broad and balanced curriculum could be a subject in which a child excels or that he or she enjoys. This may be a non-core subject but it could contribute to the child's sense of achievement and self esteem so that he or she develops more confidence in tackling other subject areas, including core subjects.

Similar arguments to the 'basics view' can be put forward to limit the curriculum offered to pupils for whom English is an additional language (see also 'English as an additional language'). Why teach them history when they cannot speak English properly? Similarly, it is sometimes argued that for pupils with special educational needs, the curriculum should be narrowed. Why teach a modern foreign language when they cannot yet feed themselves? The benefits of the broad and balanced curriculum are again overlooked.

In line with the approach of concentrating on the basics, which had been pursued by the Conservative government, the Labour government introduced a National Literacy Strategy to be followed in 1999 by the implementation of a National Numeracy Strategy. This recommended a daily literacy hour from 1998 and, for mathematics, 50 minutes at Key Stage 2 and 45 minutes for Key Stage 1 from 1999.

Schools were expected to spend the same time that they normally would on science, information technology, and religious education. The Secretary of State lifted the statutory requirement for schools to follow the Key Stage 1 and 2 programmes of study in the non-core National Curriculum subjects of design technology, history, geography, art, music and physical education. This would apply for two years from September 1998 until a revised National Curriculum is brought in from September 2000. There was the opportunity also to offer other non-core subjects. The Office for Standards in Education introduced a new focus to inspections which took account of the changes in the statutory basis of the curriculum.

There are some signs that the value of non-core curriculum subjects may be recognised more fully. In 1997, the then School Curriculum and Assessment Authority (SCAA) held a national consultation as part of its review of the National Curriculum leading up to the year 2000 when a revised National Curriculum will be implemented. Schools were asked for their views regarding a set of aims and priorities for the school curriculum at each key stage. The consultation involved consideration of whether the existing statutory requirements represent a suitable framework to meet present aims and priorities. These statutory requirements are set out in core and foundation subjects (and sex education in Key Stages 3 and 4).

The interest in lifelong learning could also underline the importance of a broad and balanced curriculum. Reports (e.g. Ball, 1994) have shown the importance of early learning to lifelong achievement. The most important learning in the early years is thought to relate to the so called 'super skills' of learning such as self esteem, confidence, aspiration, motivation and socialisation. These skills appear to aid success in long term progress and achievement.

If learning how to learn sufficiently influences the content of the curriculum for initial teacher training and in-service education and training, it may work against the apparent tendency towards a narrower curriculum. In a sense the content of what is focused on is less relevant than learning to learn. But in reality, the way in which we learn different areas of learning are influenced by the content. The way we learn physical education is different to the way we learn mathematics.

There is a great emphasis in many independent schools on a broadly based curriculum not only in the more obviously accepted academic subjects but also in drama, music, art and sport, which are all given high status. A wide range of subjects help to enhance the status of the school through such means as drama and musical performances, art exhibitions and inter-school sports successes.

The architecture of the school curriculum is enormously important. The seventeenth-century scholar Sir Henry Wooton expressed the necessary conditions of architecture as, 'firmness, commodity and delight'. Applied to the school curriculum, 'firmness' would be the method of support and construction of the structure and the way it holds together. 'Commodity' refers to the appropriateness of the design to the purpose. 'Delight' is the emotional response to the execution of the architecture. In this analogy, the 'basics' curriculum is in danger of providing a one-room squat when children should be exploring the Parthenon.

Schools should:

• be aware of the disadvantages of reducing the curriculum to a narrow core of 'basics'
• recognise and encourage others to see the contribution of non-core subjects both for their own value and for their contribution to core subjects
• be especially aware of these issues in relation to particular groups of pupils such as those for whom English is an additional language
• consider ways of recognising and structuring the skills of self esteem, confidence, aspiration, motivation and socialisation.

References

Ball, Sir C. (1994) *Start Right: The Importance of Early Learning*, London, The Royal Society for the Encouragement of Arts, Manufacture and Commerce.

Campbell, J. (1993) 'A dream at conception: a nightmare at delivery' in J. Campbell (ed.) *Breadth and Balance in the Primary Curriculum*, London, Falmer.

Dearing, Sir R. (1993) *The National Curriculum and its Assessment: A Final Report*, London, School Curriculum and Assessment Authority.

Address

Qualifications and Curriculum Authority (QCA), National Curriculum Review Division, 29 Bolton Street, London W1Y 7PD, tel: 0171 229 1234, fax: 0171 229 8526, e-mail: info@qca.org.uk.

Differentiation

The importance of planning

In films like *Top Hat*, *Shall We Dance* and *The Gay Divorcee* many witnessed the wonderful matching of Fred Astaire and Ginger Rogers, exquisite because, as Katherine Hepburn said, 'Astaire gave Rogers class and she gave him sex appeal'. In education differentiation is about creating the closest matching between activities and the capabilities of children.

Differentiation is a planned process of organisation and intervention in the classroom to help to ensure that school work is well matched to the individual characteristics of pupils. It is a whole-school issue relevant to pupils of all abilities. It involves using a range of teaching and learning styles which can build on the interests and experiences of all pupils in the class; matching tasks to the learning needs of pupils; linking planning, learning, teaching and assessment into a cycle to identify and match tasks to needs; and recognising individual entitlement and access to the National Curriculum (National Curriculum Council, 1993).

Differentiation can be achieved in many ways and some very complex approaches suggesting numerous ways of differentiating can be devised. However, the main ways of differentiating can be brought together in six approaches. These are: differentiation by outcome, task, support, classroom organisation, resources, and extension.

Where differentiation is provided by outcome, the whole class may be engaged in the same activity. The activity may be open ended, such as a piece of extended writing where pupils could succeed at various levels. The teacher needs to be fully aware of the different levels of ability of pupils and should communicate appropriately high expectations at each level. Care needs to be taken that different expectations do not convey to pupils different senses of personal worth. Where this approach is not carefully planned, different outcomes tend to occur anyway but may well not match the different levels of pupil ability. Because of this, differentiation by outcome has sometimes been misinterpreted as the easiest form which requires no teacher skill and happens by accident. This is far from the truth and planned differentiation by outcome requires the same balance of knowledge about the children and knowledge of the requirements of the subject that other forms of differentiation need.

Tasks may be differentiated so that they are set at different levels of pupil ability according to the teacher's judgement. This implies that the learning outcome is the same or very similar otherwise pupils are simply doing different tasks rather than differentiated tasks. For example, the learning outcome may be learning to spell ten specified words. This is to be assessed by the teacher saying the words and the pupils writing them down, spelled correctly. The differentiated tasks would be set according to the different abilities of pupils. Some pupils might look at the list of words and try to memorise each one. Some pupils could finger trace each word several times before writing it. In each case the learning outcome is the same but the task undertaken to achieve it is different and matched to the pupils' abilities.

Differentiation by support involves giving some pupils more attention than others in a particular lesson. This is usually taken to mean adult support rather than the support of pupils for their peers. These adults may be the class teacher, a support teacher, classroom assistant, parent or a student teacher. Where the class teacher gives the support, the pupils who are not receiving the support may be given self-sustaining tasks. These should be challenging activities but ones that tend not to require teacher help. This aspect of the planning needs careful thought otherwise 'self-sustaining' can become a euphemism for easy (or for colouring in).

It takes considerable skill to give support to a main group, characteristic of literacy hour organisation, and maintain awareness of the other pupils so as to be able to give them occasional help as required. Planning is crucial for many reasons. For instance, the more demanding pupils may learn to get the lion's share of teacher time, for example by being disruptive. Planning will reveal that such issues have to be addressed but will indicate that the most effective way is not by giving unplanned attention to a pupil who is being disruptive, which will reinforce the difficult behaviour.

Differentiation by organisation involves grouping pupils according to their prior learning on a particular aspect of learning. This may involve the setting of a whole-year group for perhaps mathematics or English lessons or the grouping of pupils within a classroom for a particular lesson. Grouping in this way allows the teacher or others to teach the same thing to a number of pupils for at least part of the lesson. It also allows group work, with pupils working with others whose level of understanding of the tasks is similar.

Differentiation by resources takes place when the teacher uses particular resources for some pupils to support their learning. The resources may range from a pencil grip to assist fine motor control, to suitable computer software. If resources are simply being rotated around several groups because there are insufficient resources for the whole class to use at one time, this is not differentiation by resources. It is not catering for pupils with different needs, only a strategy for sharing out resources over a period of time.

Differentiation by extension involves giving an extension task over and above what is undertaken by others to certain pupils. Extension refers to an extension of the pupil not to an extension of the time allowed for a task. It is important therefore that the pupils who are required to complete the extension task are made aware of what is expected of them and that they are expected to complete the main task and the extension task in the same time that the other pupils complete only the main task. Differentiation by extension may be seen also as differentiation by pace of writing.

The interaction of different types of differentiation in the same lesson may be complex, further emphasising the need for planning. Differentiated tasks may be carried out in different groups so that differentiation by organisation complements differentiation by task. One of the groups may be given more support than others, therefore adding differentiation by support.

Planning for differentiation takes place at all levels. At whole-school level the school's aims may include equality of access to the curriculum to which differentiation makes a contribution. Also at whole-school level such issues as setting for certain lesson is decided, approaches to differentiation may be mapped out in a policy, and the resources necessary may be decided. Yearly planning will involve deciding how certain requirements of the curriculum can best be delivered, including differentiated approaches. In each classroom planning is vital so that the teacher is able to respond to pupil differences.

Provision for differentiation will be incorporated in yearly, termly, half-termly, weekly and daily planning. It will be particularly helpful where planning specifies learning outcomes because it is on the basis of the pupil's progress that future differentiation is built. Teacher assessment, recording and reporting all feed into the process of differentiation. This will include individual education plans for pupils with special educational needs.

The Government (Department for Education and Employment, 1997) is keen to see more examples of particular forms of differentiation, including target grouping, fast tracking and accelerated learning.

Target grouping involves grouping pupils by ability for part of the week. Groups are not static but are changed according to the results of regular assessments. Fast tracking involves encouraging pupils to learn and to take qualifications in advance of their age peers. Accelerated learning enables pupils to progress faster and with greater understanding.

Schools should:

- ensure that all staff are aware of and are competent in differentiation by outcome, task, support, classroom organisation, resources, and extension
- plan carefully for differentiation at whole-school and classroom levels
- consider structural approaches to differentiation such as fast tracking.

References

Bearne, E. (ed.) (1996) *Differentiation and Diversity in the Primary School*, London, Routledge.

Department for Education and Employment (1997) *Excellence in Schools*, London, DfEE.

National Curriculum Council (1993) *An Introduction to Teaching Geography at Key Stages 1 and 2*, National Curriculum Council In-service Education and Training Resources, London, NCC.

Direct teaching

Some strengths and weaknesses

Leaving a New York hotel, Noel Coward was approached by an over-eager admirer. The woman cried, 'You remember me. I met you with Douglas Fairbanks'. Coward responded, 'Madam, I don't even remember Douglas Fairbanks'. But few could be more direct than Arthur Wellesley, Duke of Wellington, the 'Iron Duke' . A fawning man who had been presented to him had said, 'This is the proudest moment of my life my lord'. Wellesley's reply was, 'Don't be a fool sir'. Such directness, while unpleasant for the recipient, is refreshing in a world where so much is oblique. Direct teaching therefore starts with the advantage of being positively named.

Among the observations of the Office for Standards in Education when considering the teaching of reading (Office for Standards in Education, 1996) and the teaching of number (1997) was that there was insufficient effective use of direct teaching. Direct teaching is also known as direct instruction or the didactic method.

Direct teaching may be used with small groups but is often associated with whole-class teaching. As such, it may be seen as one of the ways of teaching, along with group work and individual work. The main features of individual, group and class work have been outlined by Pollard (1997). Individual work is seen as useful in developing the ability to work independently and autonomously. Group work (see Group work: learning together) can develop social and language skills and can extend learning through its social setting. Class work is seen as useful for starting and ending the day, for administrative matters such as registration, for introducing work, directly teaching, extending work and reviewing progress.

It is suitable for activities which contribute towards a feeling of belonging to a class. These include class discussions and debates, singing, drama, parachute games, circle time and many more. The feeling of corporate identity can contribute to raising self esteem and the general security of the child.

It may involve a significant amount of teacher talk, but this can be balanced by ensuring that children are encouraged to speak too and are listened to with respect by the teacher and other children.

With direct teaching, the teacher is involved pro-actively, not only when pupils are stuck. There is regular interaction with pupils and perceptive questioning of them by the teacher. The teacher is quick to recognise any misconceptions which the pupils may have and give direct and useful help.

Direct teaching need not be associated with simply telling the child what she or he would learn more effectively by finding out for themselves. Such a view misses the subtleties of direct teaching and the skilful use of questioning which can lead the child to make information and ideas their own and not simply soak in without question what the teacher says.

The strengths and weaknesses of direct teaching may be considered by comparing it with individual teaching. One approach to individual teaching is the use of published schemes of work. The advantage of a scheme, let us say a mathematics scheme, is that it offers a range of work matched to pupils' ability. Thirty pupils can be working at their own pace and in their own way on the scheme. The teacher is available to step in and help individual children as they need it.

A disadvantage of this approach is that it can be difficult for the teacher to call the class together for a common lesson in any meaningful way because so many pupils are working on different tasks. Pupils tend not to talk to each other or to the teacher except when they are in difficulty. There tends to be an over-emphasis on the written word and speaking and listening tend to be reduced. Consequently, opportunities to consolidate understanding and extend it through comment and discussion are diminished.

Furthermore, the pupils who respond best to group and class co-operation may have less opportunity to join in any corporate work. They may continue to work in relative isolation to their peers, possibly at a much slower pace than they would if given the opportunity to share and discuss. It is important, of course, to discuss the aspects of a subject which are understood and enjoyed and not just the parts where there is difficulty. Another issue with published individually used schemes is that it is very difficult for the teacher to know if a pupil is working at a pace which is appropriately challenging for him or her.

In contrast, direct teaching involves the whole class or groups within it. It gives the teacher the opportunity to set the pace of a lesson and ensure that it is fittingly brisk. The pace is of course modified if it becomes clear that pupils are failing to grasp key points. Such teaching generally ensures a better pace than the individual working through a scheme. There are schemes which are intended to avoid such disadvantages and which, when followed with discretion, avoid the disadvantages of a separated class of individual learners.

One possible structure is to use the beginning of the lesson to directly teach the whole class. The main part of the lesson may involve group or individual work but on a common theme. There would be a manageable number of groups and all of the groups would be doing the same curriculum subject. The end of the lesson would be an opportunity to draw together the work that different groups may have been doing and to reinforce some main teaching and learning points that the lesson sought to get across. This model is the basis of the literacy hour.

Direct teaching does not have to involve the teacher dominating the talking. The class should be very actively involved and their involvement should be providing for the teacher the constant feedback which will enable him or her to modify the planned lesson as necessary to ensure that the learning objectives are achieved. This is formative assessment in action.

Where whole-class direct teaching is taking place it is important that the role of classroom assistants is made clear. The assistant may help in setting high standards of behaviour through the occasional quiet word with a child who is off task. The assistant may quietly reinterpret what has been said by the teacher to a child who may have missed a teaching point. But above all, the classroom assistant is an integral part of the lesson, not merely a passive spectator.

Planning should be shared and it should be clear to the assistant what her/his task is in the main part of the lesson. Not only should the activity be clear but the learning outcome which is expected of the pupils with whom the assistant is working should be plain.

Direct teaching may involve the teacher using concrete objects to aid learning and encouraging children to learn from handling objects and materials. The use of direct teaching can successfully follow sessions of more concrete work and can help consolidate such work in a more abstract form.

Direct teaching is best considered for its fitness for purpose along with other demonstrably effective methods of teaching, such as carefully planned and structured guided discovery, paired reading and small group activities. The match of the method of teaching with the content of what is to be taught and the learning needs of children should ensure variety in teaching styles which will be more stimulating for the pupils and more rewarding for the teacher than the over-reliance on one method.

The school should:

- ensure that the concept of direct teaching is fully understood by staff
- encourage its appropriate use along with a range of other successful teaching strategies.

References

Office for Standards in Education (1996) *The Teaching of Reading*, London, OFSTED.
—— (1997) *The Teaching of Number*, OFSTED.
Pollard, A. (1997) *Reflective Teaching in the Primary School: A Handbook for The Classroom Third Edition*, London, Cassell.

Early years

Nursery developments and reception classes

For Edmund Burke, good order was the foundation of all things. In education, the bedrock of later achievement is provision for pupils in the early years. Recognising the importance of nursery education the previous Conservative government, and subsequently the Labour government elected in 1997, promised a free nursery place for every child of 4 years old whose parents wish it.

'Desirable outcomes' for children's learning (School Curriculum and Assessment Authority, 1996) have been established as goals for learning for children by the time they enter compulsory education (which begins the term after the child's fifth birthday). These imply particular foci for teaching in the nursery. The desirable outcomes relate to language and literacy, mathematics, knowledge and understanding of the world, physical development, and creative development. Desirable outcomes are intended to provide a foundation for Key Stage 1 of the National Curriculum. An important principle is that effective partnership between each setting and home should be developed as fully as possible.

The influence of this document in schools is to help ensure that the teacher keeps in view the learning outcomes of the children. As these are monitored, it becomes possible to seek reasons when children are not achieving as well as the average or not progressing as expected. These reasons will help provide the strategies to ensure that early support is given and that early success in education is provided wherever possible. An inspection system has been set up by the Office for Standards in Education (OFSTED) to monitor nursery provision (in non-school settings) which complements the inspection of school nurseries through the school inspection system.

David Blunkett, when shadow education and employment secretary, in a speech to the 'Excellence in the Early Years' Conference in London in January 1997, set out a six-point plan for family learning. These initiatives were intended to support parents in getting their child off to a good educational start.

1   Developments would build on the home start programme to support the early educational development of young children in disadvantaged communities. Learning materials would be developed for volunteers to use with parents, for example to develop literacy skills through play.
2   Retired members of the community ('foster grandparents') would link up with young children and their families.
3   Health visitors would give advice on early child development and make learning materials available for new parents.
4   As part of a revised National Curriculum, parenting skills would be taught in secondary schools.
5   Nursery education for 4-year-olds would be developed through local partnerships between public, voluntary and private sector providers. There would be free places for all 4-year-olds.
6   The pilot programme of 25 Early Excellence Centres (EEC) would help to stimulate the development of integrated facilities and raise standards in their areas. Each EEC would combine nursery education and child care, adult education, parenting classes and wider family services and training opportunities for local providers.

Peter Moss, a researcher at the Thomas Coram Research Unit, London University, speaking at the same conference, presented a vision as part of which five areas needed particular attention. The first three of these were a national early years policy, a legal framework, and a funding base which was coherent, equitable, assured and adequate. Fourth, there should be staffing and training which would involve the introduction of a new qualification as an early childhood teacher trained to work with children from 0 to 6 years old in a multi-functional service. Finally, there should be a national development fund to create at least one 'model' early years service in each local authority area, and new models of school-based early years provision as alternatives to nursery classes.

In the Government White Paper, *Excellence in Schools* (Department for Education and Employment, 1997a), early years are the concern of the chapter, 'A sound beginning'. The government intends to offer:

• early years education alongside child care and family learning 'where appropriate'
• assessment of children when they start primary school
• smaller infant classes
• a national programme to raise numeracy and literacy standards and develop positive attitudes to learning.

Each local authority has been required to set up an Early Years Forum with local private and voluntary providers. It represents the range of providers and users of early years education. The forum draws up early years development plans. The initial focus is on how to achieve the aim of offering a school place to every 4-year-old whose parent wish for one. The plans show how co-operation between private nurseries, voluntary pre-schools and play groups and schools can best meet the needs of parents and children. To support these initiatives, it is proposed to focus on staff training and qualifications including early years training for qualified teachers; and having common standards of regulation and inspection.

The 'Desirable Learning Outcomes' (School Curriculum and Assessment Authority, 1996) were recognised as providing national standards for early years education. The National Framework for baseline assessment published by the then Schools Curriculum and Assessment Authority (SCAA) would enable schools and local education authorities (LEAs) to use schemes which met the SCAA requirements.

Class sizes for 5-, 6- and 7-year-olds are to be reduced to 30 or below before the year 2002. This was to involve working closely with LEAs and schools to ensure that this was managed smoothly. LEAs would draw up action plans to show how these reductions would be achieved to meet the government target. The abolition of the Assisted Places Scheme (by which financial support was given to enable certain pupils to attend independent schools) is intended to release funds to help achieve the class reductions.

Raising standards in literacy and numeracy would be achieved through the setting of national targets in literacy and numeracy and through a national literacy strategy and a numeracy strategy. There would be a sharper focus on literacy and numeracy in the curriculum. The training provided for all primary teachers is intended to help raise the standards of literacy for all pupils.

The White Paper recognised the importance of involving parents and that the best early years centres offer support and learning opportunities for parents to learn beside their children. Such parental learning may be provided as workshops to teach parents how best to support their children's learning, or parental language classes for those for whom English is an additional language.

By 1998, some progress had been made towards achieving the government's policy objectives for nursery education. For example, in March 1998, the government launched a consultation paper on the 'Regulations of Early Education and Day Care', aiming to create a more uniform regulatory regime for all early years settings, including reception classes, providing nursery education and day care. By 1998, all LEAs had an Early Years Development Partnership in place (previously referred to as the Early Years Forum). By mid-1998, some 148 LEAs had Early Years Development Plans in place which showed how every 4-year-old in their area would have access to a good quality nursery place by September 1998. (As they develop, plans will also set targets for the expansion of places for 3-year-olds and consider how other services such as child care and family support services can be integrated.) The QCA had been asked to work with National Training Organisations to establish a clear, comprehensive framework of training and qualifications for the early years and play-work sectors which would enable workers to add to their skills and progress in their chosen careers. The QCA also undertook to review the desirable learning outcomes.

The Government Green Paper *Excellence for All Children* (Department for Education and Employment, 1997b) takes a similar view of the importance of early years. Early intervention and early identification of special educational needs is seen as important and economical. Of course, the early identification of SEN is not restricted to identification in the early years, as difficulties can emerge when the child is older. Early intervention may save more intensive and more expensive intervention later on. Multi-agency support for children with special educational needs was to be a priority in the government's pilot programme for early excellence centres.

The school should:

- establish practical strategies for productively involving parents, and monitor the effectiveness of these in enhancing the child's education
- monitor progress in relation to desirable learning outcomes so that focused early intervention can take place if necessary where progress is slow
- co-operate with private nurseries, pre-schools and play groups (and others) in clearly specified and practical ways which have tangible benefits for the education of children (for example shared training).

References

Department for Education and Employment (1997a) *Excellence in Schools*, London, DfEE.
—— (1997b) *Excellence for All Children: Meeting Special Educational Needs*, London, DfEE.
School Curriculum and Assessment Authority (1996) *Nursery Education: Desirable Outcomes for Children's Learning on Entering Compulsory Education*, London, SCAA.

Address

Under Fives Policy Development Team, Department for Education and Employment, Sanctuary Buildings, Great Smith Street, Westminster, London SW1P 3BT, tel: 0171 925 5203, fax: 0171 925 5079.

Efficiency of the school and how it may be improved

'There are only two qualities in the world,' said George Bernard Shaw, 'efficiency and inefficiency; and only two sorts of people; the efficient and the inefficient.' The focus on the concept of 'efficiency' is relatively recent in primary school management, having been encouraged by developments such as the Local Management of Schools (LMS). Efficiency has been brought into particular prominence by the Office for Standards in Education (OFSTED) inspection system.

The Office for Standards in Education (1995) provides a useful framework from which the efficiency of a school in the primary sector can be judged. It starts from the premise that an efficient school makes good use of all its resources to achieve the best educational outcomes for all its pupils. In doing this, the school provides excellent value for money.

Inspectors evaluate the efficiency and effectiveness with which resources made available to the school are managed. This includes the use made of specific grants and the allocation and use of money for pupils with special educational needs. The inspectors must also evaluate the extent to which the school provides value for money.

Judgements are to be made according to the extent to which staff, accommodation and learning resources are effectively used, financial control and school administration are efficient and careful financial planning supports educational developments. Value for money judgements are made about the educational standards achieved and quality of education provided in relation to the school's context and income.

Regarding effective use of staff, accommodation and learning resources, this includes the deployment of support staff for pupils with special educational needs and for pupils for whom English is an additional language. This will take into consideration any staff funded through particular grants.

Turning to efficient finance and school administration, schools should refer to the document *Keeping Your Balance: Standards for Financial Administration in Schools* (Office for Standards in Education/ Audit Commission, 1996). Financial administration needs to be sound and should occupy the minimum of management time while ensuring that information is available to governors and the head teacher and that finances are in good order. Administrative procedures should be flexible, support the aims of the school and lead to efficient day-to-day organisation.

Educational development should be supported through careful financial planning. A key factor in ensuring this is the management of the budget. To manage budgets effectively, schools need to be aware of the present sources of their income and of potential sources of income, and plan and monitor expenditure in the most transparent way possible.

Governing bodies have responsibility for oversight of financial management. It is important therefore that governors ensure that the school is able to account for any expenditure to which it is committed, budgets systematically for new expenditure, and regularly analyses the use of resources.

The school should list clearly the income from all sources. This will include the delegated local management formula budget share (for community schools). Foundation schools will not receive an annual maintenance grant but funding based on a replication of Local Management for Schools (LMS). Also included will be Standards Fund income, Single Regeneration Budget, Section 11 schemes and other sources. All funding for special educational needs should be clearly set out. Brief annotation could explain anything that was not immediately apparent from the figures and headings.

The main elements of a school's expenditure will be on staffing, learning resources, curriculum, premises and services. Central to the task of ensuring that educational developments are supported by financial planning is a clear school development plan in which developments are costed and allocated a time for completion. Although most of the expenditure may go on items like staffing, there should be careful consideration of the structure and deployment of staff and alternative staffing arrangements should be considered and appraised. In other areas, there is likely to be more flexibility and the school should be able to demonstrate that it has considered alternative ways of achieving its educational aims. For example the use of alternative equipment should be considered before it is decided to purchase a set of materials.

The touchstone of efficiency will be the way and the degree to which spending is reasonably expected to improve educational outcomes such as attainment, progress and attitudes to learning. The school development plan will cover the coming year in detail and subsequent years in less detail and will normally embrace three to five years ahead.

Once decisions about expenditure have been taken, particularly if large sums are involved, there should be an assessment of how effective the expenditure has been in improving educational outcomes. Did the new mathematics scheme raise achievement? Did the approach to behaviour management raise the standard of behaviour?

Developments in the support of literacy and numeracy are attracting resources to schools in the form of specific funding for books, training and other support. The efficiency of the way in which this funding is used should be carefully monitored.

It is important that the funding for special education can be shown to be going directly to the pupils concerned. Also the Standards Fund must demonstrably be spent for the purposes for which it is intended. It may be useful to imagine the budget is to be shown as partial evidence to someone who begins with the conviction that the school is not spending earmarked money as it should. The budget should clearly and unequivocally demonstrate that this is not so.

If the socio-economic circumstances of pupils are unfavourable and the attainment of pupils on entry are low, yet pupil attainment and progress, attitudes, behaviour and personal development, and quality of education is high and the unit cost is average, the school will be providing very good value for money. If on the other hand the socio-economic circumstances of pupils are favourable and the attainment of pupils on entry is high, yet pupil attainment and progress, attitudes, behaviour and personal development, and quality of education is low and the unit cost is high, the school will be providing very poor value for money.

A sometimes overlooked way of increasing the efficiency of the school is through networking and the resulting pooling of resources – human, physical, and in terms of time. Networking has many meanings but here it is taken to be the forming of close and mutually beneficial relationships between schools in the primary sector through regular contact in order to improve efficiency.

For some independent pre-preparatory schools and preparatory schools, networking is nothing new. Also, for LEA schools, with their comparative independence brought about by LMS developments and other factors, networking is also important.

In order to share and therefore use professional expertise more economically, schools can arrange joint training or can arrange time outside school for particular members of staff such as a specified subject co-ordinator to attend professional groups with colleagues from other schools. So called 'cluster' groups are formed by head teachers to discuss, support and share their work.

Yet, where networking has not been harnessed to improve efficiency, it is still not difficult to find several schools perhaps only a short distance apart developing similar policies, unaware that nearby their work is being duplicated. In such cases much work can be saved if the work is shared or developed jointly. Of course, in developing something like a policy, it is important that staff in a particular school contribute to it, discuss it and feel that the policy is theirs. Even allowing for this it is still feasible to jointly draft a first discussion document which each school could then mould in its own way.

Curriculum development is another example where the initial

documentation is likely to be similar for many schools. So why not arrange for the relevant subject co-ordinators from several schools to meet and prepare a joint initial document pooling their expertise? This again could be distinctively developed by the individual schools.

Physical resources can be jointly bought and shared according to written agreements. The use of facilities can be shared or traded for the use of the facilities in another school. For example, a school with a swimming pool can trade sessions in this for sessions in another school's basketball court where each school lacks the facilities of the other.

As part of the process of benchmarking, target setting and the sharing of best practice, all imported from business, the use of networking is paramount. Schools which are 'statistical neighbours' will want to network to learn from each other. At the centre of the networking hub will be the school which has several similar statistical neighbours and which performs better than these in terms of reaching high standards.

Where such a school is some distance from others, visits may be possible but the use of information and communications technology should help ensure that contact and sharing documents and ideas is realistic.

Perhaps recent trends have been towards competition among schools but the power of co-operation to increase efficiency should not be overlooked.

Schools should:

- use networks to avoid duplicating work which can be shared with other schools
- share resources where practicable to maximise their use
- develop efficiency through co-operation with statistical neighbours.

References

Office for Standards in Education (1995) *The OFSTED Handbook: Guidance on the Inspection of Nursery and Primary Schools*, London, HMSO.
Office for Standards in Education/Audit Commission (1996) *Keeping Your Balance*, London, OFSTED/AC.

Address

Management Unit (4R), Standards and Effectiveness Unit, Department for Education and Employment, Sanctuary Buildings, Great Smith Street, Westminster, London SW1P 3BT, tel: 0171 925 6458, fax: 0171 925 6001.

Emotional and behavioural difficulties

'Difficulties' is a tame word. This is reflected in Prime Minister Harold Macmillan's ironic comments about the resignation of treasury ministers, 'I thought the best thing to do was to settle up these little local difficulties, and then to turn to the wider vision of the Commonwealth'. Certainly, the word 'difficulties' hardly conveys the severity and complexities of some levels of emotional and behavioural disturbance. Emotional and behavioural difficulties (EBD) refer to a range of difficulties including neurosis, anti-social behaviour and, very rarely, in residential special provision, psychosis.

The *Code of Practice on the Identification and Assessment of Special Educational Needs* (Department for Education, 1994a) considers that pupils with EBD have a learning difficulty as defined by the Education Act 1996. The learning difficulty may be seen as children having not 'learned', in the very broadest sense, accepted personal, emotional and social development. Also, general learning including school studies tends to be inhibited by EBD. This may be for instance because the child is disruptive or absents him- or herself from school, or because he or she has difficulty concentrating.

Children with EBD may disrupt the education of others, although some children with EBD may be overly quiet and withdrawn. Among the factors associated with EBD are neglect or abuse, physical or mental illness, sensory or physical impairment or physical trauma. EBD may be associated with other forms of learning difficulty. For example, a child with EBD may also have moderate learning difficulties.

The range of educational settings associated with EBD is wide as *Circular 9/ 94: The Education of Children with Emotional and Behavioural Difficulties* (Department for Education, 1994b) indicates. The document covers:

* school-based provision and assessment in ordinary schools (the Code of Practice stages 1 to 3)
* the subsequent stages and provision and assessment in ordinary schools (the Code of Practice stages 4 and 5)
* special schools

- residential provision for pupils with statements of special educational needs (SEN)
- children and young people requiring psychiatric care.

The Government Green Paper *Excellence for All Children: Meeting Special Educational Needs* seeks to exemplify the policies and action proposed throughout the Green Paper for children with EBD.

The government aims to shift resources over time from remedial action to preventive work. It argues that there needs to be the closest co-operation between the education service and other agencies, and co-ordinated action at school, local and national level. Foundations of an overall strategy include:

- early identification and intervention, with schools and other agencies working with the families of children with EBD
- effective behaviour policies in schools and local education authorities (LEAs)
- a range of specialist support to meet the varied needs of pupils within this broad group.

The National Advisory Group on Special Educational Needs (SEN) has set up a sub-group to examine ways of improving provision for pupils with EBD.

The government believes that its policies for improving performance in basic skills and for working with parents should 'help to forestall the emergence of EBD in many children who might develop EBD as a consequence of early failure at school'. The government proposed to support the development and wider dissemination of the number of assessment techniques already in use.

The framework of the SEN *Code of Practice on the Identification and Assessment of Special Educational Needs* (Department for Education and Employment, 1994) helps schools to tackle children's behaviour problems in a systematic way. For children with more complex difficulties, intervention in the primary years is important, using collaborative approaches with key roles for social services departments, health authorities and parents. The Department for Education and Employment (DfEE) and the Department of Health will work together to establish a national programme of early intervention projects for nursery and primary age children identified as having EBD.

Such approaches are important but it is unlikely that short term intervention will be successful in all cases. Financial and other resources for longer term support will also be necessary. Also, EBD sometimes confounds intervention with young children. It may arise in adolescence, for example, precipitated by family circumstances. Or the child may have exhibited violent behaviour as a young child which was physically manageable while the child was small but which became increasingly difficult to contain as the child grew older, larger and stronger.

The policies on inclusion (see 'Inclusion: ideology or pragmatism?') present schools with a particular challenge. The government will consider how to promote good practice in providing for EBD in mainstream schools, drawing on a project being carried out by the University of Birmingham. What should not be overlooked in this is the whole-school effect that a good special school has on pupils with EBD. Such a school is more than the simple accumulation of the approaches used there. There is a whole-school containment both physical and psychological in the best special schools.

The Qualifications and Curriculum Authority (QCA) is carrying out a project exploring curriculum factors leading to the exclusion of children with EBD. In some cases schools and LEAs should consider establishing in-school units.

By April 1998, LEAs had to prepare behaviour support plans setting out arrangements for the education of children with behavioural difficulties, including those with SEN. Effective co-ordination between local agencies should ensure that behaviour support plans dovetail with Children's Service Plans and other activities such as the work of the proposed Youth Offender Teams on Final Warnings.

It has been proposed to promote SEN issues in initial, induction and in-service training, and within the framework of behaviour support plans. LEAs will set out the training available to help staff manage pupil behaviour more effectively. Government will seek to ensure that the development of training for specialist staff working with EBD is a priority in proposed regional arrangements.

Where difficulties are severe, children may need to be educated outside mainstream schools, perhaps in a residential setting. The regional planning mechanisms are intended to aid the match between provision and needs. The aim should be for children to return to mainstream as soon as they are ready. It is proposed that EBD special schools begin to provide support to mainstream schools. This may be appropriate in some instances. But it would be naive to think that the provision offered in a good special school for pupils with EBD can simply be lifted out of the setting as a set of skills and techniques.

The DfEE will run workshops, with the support of the Office for Standards in Education (OFSTED), on effective practice in EBD schools. The government intends to build on these workshops to develop a programme of consultancy support to EBD special schools.

Two aspects of government intentions aimed mainly at secondary-age pupils may have some application to primary-age pupils with EBD. First, there could be wider use of pupil referral units with expertise in aspects of EBD provision to work in partnership with schools regarding exclusions.

Second, the QCA is studying how to make the National Curriculum more accessible to students with EBD.

Whatever the developments that emerge from the Green Paper, there is already a strong body of practice to draw on in relation to pupils with EBD.

Various forms of therapeutic approaches may form part of the provision. These may include counselling, psychotherapy, play therapy, behaviour therapy, art therapy, music therapy or drama therapy. Aspects of the curriculum which allow expression can be beneficial; these include music, drama and role play, physical education, dance and art.

One approach which can refreshingly encourage teachers and others to avoid thinking in terms of EBD being within the child is an ecosystemic approach. In this perspective, the child's behaviour is seen as a result of interactions between a set of 'systems'.

These systems are:

• the child him- or herself
• the child, the teacher and the classroom group
• the child and his or her relationship with the whole school, parents and external agencies
• the child in relation to the cultural, social and educational beliefs of society.

Difficult behaviour occurs when there is a dysfunction between these systems. Productive and positive interactions between teacher and pupil, and between school and parents benefit the whole system. Co-operation between professionals is imperative.

The school should ensure that:

• it is the appropriate venue for the child's education
• a full assessment of the needs of the child informs provision
• a pragmatic view is taken as to whether provision is in a special school or an ordinary school
• any other learning difficulties are assessed and addressed
• partnership with parents is sought even with parents who may be unable or unwilling to support the child.

(See also the chapter: 'Inclusion: ideology or pragmatism?'.)

References

Department for Education (1994a) *Code of Practice on the Identification and Assessment of Special Educational Needs*, London, DfE.
—— (1994b) *Circular 9/194: The Education of Children with Emotional and Behavioural Difficulties*, London, DfE.

Department for Education and Employment (1997a) *Excellence in Schools*, London, DfEE.
—— (1997) *Excellence for All Children: Meeting Special Educational Needs*, London, DfEE.

Address

Association of Workers for Children with Emotional and Behavioural Difficulties, Charleton Court, Maidstone, Kent ME17 3DQ, tel: 01622 843 104, fax: 01622 844 220.

English as an additional Language (EAL)

Guidelines and confusions

Even for those fluent in the English language, there are unforeseen pitfalls. Television presenter MacDonald Hobley, introducing Sir Stafford Cripps, Chancellor of the Exchequer, turned to the camera and intoned, 'Sir Stifford Crapps'. The infelicitous quotations from *Punch* magazine illustrated the banana skins waiting for those who sought to quote 'Literature' with an imperfect knowledge, as when a dinner guest smilingly thanked his host by drawing on Othello, saying, 'I have eaten wisely but not too well'.

But for those children for whom English is an additional language, great skill and care is needed to develop their skills and confidence.

The Schools Curriculum and Assessment Authority (SCAA) (1996) offered guidelines and a framework to help schools carry out an audit of provision for teaching EAL. To underpin such work, five principles are provided:

- developing whole school policies
- fully using the National Curriculum programmes of study
- ensuring effective teaching and planning
- using resources to meet individual needs
- linking outcomes from different types of assessment.

The guidelines develop each of these principles as follows.

Whole-school policies for teaching EAL should be founded on a sound knowledge of pupils' needs and attainments. A way of achieving this is a manageable audit of such information as previous schooling, educational history, literacy in another language, the extent to which English is understood and spoken at home; and (where appropriate) length of residence in the United Kingdom. This information would inform the planning of teaching and help to assess progress. Policies should include ways of monitoring the effectiveness of the overall provision.

Pupils learning EAL are entitled to the National Curriculum programmes of study to the same degree as other children and all their teachers have responsibility for teaching English as well as the subject content of other

The three common requirements of the National Curriculum orders concern access to the programme of study, the use of ... and the use of information technology. These have particular ... ce for pupils for whom English is an additional language. For some ... vers the access statements mean that materials from earlier key ... ay be selected in ways suitable for the ability of the pupils. The ... of spoken and written English needs to be embedded in the ... and learning of the subject content. Communication in all subjects ... nclude the use of electronic media.

... achers should organise and structure lessons appropriately and use ... e in a way which supports and stimulates developments in English to meet the particular needs of pupils for whom English is an additional language. This applies to all staff involved in teaching, instruction, or providing support for learning. Effective planning when teaching EAL includes:

- involving in planning and review sessions bilingual staff, Section 11 staff and (where they are appropriately involved) special educational needs assistants
- ensuring a range of language experiences
- making use of information technology and text on screen to support the individual pupil's development in English.

Using written resources effectively in the classroom includes providing a range of materials to offer different points of access to a topic and the use of good quality dual language materials where they are available. Talk in the classroom is effective when, among other things, key language features are identified in lesson planning, and the teacher paraphrases into English to indicate alternative ways of expressing the same meaning. Writing in the classroom is effective when certain features exist, such as when the purpose of the writing is made clear to pupils, and when opportunities and support are given for writing extended texts in English.

The resources of the school should be organised and deployed to support the teaching of EAL. Plans should show how learning targets for pupils are to be achieved and should identify the financial commitments necessary.

The assessment policy of the school should link two assessments. These are statutory assessments and any additional assessments of a pupil's acquisition of English. This should provide accurate recognition of pupils' attainments, progress and needs.

The SCAA guidelines offer sound advice and deserve to be consulted in full. However, two issues can cause particular concern for schools: trying to determine whether a pupil who has EAL has special educational needs, and whether it would be appropriate to concentrate more on teaching English at the expense of a broader and more balanced curriculum.

The definition of special educational needs as expressed in the Education Act 1996 is as follows:

> A child has 'special educational needs'...if he [sic] has a learning difficulty which calls for special educational provision to be made for him.
>
> A child has a learning difficulty if he [sic] has: 'a significantly greater difficulty in learning than the majority of children of his age' or has 'a disability which either prevents or hinders him from making use of educational facilities of a kind generally provided for children of his age in schools within the area of the local education authority'.

The Act is careful to distinguish pupils for whom English is an additional language. A child must not be taken as having a learning difficulty, 'solely because the language (or form of language) in which he is, or will be, taught is different from a language (or form of language) which has at any time been spoken in his home'.

Staff who work with pupils with special educational needs should understand the role of staff who work supporting pupils for whom English is an additional language, and vice versa. There will be times when these staff will need to work particularly closely together when a pupil for whom English is an additional language also has special educational needs. Individual assessment of pupils' needs will be used carefully to establish the degree of overlap between the areas of special educational needs and EAL.

Care needs to be taken that more able pupils for whom English is an additional language are assessed and the appropriate provision made for them which will sufficiently challenge them.

In assessments, including national tests and tasks, it should be ensured that the necessary steps are taken to ensure that the pupil's full ability is being recognised.

In restricting the breadth and balance of a curriculum, one reduces the opportunities for pupils to learn language which is particular to certain subjects. Some of these words have distinctive meanings from the same word used in an every day sense. So, for example, a pupil learns that the word 'area' has several meanings including a mathematical and a geographical one.

Other subjects will give many opportunities to practice and understand general terms which happen also to be the currency of the subject. In history, for instance, words such as before, after, past, present, recent and ancient will tend to be used frequently.

In some subjects, such as science, opportunities to use third person language are offered. These will need to be explicitly taught and are an important part of formal discourse.

Art, music, physical education and some aspects of mathematics are among subjects which, being less dependent on the English language, can offer opportunities for success and a chance to build self esteem for pupils with EAL.

The learning of a modern foreign language may give the pupil with EAL the opportunity to do well, particularly if the language is the language which the pupil speaks at home. This success can in turn further motivate the pupil to learn English.

Two further points deserve emphasis. First, there may be a discontinuity between the home and school experiences of a child for whom English is an additional language. Therefore, it is particularly important for the school to build on the child's linguistic and cultural background. This includes valuing the child's background and also using that background as an educational foundation, for example, through the sensitive use of appropriate materials.

Second, a child's first language should be acknowledged where possible. A strong grounding in a first language tends to enhance learning in the second language, for example, because the understanding of concepts transfers across languages.

To improve their provision for pupils for whom English is an additional language schools should:

- develop whole-school policies
- fully use the National Curriculum programmes of study and consider particularly carefully the benefits of a broad curriculum
- ensure effective teaching and planning
- use resources to meet individual needs
- link outcomes from different types of assessment
- avoid confusing pupils who have English as an additional language with those who have special educational needs
- value the child's linguistic and cultural background.

References

Schools Curriculum and Assessment Authority (1996) *Teaching English as an Additional Language: A Framework for Policy*, London, SCAA.

Address

National Association for Language Development in the Curriculum (NALDIC), S-W Herts LCSC, Holywell JMI School Site, Tolpits Lane, Watford, Herts WD1 8NT, tel: 01923 231 855, fax: 01923 225 130.

Equal opportunities
Beyond the platitudes

Many memorable incidents in the past have hinged upon social or other distinctions. The actor Donald Woolfit's ceremonial obeisance after a performance before provincial audiences was probably tinged with inverted snobbery. To take another example, a universe of social stratification lay behind Rebecca West's comment that a man she knew was, 'Every other inch a gentleman'.

Yet in a society that seeks to be increasingly a meritocracy, the notion of equal opportunity is widely accepted although it often means different things to different people. It can be little more than platitudes to some, a sort of politically correct mantra. At a more meaningful level, it can refer to the following:

- equality of access, that is, ensuring that people have the same opportunities as are available to others
- equality of outcome, in which there is an attempt to ensure that a particular group (e.g. boys) reach levels of achievement equal to another group (e.g. girls)
- equivalent experience, enabling each person to fulfil their potential
- overcoming limitations on learning and experience owing to earlier experiences of stereotyping.

Clearly, there is not equality of access to the independent school sector. However, many parents are 'first time buyers' and tend to choose schools carefully rather than, for example, always following a family tradition of links with a particular school.

Equality of opportunity in a school will be reflected in a wide range of features: school aims and objectives, policies, staffing structures, curricular plans and organisation, pupil groupings and pupil records and relationships within the school.

That there should be equal opportunities for pupils irrespective of various aspects of their identity is widely accepted. These factors include age, prior attainment, gender, special educational need, social class, ethnic background and speaking English as an additional language. The school should monitor standards of achievement according to these factors to check fair provision. Standards (or outcomes) include pupil achievement, progress, attitudes, behaviour and personal development, and attendance.

Office for Standards in Education inspectors are required to highlight any significant variations in attainment among pupils of different gender, social background or ethnicity (Office for Standards in Education, 1996).

Achievement related to gender concerns the issue of when boys or girls do better than one another in areas of the curriculum, where there is no apparent reason. A school finding significant discrepancies according to gender in, for example, the national test results would want to explore possible reasons why. The school would come up with hypotheses that would seek to bring the achievement of pupils of one gender up to the level of that of the other gender. For example, it might be that the content of the subject was being presented in a way that did not motivate, say, boys as much as girls.

Where social background is found to correlate with poorer performance, the school will want to examine the reasons. Does the content of some subjects appeal to pupils of one social background and not another? Are messages being inadvertently conveyed to pupils of some social backgrounds that less is expected of them or that they are less valued than others? Do the expectations of the school put at a disadvantage pupils of one social background and not another? For example, the expectation that all pupils do homework may disadvantage pupils whose home circumstances are not conducive to homework.

Where ethnicity is perceived to be a factor in lower achievement, the picture is complicated because of the interaction of ethnicity and social class in some cases. For example, if social class is statistically accounted for in comparisons of one ethnic group with another, does the difference in achievement still appear?

Another issue relating to equal opportunities is progress. *The OFSTED Handbook* (Office for Standards in Education, 1996) reminds inspectors that is important to examine the progress of different groups, for instance according to gender or ethnicity. It is recognised that certain schools provide more effectively for some groups of pupils than for others. Any significant variations, and the reasons why they exist, are important. Inspectors also check whether the school monitors the performance of different groups and, if it does, what the data indicates and how the school responds.

Concerning attitudes, behaviour and personal development, equality of opportunity relates to the expectation that for all pupils these standards would be similar irrespective of gender, ethnicity or social background. Where standards of pupil attitudes, behaviour and personal development vary according to equal opportunity factors, the school should look carefully to see if there is any aspect of provision which leads to this. At the same time there are expectations that the provision relating to attitudes, behaviour and personal development fosters the equal valuing of all groups. Inspectors must evaluate and report on pupils' response to the teaching and other provision made by the school. They must highlight strengths and weaknesses as shown by, 'the quality of relationships in the school including the degree of racial harmony, where applicable'.

Attendance is another standard which can be analysed in terms of equal opportunities. Any group discrepancies will require analysing to ensure that provision is not affecting the standards of attendance.

Regarding teaching, the judgements of inspectors about the quality of teaching are based on the extent to which (among other things) teachers use 'methods and organisational strategies which match curricular objectives and the needs of all pupils'. If it appears that methods and organisational strategies are being used which match the needs of some groups of pupils and not others, then these need to be examined.

Turning to the curriculum and assessment, inspectors have to evaluate and report on strengths and weaknesses in various issues. These include the planning and content of the curriculum and the contribution it makes to the educational standards achieved by all pupils, 'taking account of their age, capability, gender, ethnicity, background and special educational need'.

Among the criteria on which judgements are based is the extent to which the curriculum provides equality of access and opportunity for pupils to learn and make progress. Inspectors have to judge how the 'curriculum planning and implementation take account of pupils' age, attainment, gender, ethnicity and competence in English as an additional language or special educational need, through the provision of appropriate teaching methods and materials'. The curriculum 'should respond to the cultural heritage of pupils and promote equality of opportunity', and pupil organisation in class and teaching groups 'should help ensure equality of access and opportunity' (Office for Standards in Education, 1996, p. 77).

In evaluating the quality of leadership and management, inspectors have to determine whether the school has a positive ethos which reflects equality of opportunity for all pupils. The ethos of the school should value the backgrounds of all pupils and should reflect the fact that the school sees the importance of equality of opportunity.

The school's leadership and management should be effective in seeing that policies are formed and implemented to promote equality of opportunity and high achievement for all pupils. There should be a policy on equality of opportunity and this should be reflected in subject policies and other policies. All policies should be focused and practical.

The school should comply with relevant legislation and case law including the Sex Discrimination Act 1975, the Race Relations Act 1976, the Education Acts 1981 and 1986, the Children Act 1989, and the Education Reform Act 1988. (For a summary of these Acts and other legislation see Farrell, Kerry and Kerry, 1996.)

Leadership and management should effectively promote equal access by all pupils to the full range of opportunities for achievement provided by the school. For example, equality of opportunity should be evident in staff distribution and in staffing and management structures. In this way pupils can have relevant role models. For example, in the area of ethnicity, a school which does not have staff whose ethnicity reflects that of pupils may be able to recruit visiting staff from ethnic minority groups so that pupils can see members of their own ethnic group in positions of authority. Equal opportunities for all the staff in the school are important not only for the effect on staff but also for the integrity of the school.

Also, out-of-school visits by pupils and visitors to school can provide opportunities for pupils to see other cultures in a positive light.

The school should :

- define clearly what it means by equal opportunities
- ensure that equal opportunities permeate school aims and objectives, policies, staffing structures, curricular plans and organisation, pupils grouping and pupil records, and relationships within the school
- review equality of opportunity in achievement, progress, attitudes, behaviour and personal development, attendance, the quality of teaching, curriculum and assessment, and leadership and management.

References

Farrell, M., Kerry, T. and Kerry, C. (1996) *The Blackwell Handbook of Education*, Oxford, Blackwell.

Office for Standards in Education (1996) *The OFSTED Handbook: Guidance on the Inspection of Nursery and Primary Schools*, London, HMSO.

Further reading

Equal Opportunities Commission (1991) *Sex Discrimination in Schools: A Guide for Governors*, London, EOC.

—— (1994) *An Equal Start: Guidelines on Equal Treatment for the Under-eights*, London, EOC.

Addresses

Education and Training Unit, Equal Opportunities Commission, Overseas House, Quay Street, Manchester M3 3HN, tel: 0161 838 8285, fax: 0161 835 1657, e-mail: info@eoc.org.uk.

Equal Opportunities Commission (Wales), Windsor House, Windsor Lane, Cardiff CF1 3DE, tel: 01222 343 552, fax: 01222 641 079.

Governing bodies
Clarity about their role

Caricaturing the acrimony that was supposed to exist between two Conservative politicians, Harold Wilson said that whenever Harold Macmillan had been out of the country, his colleague R. A. 'Rab' Butler would meet him at the airport and shake him warmly by the throat. Such a rift has no place in the relationship between head teacher and governors and every effort should be made to ensure that the partnership is as trusting and productive as possible.

But even before the issue of building a close working relationship between the head teacher and the governing body arises, for some schools a more urgent and basic issue presents itself. How can the school recruit committed and competent governors to begin with? Here, unfortunately, there are no easy answers and the schools who already have good governors seem to find it easier to recruit new ones. Yet even from a very low starting point progress can be made.

Writing to all parents and following this up with meetings and individual discussion may be time consuming but often in the longer term reaps rewards. Advertising in the local press or, for community schools, approaching local education authority officers who may be able to help with recruitment can be a good starting point. Local churches and voluntary organisations may be recruiting grounds for potentially good governors.

Governor training is an important aspect of attracting governors who may initially feel diffident. The knowledge that they will receive training to support them in their work will be reassuring. Good quality training also contributes to retaining governors once they are in place. It also increases the competence of governors and therefore their confidence, so that they can tackle educational issues in their meetings. Local education authorities offer governor training to governors as part of the buy-back arrangements for community schools and voluntary controlled schools. In the case of foundation governors of voluntary controlled schools, the Diocesan Authority may provide training. Other organisations provide governor training, for which they charge.

One useful resource for head teachers and governors is *School Governors:*

A Guide to the Law (Department for Education and Employment, 1997). A summary chart in that publication usefully sets out the respective duties of the head teacher and the governing body as regards meetings; the curriculum; religious education and collective worship; special educational needs; finance; staff (teaching and non-teaching); admissions; equal opportunities; discipline and attendance; providing information; inspection; health, safety and welfare; charging for school activities; and the school building.

Guidance on Good Governance (Department for Education and Employment, 1996) provides advice for governing bodies and head teachers. The document has three sections (good practice, who does what, and the main work) and annexes on handling complaints, committees and working parties, and a checklist of information and advice on reports given by the head teacher to the governing body.

It is important that governors are familiar with the legally required policies. Some of the legal requirements apply to all schools while others apply only to certain types of school.

In the case of all schools, governors must ensure that an action plan is written to further develop the school following an inspection of the school by Office for Standards in Education (OFSTED) inspectors. Governors are responsible for a prospectus; a written statement of general principles regarding behaviour and discipline; and for rules and governance procedure on staff discipline. Governors have to provide an annual governor's report to parents. They must have a policy on special educational needs and also a policy on charging.

Policies relating to admissions, the curriculum, health and safety, standing orders and sex education apply in different ways to different types of school.

An admissions policy must be produced for voluntary aided and foundation schools and for community and voluntary controlled schools if the local education authority has transferred responsibility to them.

Regarding the curriculum, governors of community schools, voluntary controlled schools and community special schools have to keep a written statement of their curriculum aims. In the case of foundation schools governors must have a curriculum complaints procedure.

Governors must have a health and safety policy in the case of voluntary aided and foundation schools.

They must make standing orders if their school is a foundation school whose instruments and articles of government were made by Regulations.

Regarding sex education, governors of community, foundation and voluntary aided and voluntary controlled primary schools have to decide whether to include sex education in the curriculum and must keep a written record.

It is important to ensure that governors discuss the main educational issues of the school, including the curriculum and major policies such as those on special educational needs, charging, and others. Some governors may initially feel on stronger ground making judgements on tangible things such as buildings and materials but their views and decisions are necessary in other less tangible areas.

Governors must decide the aims and policies of the school and how standards of education can be improved. This will be done in consultation with the head teacher and as appropriate with the local education authority. They also decide how the school should be run in broad terms.

They will help to draft a school development plan with the head teacher and staff. Governors decide how to spend the school budget. They take due regard of the Local Management of Schools scheme and any powers which they delegate to the head teacher.

The school's governors ensure that the National Curriculum and religious education are taught and they report on the National Curriculum assessments. The governing body selects the head teacher and the deputy head teacher.

The governors appoint, promote, support and discipline other school staff in consultation with the head teacher. They form a link between the local community and the school.

The school's articles of government will set out the way in which the respective responsibilities of the head teacher and governors are shared out in the school. The School Teachers' Pay and Conditions of Employment Document (annually revised) gives the conditions of employment for the head teacher.

The essential feature of partnership between the school and the governing body is for the participants to know and understand their own role and that of others. The role of governors is to determine the school strategy and to monitor the school. The role of the head teacher is to carry out the day-to-day management of the school.

Governors are responsible to the local education authority and parents for how the school is run. They ensure that, broadly, the school is effectively run, bearing in mind relevant legislation and any local education authority policies. In doing this governors seek to ensure that the school gives the best possible education to its pupils.

Day-to-day decisions affecting the school are made by the head teacher who will discuss central issues with the governing body, seeking their guidance and support. The head teacher is responsible to the governing body.

The head teacher has certain legal powers because of his or her role. Other powers may be delegated to the head teacher by the governing body, giving the head teacher tasks to carry out for which the governors are ultimately responsible. An example is appointing junior staff. Such tasks should be carried out in accordance with the guidance which the governing body has laid down.

Also, the head teacher must keep governors informed of what is happening in the school and must provide governors with any information which they request about how the school is run.

This will assist them in making judgements and in deciding strategies which will ensure that the school provides good education. Well informed governors can also advise the head teacher more effectively. A common way of keeping governors informed is through the head teacher's written report presented at governing body meetings. Should the head teacher provide an oral report, this should be carefully minuted.

Schools should:

- be absolutely clear about the respective roles of the head teacher and the governing body
- assist the recruitment of effective governors as necessary and ensure that training is provided.

References

Department for Education and Employment (1996) *Guidance on Good Governance*, London, DfEE.

—— (1997) *School Governors: A Guide to the Law (County and Controlled Schools)*, June 1997 edition, London, DfEE.

Addresses

Department for Education and Employment School Government Team, Department for Education and Employment , Sanctuary Buildings, Great Smith Street, Westminster, London SW1P 3BT

Community Schools, tel: 0171 925 5592/ 6336, fax: 0171 925 6374.

Voluntary and Foundation Schools, tel: 01325 39 1100/1184, fax: 01325 391 184.

National Governors Council, Glebe House, Church Street, Crediton, Devon EX17 2AF, tel: 01363 774 377, fax: 01363 776 007.

Group work

Learning together

'Group work' is one of the trinity of primary school teaching methods, along with whole-class and individual work, which is endorsed in many official publications. One of the benefits of group work is that it can offer the opportunity for participants to develop social and language skills. Perhaps such benefits were never available to the prisoner who stayed in the court cells while his lawyer presented a dock brief. During the case the lawyer was sent below to interview his client and returned to the court to inform the judge, 'My Lord, my client is a man of few words and so far he has favoured me with only two'.

Learning in a social context and relating to others is an aspect of social constructivist approaches such as those of Vigotsky (1962, 1978). The meaningfulness of the social context in which the learner acts is important. The relevance of Vigotsky's work to education has been eloquently shown by such writers as Bruner (1986). To take only one example, Vigotsky's notion of 'zone of proximal development' relates to a child's problem solving. It concerns the area between the child's present developmental level and the potential developmental level in collaboration with or under the guidance of other people who are more capable. From his or her present state of understanding, the child is able to further extend understanding, given meaningful, suitable support from others, than if he or she was not given such support.

The support may be given by a teacher or parent who may explain or discuss with the child. But it may also be provided by a group setting, for example as a group of children work on a problem to be solved or a task which has to be completed. This sort of collaborative group work may be aided by judicious teacher interventions. All this has the effect of bridging the distance between a child's present and potential understanding. Language and discussion are important features of this perspective of learning.

When deciding on group work, the teacher will have reasons for choosing it in preference to a whole-class approach or individual work. Group work, as with any other approach will be justifiable by being 'fit for its purpose'

(Alexander *et al.*, 1992). This judgement may be informed by practical constraints such as the size and shape of the classroom, the furniture and available resources. It will also be influenced by the teacher's aims. Group work may be considered appropriate if the teacher wishes to encourage pupils to work in co-operation, to enable them to learn from each other, and to encourage pupils to be independent in learning. It would also be fitting if the teacher's aim was to encourage language skills and social skills. Problem solving and creative work can be encouraged by group work.

Groups can take many forms but can be categorised broadly into four types (Pollard, 1997): groups considered according to task allocation, teaching groups, seating groups and collaborative groups. Task allocation groupings relate to the task being set but the grouping may exist in the teacher's mind and does not have to be reflected in the physical grouping of pupils. Teaching groups involve the teacher instructing a group of pupils who are at the same level, doing the same activity at the same time. Seating groups may be formed around a table where pupils can work individually and have the opportunity to socialise. Such groups may be used for work on a group activity as the situation demands. Collaborative groups involve a shared group aim, collaborative work and a result which reflects the group working together.

Among the criteria for forming groups are those of attainment, friendship and interests. Attainment groups are useful as temporary formations for children working on particular tasks at the same level. Where attainment groups are permanent or long term this restricts the opportunity for pupils to benefit from other forms of grouping.

Friendship groups may aid social development and may enable the teacher to notice children who may be isolated or who may use their popularity unhelpfully, for example to ostracise others. This would suggest sensitive interventions by the teacher to assure equitable valuing of all children. The popularity with pupils of friendship groupings indicates a potential difficulty with collaborative group work. If collaborative group work coincides with friendship groups or if friendships develop in collaborative groups, then the socialising side of friendships can get in the way of the work.

Children may be 'off task' because they see the groups as an opportunity to socialise. Also, the teacher may feel constrained from intervening too early in groups where the intention is to encourage children to support each other's learning and to work together without too much assistance from the teacher. One way of approaching this dilemma is for the teacher to make pupils aware of the time allocated to group work and for the teacher to have a clear notion of what outcomes would represent a reasonable 'on task' period of work for a particular group. The teacher can also listen in to group discussion once children are used to it without too much distorting the interactions between children. Of course, the teacher will also want from time to time to intervene to explain a point or encourage further debate. This would fit in well with Vigotsky's concept of a 'zone of proximal development' assisted by pupils in the group and by the teacher.

Interest groups may be motivating as children gather to share enthusiasms. They may have the effect of bringing together pupils of different social backgrounds and different ethnic groups. They may alternatively bring together pupils of very similar backgrounds with interests associated with a particular social or ethnic group. The degree to which a teacher would feel it was appropriate to intervene in the formation of these groups would depend on the extent to which various interest groups over a period of time led to different fruitful groupings.

It may be necessary for the teacher to actively teach the children some of the skills of group working where these are not developing 'naturally', otherwise the lack of such skills may frustrate attempts to develop a group approach to learning. This may involve the teacher setting up training tasks for pupils which demand co-operation, activities to promote self-monitoring skills, and activities to promote self-evaluation skills (Bennett and Dunne, 1992).

The different roles and personalities of children may need to be taken into account in group work. The interaction of children who lead, those who follow, those who do not participate and others will be monitored to ensure that group processes do not inordinately obstruct the learning tasks of the group. This too is a matter of balance because it is through the group processes that the various roles of the group begin to be established. This may be considered, depending on the aims of the teacher, as a legitimate part of the social learning within the group.

The teacher will need to be aware of the relative merits of directing groups on the one hand and of leaving choices to children on the other. The degree to which the teacher directs such parameters as the number of pupils in each group and which pupils constitute the group will depend on circumstances. They may vary according to the tasks or the development of relationships between pupils within the whole class.

One social aim of grouping pupils could be to help ensure that pupils have the opportunity to work with and get to know other pupils whom they might otherwise not get to know. This would be aimed at encouraging pupils to be able to relate to a wide range of others not necessarily, for instance, only pupils who share their interests.

Children may be asked to share the outcomes of their group work with the whole class after the group sessions. This can be beneficial in that it can motivate pupils to stay 'on task' in the group setting. The teacher will need to think through carefully how the feedback is to be managed. Will children in each group be asked to volunteer information or will there be a group 'spokesperson'? Would it help if the teacher checked before the feedback that each group had got something to say? How much time would be necessary for feedback to ensure that each group was able to make a useful contribution?

As well as the importance of group work to the development of language and social skills and as a powerful way of learning, its importance as a preparation for later life should not be overlooked. In many adult settings, industry and commerce and elsewhere, the importance of being able to participate productively in group activities is greatly valued.

Schools should:

- recognise the potential of group work for developing learning, including offering the opportunity to develop language and social skills
- ensure that group work, along with whole-class and individual approaches, is fit for its purpose
- monitor the social learning and other learning consequences of different types of grouping.

References

Alexander, R. J., Rose, J. and Woodhead, C. (1992) *Curriculum Organisation and Classroom Practice in Primary Schools: A Discussion Paper*, London, Department of Education and Science.

Bennett, N. and Dunne, E. (1992) *Managing Classroom Groups*, London, Simon and Schuster Education.

Bruner, J. (1986) *Actual Minds: Possible Worlds*, Cambridge, Mass.: Harvard University Press.

Pollard, A. (1997) *Reflective Teaching in the Primary School: A Handbook for the Classroom*, third edition, London, Cassell Education.

Vigotsky, L. S. (1962) *Thought and Language*, Cambridge, Mass.: Massachusetts Institute of Technology.

—— (1978) *Mind in Society: The Development of Higher Psychological Processes*, Cambridge, Mass.: Harvard University Press.

Further reading

Galton, M. and Williamson, J. (1992) *Group Work in the Primary Classroom*, London, Routledge.

Head teachers

Leadership and management

H. L. Mencken said that a cynic was someone who, when he smelled flowers, looked round for the coffin. When applied to leadership, the cynical view is that the prospective leader sees which way the crowd is going, runs to the front of it and shouts, 'Follow me!' But there are many examples of schools where good leadership has positively influenced the lives of those who have been there.

Certainly, leadership is central to the head teacher's role. The deputy head teacher leads but ideally in the context of a strong relationship with the head teacher. Governors lead, having been given increasing authority by legislation in recent years, but often look to the head teacher for advice and guidance.

Leadership gives the school a sense of direction. Leaders may not necessarily excel at administration and managing resources, but they should be good at inspiring others, creating a vision, translating it into action and maintaining impetus. Management is associated with systems and is strong on the idea of controlling, particularly financial control. The head teacher has to combine the roles of leader and manager.

In 1994 The Office for Standards in Education (OFSTED) commissioned a review of research by the International School Effectiveness and Improvement Centre at the Institute of Education, London University. This review looked at factors identified in the literature as being important to a better understanding of effectiveness. It analysed the key determinants of school effectiveness in primary and secondary schools (Sammons, Hillman and Mortimore, 1995).

Effectiveness was defined narrowly in terms of pupil outcomes in, for example, mathematics, English and public examination results. The main determinants included professional leadership and shared vision and goals.

The review noted that good professional leadership was proactive. For example, it involved the vigorous selection and replacement of teachers, especially early in a new head teacher's tenure. It encompassed successful efforts to obtain extra resources such as grants, and contributions from local businesses. Good leadership included sustaining regular contact with relevant outside contacts such as local education authority networks. The senior management team and other staff were involved in decision making, and authority was delegated to others.

Effective leadership was characterised by clarity of purpose and of communications. Both autocratic or over-democratic ways of working were avoided. There was careful judgement of when to make an autonomous decision and when to involve others. The leadership demonstrated professional authority in the process of teaching and learning. This did not mean simply being the most senior administrator or manager but also being the leading professional. This in turn meant involvement in and knowledge of what goes on in the classroom, the curriculum, teaching strategies, and monitoring of pupil progress, providing support to teachers, having a high profile in school, and assessing the way teachers function.

The review of research suggested that the head teacher also had an impact on pupil achievement levels indirectly by influencing school and staff culture, attitudes and behaviour which, in turn, affect classroom practice and the quality of teaching and learning.

The second determinant to do with school effectiveness was shared vision and goals. An important feature here was that the aims and values of the school were clear and were clearly communicated. Another factor was staff consensus on shared goals, leading to a sense of purpose. Next it was important that consensus was put into practice through consistent and collaborative ways of working and of decision making, so that the school functioned as a coherent whole. Other factors were commitment to quality in all aspects of school life, clear sets of organisational priorities, and collegiality and collaboration.

The TTA *National Standards for Head Teachers* (Teacher Training Agency, 1998) set out the knowledge, skills, understanding and attributes relating to the key areas of headship. They define expertise in headship and are intended to inform the planning of professional development for aspiring and serving head teachers. All head teachers are expected to exhibit leadership and management 'which secures high quality teaching and learning and raises standards of achievement'.

The standards are in five parts:

1   the core purpose of the head teacher
2   the key outcomes of headship
3   professional knowledge and understanding
4   skills and attributes
5   key areas of headship.

The core purpose of the head teacher is to give professional leadership to the school. This should be such that it secures the school's success and improvement, ensures high quality education and better standards of achievement for pupils.

The key outcomes of headship are concerned with the results of effective headship in schools. These relate to ethos; teachers; pupils; parents; governors; and staff, accommodation and resources. Ethos, for example, is expected to be positive, reflecting the school's commitment to high achievement, effective teaching and learning and good relationships.

To carry out their responsibilities effectively, head teachers need specific professional knowledge and judgement and a range of leadership, management and personal skill attributes applied to each of five key areas of headship responsibility (see below). For example, head teachers need to know and understand what constitutes quality in educational provision and the characteristics of effective schools.

The fourth part of the standards concerns the skills and attributes which the head teacher is expected to apply to the five key areas of headship responsibility (see below). One aspect is leadership skills, attributes and professional competence linked with the ability to lead and manage people to work as individuals and as a team towards a common goal.

The fifth part of the standards concern the five key areas of headship responsibility referred to earlier. School leadership and management tasks are set out for each of the five key areas of headship:

- strategic direction and development of the school
- teaching and learning
- leading and managing staff
- efficient and effective deployment of staff and resources
- accountability.

Expertise in headship is shown by the ability to apply professional knowledge, understanding and skills and attributes to bring about expected outcomes. The head teacher is expected to work with the governing body, the senior management team and other colleagues in relation to all five areas.

The TTA launched the National Professional Qualification for Headship (NPQH) in 1997. Aimed at those preparing for headship, it complements the national standards for head teachers and can be taken over a period of between two terms and three years. The training and development programme leading to the NPQH comprises elements which relate to the five key areas of headship responsibility. There is a compulsory module: strategic leadership and accountability. The three further optional modules are: teaching and learning; leading and managing staff; efficient and effective deployment of staff and resources.

One principle of the NPQH was that the qualification should assure governors and others that a newly appointed head teacher has the necessary foundation of school leadership and management knowledge, understanding, skills and attributes to perform successfully against national standards. It should provide a baseline from which a newly appointed head teacher could subsequently, in the context of their new school, continue to develop his or her leadership and management abilities through, for example, the HEADLAMP initiative.

Each head teacher's training programme has to focus on one or more leadership and management task which aims to promote high standards and effective teaching and learning in the school. For example, one task is defining the aims and objectives of the school. Additionally, and in relation to the selected tasks, each head teacher's training programme must focus on one or more of a range of leadership and management abilities.

It is not easy to make judgements about the effectiveness of a head teacher without knowing the context of the particular school concerned. The time a head teacher has been in post will affect the balance of judgement about what can be laid at the door of the previous incumbent and what any comparatively new post holder should have achieved.

The circumstances of the school and its previous standards will be influential. But a new head teacher is expected to make a fairly rapid impact on key areas of school life. A particular circumstance is the head teacher appointed to a school which has been judged by OFSTED inspectors to be failing or requiring special measures. Here the head teacher has, on the one hand, the disadvantage that there are problems with standards and provision, but on the other hand the opportunity to bring to bear outside pressures for change, from government, parents and others.

But at a more practical level, it is more informative if one can track the influence of the head teacher, new or established, on particular aspects of the school. The influence may be direct or indirect.

The ethos might be traced to the style of the head teacher and it might have been noticeable that the previous ethos changed for the better when the incumbent head teacher was first appointed. A less direct influence might be on the improving standards, say in mathematics. This might be traceable through the decision of the head teacher to allow the mathematics co-ordinator non-contact time to attend courses and to use these to train other teachers back in the school.

When governors are called upon to judge whether the leadership and management provided by a head teacher has been successful, for example when a pay review is taking place, it is helpful if they have set clear targets agreed with the head teacher on which the judgement should be based. They may also seek professional advice as to what these targets should be and how the outcome should be evaluated.

References

Sammons, P., Hillman, J. and Mortimore, P. (1995) *Key Characteristics of Effective Schools: a Review of School Effectiveness Research Report*, commissioned by the Office for Standards in Education, London, Institute of Education and OFSTED.

Teacher Training Agency (1998) *National Standards for Head Teachers*, London, TTA.

Address

Teacher Training Agency, Portland House, Stag Place, London SE1E 5TT, tel: 0171 925 3700, fax: 0171 925 3792, e-mail: TTA@GTNET.GOV.UK.

Health and safety

A manageable framework

There are times when activity is tedious. Peter Ustinov, directing a movie, became so exasperated by the over-activity of an infuriating method actor that he eventually cried, 'Don't just do something. Stand there!'. But the school's approach to health and safety cannot be passive: it must be proactive. The school should never put itself in a position where someone could fairly say that an accident was one of those that was 'waiting to happen'. It must seek out and counter-balance potential dangers. It should also be borne in mind that the area of health and safety is particularly complicated.

One particular aspect of health and safety which has been highlighted by tragic events in recent years is school security (see 'Security of the school').

Under the *Health and Safety at Work, etc. Act* 1974, an employer has responsibility for the health and safety of all employees and for anyone else who comes on to the employer's premises or is affected by what they do. For schools there are also responsibilities to pupils, parents and other visitors to the site. The *Management of Health and Safety at Work Regulations* 1992 require that assessments of significant risk associated with the school are made.

In the case of community schools and voluntary controlled schools the employer is the local education authority. For foundation schools, city technology colleges and voluntary aided schools the employer is the governing body. In independent schools, the governing body, proprietor or trustees are the employer.

Health and safety is largely about identifying and controlling risks. These risks may be associated with school events, activities and locations. Statutory requirements place a duty on the employer to establish, monitor and review the effectiveness of safe working procedures. The head teacher is a key person in seeing that this is done.

Risk assessment involves making more formal the decision making processes and the reasons for making certain judgements about danger and risks. As these judgements are clarified, this enables us to take control of the potentially hazardous situations. Risk is assessed by examining the potential severity of the result of an incident and relating the outcome to the likelihood of the hazard occurring.

The measures already in place to minimise hazard are also taken into account. In a school activity, factors to take into account include the age, previous experience and maturity of children. Having made this assessment, the steps indicated might be the further controlling of the situation and the educating of those involved to further increase their competence.

A simple model of risk assessment (Griffin and Woolley, 1997) involves asking a series of questions:

- is there a danger? (recognising the hazard)
- how likely is it that the danger will happen? (identifying the risk)
- how serious would it be? (possible outcome)
- what if anything can be done to minimise the likelihood or the severity? (choices for control)
- how is the order of priorities for control to be decided? (priorities)
- what is going to be done and who will do it? (record/plan the action necessary)
- is the risk acceptable after these changes and will this state continue? (evaluation, monitoring and review)
- does the process work for different activities? (transferability).

Such a model may be used by staff and, adapted according to age and understanding, to pupils when teaching them risk assessment.

Staff competence in the area of health and safety can be increased in several ways. Legally, staff must be provided with adequate information, instruction, supervision and training. Staff with particular responsibilities should receive health and safety training such as first aid, the uses of certain materials and equipment and the supervision of outdoor activities. The school should keep a record of training, of any health and safety concerns and the short term action taken to 'make safe' and the long term action planned.

Staff should be conversant with health and safety procedures and act accordingly. Health and safety are evident in the way pupils behave, in the school accommodation and site, learning resources, the teaching and educational activities, including visits.

The school should have a clear written policy and procedures to identify, control, manage, record and report health and safety risks. It should educate and train pupils in safety procedures to empower them regarding their own safety.

There should be a written statement of health and safety policy and one or more members of staff should hold formal responsibility for co-ordinating the implementation of the policy. Procedures for monitoring and reporting should be in place and there should be arrangements for dealing with accidents and emergencies.

In the health and safety conscious school, practices will be as safe as is reasonably practicable in all areas including play areas and specialist areas. Pupils will know about safe working procedures. In preparing and conducting visits out of school, health and safety will be given due attention. The environment, including the layout, placement of equipment and materials and the condition of floors and play areas, should be designed with safety in mind. Equipment will be in a safe condition and well maintained. Floors and surfaces will be clean and there will be clean and appropriate arrangements for eating food. There will be appropriate arrangements for providing, storing, administering and recording first aid equipment and medication.

Specific subjects have particular health and safety procedures. For example, play equipment for young children will be safe and well maintained. In drama, procedures and any items used will be safe. Kilns will be guarded to stop pupils touching the hot surfaces. In physical education there will be procedures for using equipment and facilities. More generally, potentially harmful cleaning materials used in the school will be safely stored.

Risk assessment approaches can be introduced across the curriculum without distorting the normal content. Indeed, it can use the existing content while drawing on health and safety themes. In history, for example, the comparative risks of taking certain military decisions can be examined, or the changes to health over the centuries resulting from improvements in diet and hygiene can be focused upon. Geography can cover the risks associated with living in different parts of the world, perhaps from natural disasters such as flood or famine.

In developing and agreeing school rules, the use of risk assessment informs the process and helps make the rules more comprehensible to pupils. The greater the degree to which rules are seen as sensible and reasonable, the greater the likelihood of pupils complying with them.

Regarding the administration of medicines to pupils, the Education Act 1993 requires health authorities to assist local education authorities with pupils who have special educational needs, including medical needs. But teachers are not contractually required to administer medicine or to carry out medical practices with their pupils other than those required 'in loco parentis'. Medicines are best administered by parents but this is not always practicable.

Circular 14/96: Supporting Pupils with Medical Needs in School (Department for Education and Employment, 1996a) addresses the issue of medicines in schools. This should be read with particular care. The circular is concerned with two issues. First, that all schools have policies and procedures to support children with medical needs. Second, that there are care plans for pupils requiring medical practices while at school. Also published is a good practice guide, *Supporting Children with Medical Needs* (Department for Education and Employment, 1996b). Head teachers should obtain written confirmation from the employer (LEA or governing body as appropriate) indicating that there is adequate insurance cover for teachers willing to undertake medical support. (The position of other members of staff may vary according to their job description.)

Issues arise for staff training, developing school policy, record keeping and the role of various staff including the head teacher.

Schools should:

- if they are local authority schools, be fully conversant with the requirements of their LEA safety systems
- understand the implications of the relevant legislation including the *Health and Safety at Work, etc. Act* 1974 and the *Management of Health and Safety at Work Regulations* 1992
- carry out risk assessment for activities relating to the work of the school
- take the steps indicated by the risk assessment, such as further controlling the situation and the educating of those involved to further increase their competence
- have a clear written policy and procedures to identify, manage, control, record and report health and safety risks
- have a written statement of health and safety policy and one or more members of staff responsible for co-ordinating the policy
- educate and train pupils in safety procedures
- have procedures for monitoring and reporting and arrangements for dealing with accidents and emergencies.

References

Department for Education and Employment (1996a) *Circular 14/96: Supporting Pupils with Medical Needs in School*, London, DfEE.
—— (1996b) *Supporting Children with Medical Needs*, London, DfEE.
Griffin, M. and Woolley, A. (1997) 'Risk Assessment for Pupils and Schools', *The Head Teachers' Legal Guide Bulletin* 29: July.
Merlin Publications *The School Health and Safety Management Pack* (for head teachers, governors and staff, videos and manual, priced around £200).

Address

Merlin Publications, Dyer House, 3 Dyer Street, Cirencester GL7 2PP, tel: 01285 641 851, fax: 01285 643 164.

Homework

The importance of whole-school planning

Few children would recognise the wisdom of George Bernard Shaw's observation that, 'A perpetual holiday is a good working definition of hell'. So the notion that home and work might go happily together needs to be fostered by a close partnership between parents and the school. Where home circumstances are not conducive to homework, the school may have to take on the role of the more active partner.

Overall planning is necessary for the potential of homework to be fully exploited. Homework is viewed as work which is set in lesson time and which is 'integral' to the curriculum and is done either 'at home or in curriculum extension time at school' (Department for Education and Employment, 1997). Curriculum extension refers to the variety of opportunities which are provided before or after school, voluntarily or because the teacher has requested them. These opportunities may include extra tuition and provision to do homework. As well as curricular extension, the wider provision of the school will include curricular enrichment (extra-curricular activities).

In a similar vein, the government White Paper *Excellence in Schools* regards homework not as an 'optional extra' but as an essential part of good education. Furthermore, from September 1998 national guidelines have applied to homework. These concern:

- the amount of homework which pupils of different ages should complete
- the amount of time pupils of different ages should spend on homework
- the sorts of tasks and activities which constitute good homework
- how schools can develop and carry out successful homework policies
- what is expected of schools and parents.

A report reviewing homework policy and practice in schools (Office for Standards in Education, 1995) indicates that good academic performance and high levels of participation in extra-curricular activities and homework are closely associated.

In seeking to ensure that the homework it sets is appropriate and suitable, the school should begin by reviewing its current approach. An audit of practice will reveal the amount and quality of homework set. This may be considered by year group or in various other ways. A scrutiny of the work over a period will indicate how pupils respond to the work set. The views of pupils and parents can be sought to inform the school's discussions.

The Office for Standards in Education (OFSTED) identifies aspects of the most informative aspects of written homework policies in primary schools. These:

- extend existing lesson time
- give opportunities for independent work
- check that pupils have understood their class work
- help pupils to see the connection between good study habits and higher achievement
- consolidate or extend work done in school
- prepare the ground for subsequent lessons.

Like other school policies, the policy on homework and its effects needs to be monitored. This will help ensure that the policy can be modified as necessary if it is not having the desired effect of improving the quality and effectiveness of homework. Monitoring will indicate whether the homework policy is being followed throughout the school. It will show whether there are any differences in the response to homework by different groups of children, such as boys or girls, children of different social backgrounds, children with special educational needs, and so on.

Monitoring arrangements should be built into the policy and it should be clear who is to monitor, to what purpose, and how the results of monitoring will be reported back and used to improve provision. In larger primary schools, the monitoring may be carried out by senior staff such as year leaders. In smaller schools, the monitoring may be done by the class teacher with extra sampling monitoring by senior staff.

A simple but robust system of monitoring is likely to be the most effective approach, rather than a massive exercise which can only be sustained infrequently. It is more realistic to have a small scale but systematic sampling regime that can be kept going. For younger children, reading folders might be sampled. For older pupils home–school homework diaries can be looked at as well as the children's work. The pupils' own assessment of their work can be useful.

While the class teacher is likely to set, mark and monitor the homework, Key Stage 1 classroom assistants can support this, for example by checking reading folders and responding to queries and comments from parents. At Key Stage 2, homework diaries can be used in the monitoring process.

Homework planning is best done when the planning of the overall work for the year or term is done at a whole-school level. It should be made clear to parents and children that homework is part of the planned learning offered by the school.

The overall planning of homework will help ensure that teachers encourage children to use the resources which can be found outside the school. These include talking to other people, perhaps older people who can help bring to life work in recent history with their personal recollections. Other resources include museums, public libraries, displays, newspapers and public gardens.

Given that homework learning and classroom learning need to be integrated, it is quite legitimate and necessary for lesson time to be set aside to explain homework and to check on and consolidate previously set homework. At Key Stage 2 particularly, the planned nature of homework will allow such practices as using data gathered in homework to contribute to a follow up lesson. Particular care is needed to ensure that pupils who were absent when the homework was set are not disadvantaged in the lesson. They could perhaps share the data collected by another child.

Again, through careful planning, the involvement of parents is more likely to be assured. Communications relating to homework are part of the work of a home–school partnership and at the same time the homework is evidence of, or a manifestation of, home and school links. It is an area in which sometimes differing expectations of pupils can be negotiated and agreed between the home and the school.

Where parents are expected to sign a homework diary, it should be made clear what they are conveying by signing, especially where this changes from time to time. The reasons for signing may be various. It may indicate that the child has been working for a specified amount of time. Signing may convey that the parent has tested the child on a piece of work to a specified standard (for example, getting all items correct). It may intimate that the parent has shared an activity such as reading with the child and noted any words which the child found difficult. These are just a few of the possible requirements, either separate or in combination, so clear communications about what is expected are essential.

Monitoring and knowledge of the child and his or her family will indicate where home circumstances make the family support of homework difficult. Parents may not themselves be able to read, there may be insufficient space in a crowded bed sitter, or there may be no quiet time with a large family and the child expected to help with other children. The school may be able to help through after school homework clubs, family literacy support and an awareness that where homework is not finished on time, strategies will be needed in follow up lessons to ensure that the child is not disadvantaged.

In April 1998, the DfEE issued a consultation draft on homework (Department for Education and Employment, 1998). The guidelines are not statutory and are intended to help schools draft and implement effective homework policies. The recommended time allocation for daily home activities is as follows:

Reception year: 10 minutes' reading and 10 minutes' other home activities
Years 1 and 2: 20 minutes' reading and 10 minutes' other home activities
Years 3 and 4: 20 minutes' reading and 20 minutes' other home activities
Years 5 and 6: 20 minutes' reading and 30 minutes' other home activities.

By September 1998, OFSTED proposed to publish a report of research and good practice which underpin the development of homework guidelines.

Homework may be positioned to overlap with sessions of study support aided by such organisations as Education Extra. Those who can benefit from study support include pupils who have been absent from school because of illness or family circumstances. Also, children who need help with basic skills so that they can access the curriculum can be helped by study support. In such settings, homework can be fitted into the overall organisation of the after or before school time. Overall planning of the organisation is indicated so that homework is not tagged on but is an important part of the organisation.

Many independent day schools/preparatory schools have opportunities for homework (or 'prep') to be done in school under teacher supervision after the end of classes. For example, there may be sessions for which parents can choose, sometimes on a daily basis, to have their child attend or not attend.

Schools should:

* bear in mind government guidelines
* integrate homework with the other aspects of school work
* have robust strategies for ensuring that a child whose home life is unconducive to homework is not disadvantaged
* be clear about the respective roles of the school, the pupil and the parent, and ensure that all involved understand arrangements
* monitor the success of the arrangements carefully.

References

Department for Education and Employment (1997) *School Performance and Extra Curricular Provision*, London, DfEE.
—— (1998) *Homework: Guidelines for Primary Schools (Draft for Consultation)*, London, DfEE.
Office for Standards in Education (1995) *Homework in Primary and Secondary Schools*, London, HMSO.

Address

Standards and Effectiveness Unit, Sanctuary Buildings, Great Smith Street, Westminster, London SW1P 3BT, tel: 0171 925 5128, fax: 0171 925 6001.

Inclusion

Ideology or pragmatism?

A Jewish businessman had become very successful and visited his mother resplendently attired in a captain's uniform. The mother asked him why he was dressed in this way, to which the proud son responded, 'Mother, I'm a captain'. The mother replied, 'To you you're a captain; to me you're a captain; but tell me, to a captain are you a captain?'.

The desire to be accepted is so powerful that it is the crux of many such anecdotes. While acceptance is seen as a universal good, it should not be confused with inclusion. The Green Paper *Excellence for All Children: Meeting Special Educational Needs*, published in October 1997, seeks to address raising standards, shifting resources to practical support and increasing inclusion.

The government clearly wants more children with special educational needs (SEN) included in 'mainstream' schools. Children should be enrolled in ordinary schools unless there are 'compelling reasons' for doing otherwise. The capacity of mainstream schools to provide for children with a wide range of needs should be progressively extended. Links between ordinary and special schools should be strengthened and the government wants to ensure that local education authority (LEA) support services are used to support mainstream placements.

Whenever possible, pupils should not only receive their education in mainstream school but also join in fully with their peers in the curriculum and life of the school. Children with SEN should generally take part in mainstream lessons rather than being in separate units. But separate provision may be necessary on occasion for specific purposes.

A report on trends in inclusion (Norwich, 1997) indicated several main features. Regarding pupils in special schools, there was a long term trend towards inclusion in ordinary schools of pupils with statements of special educational needs, which the report calls 'disabled' pupils. In 1996, the special school population was 88,849, representing 1.40 per cent of all 5- to 15-year-olds, the lowest percentage ever in England.

Special school placements have declined since 1983 when statements were first introduced, except for an increase in 1991–92. Local education authorities vary in the percentages of pupils aged 5 to 16 which they place in special schools. In 1996, Newham had the smallest percentage of pupils in special schools (0.32 per cent) while Wandsworth had the largest percentage (2.67 per cent). Between 1992 and 1996, out of 107 LEAs, 71 had reduced the percentage of pupils they placed in special schools.

Turning to pupils aged 5 to 15 with statements of special educational need in ordinary schools, in 1994, for the first time, most pupils with statements (51.70 per cent) were placed in ordinary schools in England. By 1996, 58.45 per cent of all pupils with statements were placed in ordinary schools. There was LEA variation with Newham having 89.20 per cent of its pupils with statements in ordinary schools while Coventry had 28.07 per cent.

The 1996 data did not allow analysis of statistics specifically relating to primary and secondary school aged pupils. Nor did it allow a breakdown of statements in ordinary schools into those children in special classes and those in ordinary classes. The data does not show trends for particular types of special educational needs. The report itself highlights the continuing doubts about the accuracy of its data source.

The government encourages delegation of funding for all or most SEN provision at Stage 1 to 3. In future the sources of such support should also include special schools. LEAs may retain some funding to support pupils at Stages 1 to 3. LEAs will have a role in monitoring the use of delegated funding for Stages 1 to 3. Government will consider the arguments for delegating some of the funding for statutory assessments, administration and review of statements to support approaches to inclusion. LEAs are expected to review their Local Management of Schools arrangements to clarify the amount of funding delegated to schools for SEN, and eliminate features which may be acting against children's educational interests by providing purely financial incentives for statements.

In recent years there have been calls for inclusion of all (or at least many more) pupils with special educational needs in ordinary schools. The argument is that such pupils should be seen as part of the individual variation among pupils which occurs in all schools. There is therefore no difference, for example, in the forms of assessment used for pupils with special educational needs and those used for all pupils. Furthermore, other pupils can be included in the same approaches. Pupils who are very able would benefit from the same sort of individual education plans that are currently used for pupils with special educational needs.

This has led, for example, to a confusion in some reports by Office for Standards in Education (OFSTED) inspections. Very able pupils have been considered together with pupils with special educational needs. Some journals put the very able and pupils with special educational needs together under an umbrella title such as 'exceptional children'.

This can be unhelpful. If all pupils, or more and more pupils, are to become 'special', then how are resources and expertise to be targeted at some of the most needy and vulnerable pupils in schools and elsewhere? How is the specialist knowledge and skill of staff who work with pupils with special educational needs to be best deployed if such staff are to become managers of individualised learning for an increasingly wider pool of pupils?

Another issue involves the setting of targets for achievement. The government has set national targets for English and mathematics at Key Stage 2. Each school will be expected to make its contribution towards the local targets set in turn by each LEA.

Given that the national targets are expressed in terms of the percentage of pupils who reach level 4 at the end of Key Stage 2, the tendency for schools could be to concentrate on pupils who would otherwise reach level 3 and ensure that they rise to level 4. This concentration on the pupils just below the target of level 4 could draw time and resources away from pupils with special educational needs (and possibly more able pupils) at the very time that government and others are seeking to increase the achievement of pupils with special educational needs.

Also, the setting of targets appears to assume that the cohorts for a school in different years stay similar. But if more pupils with special educational needs who were previously educated in a special school are educated by a primary school, the cohort will change and the tendency will be for the achievement to be lowered by pupils who, by definition, are achieving lower than average. This could place an extra strain on the school striving to meet its targets unless it is taken into account.

The government places some emphasis on value added measures of achievement. It argues that such measures will indicate when a school is making good progress from a low baseline. This may be intended to reassure schools who are worried about the effects on their place in the league tables of school achievement of an influx of pupils with SEN.

Such value added measures may not, however appeal to parents who may seek a school which achieves well in absolute terms. Parents may want their children to attend a school in which pupils achieve high levels in National Curriculum tests. The fact that a school has lower levels of achievement but started from a lower baseline and therefore made better progress may not be attractive to all parents.

It is interesting that few are heard speaking of inclusion into special schools. If ordinary schools are associated with inclusion then special schools are presumably associated with exclusion. Yet many special schools offer inclusion in the educational system which ordinary schools could not achieve. To over-emphasise inclusion may give the impression, unless one is very careful, that special schools are the poor relations in educational provision.

A vital factor in inclusion is that it should maintain or improve educational standards. It should be clear therefore that for a child to be placed in an ordinary school would be likely to lead to higher achievement than if the child attended a special school. This is not a general philosophical problem but an issue which has to be addressed with reference to particular ordinary schools and special schools in an area.

What is necessary is a pragmatic approach which seeks to ensure that each child is placed in an environment which is best suited to his or her needs. Any approach which begins with the assumption that an ordinary school is better for a pupil with special educational needs is failing to take such a pragmatic stance. It risks, for the sake of ideology, making judgements which may not be in the best interests of the child.

Schools should:

- support inclusion so far as it is practicable
- seek practical ways of monitoring the standards achieved by pupils with SEN in ordinary schools in comparison with pupils with similar special educational needs in special schools, to ensure that inclusion in ordinary schools is delivering higher standards than those achieved in special schools.

References

Department for Education and Employment (1997) *Excellence in Schools*, London, DfEE.

—— (1997) *Excellence for All Children: Meeting Special Educational Needs*, London, DfEE.

Norwich, B. (1997) *A Trend Towards Inclusion: Statistics on Special School Placements and Pupils with Statements in Ordinary Schools, England 1992–1996*, Bristol, Centre for Studies on Inclusive Education.

Address

Special Educational Needs Policy Division, Department for Education and Employment, Sanctuary Buildings, Great Smith Street, Westminster, London WC1, tel: 0171 925 5000, fax: 0171 925 6000.

Information and communications technology

Exciting developments

Not everyone is as scathing of modern technology as one time *Private Eye* editor Richard Ingrams, who said how thoughtful it was of people to put satellite dishes outside their house to show that inside lived people of inferior intelligence. To be fair, what he seemed to be decrying was not so much the technology as the fact that it is a channel for so much that is brain numbing.

Information technology was one of the subjects of the original National Curriculum. Standards have caused concern, for example in the 1995–96 Report of Her Majesty's Chief Inspector of Schools it was noted that standards in information technology were poor in one third of primary schools, although some improvements were noticed. Against this background, and with the increasing recognition of the importance of communications applications, such as the Internet, the subject area is now extended into 'information and communications technology' (ICT) and is one of the 'new core' subjects.

More and more children from relatively affluent families are using ICT at home as part of their studies. An increasing number of less prosperous families seem to be prepared to make sacrifices to give their children the opportunities that ICT can provide. The school has to encourage ICT as part of the National Curriculum and so the challenge is to make the provision positive and exciting. ICT should have a positive effect on learning and should be used to enhance learning.

Provision for ICT may include software such as word processing, art software, spread sheets, and generally software to individualise learning and make it more stimulating and motivating. It will include the Internet to gather information and to send and receive electronic mail. Great opportunities are also offered by compact disk-read only memory (CD-ROM) information such as encyclopaedias and reference material in sound and still and moving vision. Pupils can create their own multi-media resources. Programmable toys can stimulate the imagination and convey important ICT skills. Using a scanner, art work on paper can be scanned into the computer and used in creative designs. The possibilities are legion and arguably limitless.

All schools are expected to be connected to The National Grid for Learning by 2002. The grid will provide:

- on line versions of the curricula which are in operation in different parts of the United Kingdom
- information for parents on their child's school
- a centre for the professional development of teachers
- information allowing pupils to take part in events which would otherwise be prohibitively expensive
- a school senior managers' bulletin board.

An early example of a local education authority preparing for this mode of operation was Staffordshire local education authority. In 1997 it formed the Staffordshire Learning Network which linked 400 schools, 3 universities, 7 colleges of further education, libraries, youth and community centres and the careers service. There were some 56 Open Learning Centres mainly in secondary schools and colleges of further education.

The National Grid for Learning was launched for September 1998 and 1998 was named 'UK Net Year'. A public–private partnership encouraged industry to urgently install the equipment necessary to gain access to the Internet and the Grid. The Grid will ultimately link schools, colleges, universities, libraries, museums, galleries and adult learning institutions (Department for Education and Employment, 1997).

In schools, a curricular issue is the degree to which ICT is taught as an activity with particular knowledge and skills to be acquired or the extent to which it is integrated into other activities and aspects of the curriculum. The latter emphasis conveys the message that ICT is a part of every day life and a tool rather than an end in itself. A balance is required between these two approaches which are not, of course, mutually exclusive.

It is important to have a clear scheme of work for ICT with resources and time allocated, assessment procedures agreed and operated and a system of monitoring the policy. At the same time the policy should make it clear how ICT will be incorporated into all areas of the curriculum. The development of knowledge and skills should be established as it is in any other area of the curriculum. A baseline should be determined and targets set for pupils to achieve annually. These targets should be supplemented by staff time, resources and assessment.

Providing for information and communications technology (ICT) in the primary school which is not replete with equipment may be regarded as a challenge because of the cost of equipment. However, in the school which plans for ICT seriously, the greater cost is in establishing and maintaining staff expertise. It is better to have less equipment fully and effectively used by a highly trained staff than to have banks of equipment little used or used ineffectively by staff who lack confidence and expertise.

Staff training is essential so that staff have both the competence and the confidence to teach ICT. Courses may be offered by a local education authority or others.

Educating pupils in the use of ICT should include educating them to use effectively material gathered through ICT. Pupils need to learn from an early age that pulling material off the Internet or printing off pages of a CD-ROM encyclopaedia is only the start of research, not the end of it. The printed material obtained in this way needs to be absorbed, restructured and re-presented according to the needs of the task.

Teachers should be careful not to encourage a printing press approach to homework from pupils. For example, if a teacher asks for information on the Second World War, then this could simply involve printing off material. If on the other hand the teacher asks for a pupil-written account of one soldier's 'experience' of D-Day using historical information of the events, then the task requires the research skills that one wishes to encourage.

ICT contributes to effective school management. There are several providers of software such as SIMS.

There is software to help track timetabling and staff cover. This may provide facilities for timetable planning and costing, feasibility checks and manual and automatic scheduling. It may include scheduling tools for the management of staff substitution; create pupil lists and form reports containing information held in curriculum or user defined fields; it can link each pupil's personal curriculum to the timetable to produce pupil timetables and class lists. Curriculum planning software is able to give statements of all published National Curriculum Programmes of Study in all subjects and all strands and all Key Stages; and it allows preparation for Office for Standards in Education inspections with a detailed curriculum structure for the whole school.

Software is available to enable the user to plan and monitor school development. It records details of the school plan, broken down into projects, tasks and targets; and it includes additional details for each part of the plan such as dates, costs and staff involvement. An electronic mark book can enable the effective management of pupil assessments, allowing the school to record any type of assessment and choose how the marks are recorded.

Other software enables schools to compare their performance against national and local benchmarks. It allows schools to add their own information and put it into context using data provided annually by government and other agencies. Diagnostic software enables the school to examine Key Stage results in detail and to highlight strengths and weaknesses for further development. It facilitates the comparison of results, question by question, against national benchmarks.

ICT packages can help in the management of special educational needs

provision and review. They assist in maintaining a register for pupils identified as having special educational needs; recording details of Individual
Education Plans and monitoring their progress; and planning forthcoming
reviews including the generation of letters to participants.

The British Educational Communications and Technology Agency
(BECTA) seeks to ensure that technology supports the DfEE objectives to
improve standards and to provide the professional expertise needed by the
DfEE to support the development of the National Grid for Learning.
BECTA has a link-up site for head teachers and deputies and a directory of
video conferencing users in United Kingdom education. The Senior
Managers' Website enables schools to access guidance and support materials
for evaluating school development and information on educational research.
Users can also participate in electronic conferences and share knowledge of
good practice. The site is: http://www.becta.org.uk/teams/smanagers/
index.html. The video conferencing directory enables schools to contact
other schools with the same facility so they can exchange ideas. The site
address is: http://www.becta.org.uk/projects/vcdirectory.

Regarding the use of ICT both in the curriculum and as a school
management tool, the school should:

- be aware of the exciting possibilities of ICT
- ensure that the equipment used does the required task better and
  quicker than it could be done any other way
- train users to be competent and confident
- ensure that users remember that ICT is a tool not an end in itself
- ensure that ICT it is fully used given its expense
- ensure that teaching ICT skills includes specific skills teaching and its
  application
- recognise the importance of using and interpreting what is produced by
  ICT.

References

Department for Education and Employment (1997) *Connecting the Learning Society*,
    London, DfEE.

Address

The British Educational Communications and Technology Agency (BECTA), Mill-
    burn Hill Road, Science Park, Coventry CV4 7JJ, tel: 01203 416 994, fax: 01203
    411 418, www page: http://www.becta.org.uk.

Initial teacher training
Routes and structures

Being senior has enormous advantages. The American humorous writer S. J. Perelman, when well into later life, was about to get out of a New York cab when the driver said to him, 'Have a nice day'. Perelman scowled, 'Young man, I am 74 years old and I shall have whatever sort of day I like!'.

One slight disadvantage of seniority and perhaps of having been in a profession for some time is that preparation for that calling may change. Since the time that many senior staff in primary schools qualified as teachers themselves, the landscape of initial teacher training (ITT) has altered considerably. Although senior staff will have kept themselves aware of developments as they have arisen, it may be helpful to review the situation as it stands, and to consider the implications for schools.

To teach in a state maintained school, a teacher must have qualified teacher status (QTS) which is awarded after the successful completion of a course of ITT from an accredited ITT provider. The course may be:

- concurrent with or after the award of a first degree of a United Kingdom university (or a higher education institution with award bearing powers)
- after the award of a degree of the Council for National Academic Awards (CNAA)
- after the award of a qualification recognised as equivalent to a UK or CNAA degree.

Satisfactory completion of an induction year will be required in order for the new teacher to remain eligible for employment in a maintained school or in a non-maintained special school.

Circular 4/98 (Department for Education and Employment, 1998) sets out criteria which must be met by all courses of ITT. It specifies national curricula for ITT in English, mathematics and science and for the use of information and communications technology (ICT) in subject teaching. The national curricular for English, mathematics and science must be taught to all trainees on all courses of primary ITT (and to all trainees on courses of secondary ITT specialising in those subjects). The national curriculum for the use of information and communications technology (ICT) in subject teaching must be taught to all trainees on all courses of primary (and secondary) ITT. The criteria give the standards of knowledge, understanding and skills which all trainees must demonstrate to complete successfully a course of ITT (including through employment-based routes) to be eligible for QTS.

The Circular sets out trainee entry and selection requirements. These include that all entrants have attained the standard required to achieve at least grade C in Certificate of Secondary Education (GCSE) subjects in English and mathematics. Also, candidates born after 1 September 1979 and starting primary and Key Stage 2/3 training after 1 September 1998 are required to have attained a standard required to achieve at least a GCSE level grade C in a science subject. In two-year undergraduate courses, entrants must have satisfactorily completed the equivalent of at least one year of full time higher education studies.

The length and coverage of courses is also specified in the Circular. Courses must cover one of the following age ranges: 3 to 8, 3 or 5 to 11, 7 to 11, 7 to 14, 11 to 16 or 18, and 14 to 19.

All full time primary post-graduate courses must extend for a minimum of 38 weeks. (Partnership arrangements, time spent in schools and quality assurance requirements are all specified in Circular Annex I.)

The requirements of the Circular apply to all courses including employment-based routes to teaching such as the Graduate and Registered Teacher Programmes which include time for theoretical studies in an individualised and approved training programme (Teacher Training Agency, 1997a).

Sections of the Circular of particular concern to primary schools are those dealing with the following:

- the standards for the award of QTS (annex A)
- the ITT curriculum for the use of ICT in subject teaching (annex B)
- the ITT curriculum for primary English (annex C)
- the ITT curriculum for primary mathematics (annex D)
- the ITT curriculum for primary science (annex E)
- requirements for all courses of ITT (annex I).

Concerning the QTS standards (annex A), all trainees (except those on the final year of undergraduate courses) must meet all the standards in May 1998 and in May 1999, and by May 2000 all trainees without exception must meet the standards fully. Regarding the requirement for ICT, all courses must comply by September 1998 (except those on the final year of undergraduate courses) and by September 1999 all courses must fully comply. All courses must meet the requirements for primary English and mathematics by

September 1998 and for primary science by September 1999. For course requirements (annex I) all courses must fully comply by September 1998.

The standards for the award of QTS (annex A) are set out in terms of the necessary knowledge and understanding; planning, teaching and class management; monitoring and assessment, recording and reporting and accountability; and other professional requirements.

The requirements for the use of ICT in subject teaching (annex B) relates to effective teaching and assessment methods and to trainees' knowledge and understanding of, and competence with, ICT. The ITT national curriculum for primary English (annex C) concerns: pedagogical knowledge and understanding required by trainees to secure pupils' progress in English, effective teaching and assessment methods, and trainees knowledge and understanding of English. The ITT national curriculum for primary mathematics (annex D) and for primary science (annex E) is structured in a similar way. The requirement for all courses of ITT concerns trainee entry and selection requirements, course length and coverage, partnership requirements and quality assurance requirements.

School-based schemes are one of the ways in which primary schools are closely involved in ITT. The partnership of primary schools with higher education institutions (HEI) in connection with ITT is an aspect of this. A set of working papers produced by the Teacher Training Agency (1997b) reflects the development of partnerships between primary schools and higher education institutions. These papers concern a range of issues including roles, planning and practice, the benefits of partnership, the relationship of ITT partnerships to continuing professional development, quality assurance, and the importance of preparation.

The working papers are concerned not so much with teacher performance and standards, which are the focus of other guidance, but with the structures and the practices which are likely to improve the chances of the partnership's success.

Closeness to ITT developments in higher education can widen the perspective of the primary school. Regular and structured contact with the primary school can help staff in higher education to maintain a classroom perspective. Benefits can accrue to all parties, ultimately benefiting the trainee teacher. Important themes of successful partnership are communication, transparency, demonstrable fairness and striving for high quality.

While clarity of roles is important and each person has to play their part, a particularly crucial role in any school-based system of ITT is that of the school-based mentor. A useful analysis of the role has been made by Sampson and Yeomans (1994) who identify three dimensions: structural, supportive and professional. Within the structural dimension, the mentor acts as a planner, organiser, negotiator and inductor. The supportive dimension incorporates the roles of friend and counsellor. In the professional

dimension, are embedded the roles of educator and assessor. The complexity and subtlety of the role of mentor makes it as challenging as it is rewarding.
    Schools should:

- familiarise themselves with Department for Education and Employment Circular 4/98
- consider the benefits to the school which may be brought about by being involved in school-based ITT.

References

Department for Education and Employment (1998) *Circular 4/98 Teaching: High Status, High Standards – Requirements for Course of Initial Teacher Training*, London, DfEE.

Sampson, J. and Yeomans, R. (eds) (1994) 'Analysing the role of mentors', *Mentorship in the Primary School*, London, Falmer Press.

Teacher Training Agency (1997a) *The Graduate and Registered Teacher Programmes: Trainer's Handbook 1997–98*, London, TTA.

—— (1997b) *Effective Training Through Partnership: a Pack of Working Papers on Primary Partnership from the TTA*, London, TTA.

Addresses

Teacher Training Agency, Portland House, Stag Place, London SE1E 5TT, tel: 0171 925 3700, fax: 0171 925 3792, e-mail: TTA@GTNET.GOV.UK.

Teacher Supply, Training and Qualifications Division, Sanctuary Buildings, Great Smith Street, London SW1P 3BT, tel: 0171 925 6014, fax: 0171 925 6073.

Inspection
Getting the most from it

A few things are beyond improvement. Among my own list of perfection are the Fred Astaire–Ginger Rogers movies, especially when they are enhanced by the wonderful comic acting of Eric Blore and Edward Everett-Horton. It is hard to imagine improving on a fine Chablis or the best Sherlock Holmes stories complete with Sidney Paget illustrations. However personal and however long such a list, it is impossible that any school would be included in it. Schools constantly change and therefore constantly stand in need of improvement.

Inspection can be seen as a part of school improvement in a similar way to the within-school cycle of continuing self improvement. For preparatory schools the Incorporated Association of Preparatory Schools (IAPS) make an inspection, usually a few years after the appointment of a new head teacher, as well as such OFSTED inspections as may be carried out. The model used by OFSTED is based on published guidance documents which are open to criticism and change. It focuses on areas which are by common consent vital to a good school: for example the quality of teaching and learning, leadership, efficiency and value for money.

In Easter 1996, the new approach to the inspection of schools by Office for Standards in Education (OFSTED) inspectors was implemented. *The OFSTED Handbook: Guidance on the Inspection of Nursery and Primary School* (Office for Standards in Education, 1996) became essential reading for any school seeking to get the most from inspection. A careful reading of this handbook pays dividends as it gives a clear indication of the evidence which inspectors will draw on in assessing the school.

Part 1 covers the OFSTED Framework inspection requirements. Part 2 is 'Guidance on Inspection Requirements: the Conduct of Inspections'. It concerns such issues as gathering inspection evidence. Part 3 is 'The Inspection Schedule and Guidance on its Use'. This follows a structure that reflects the report that the inspectors produce on the school. It includes sections on educational standards achieved by pupils; the quality of education; the management and efficiency of the school; curriculum areas and subjects.

The educational standards achieved by pupils at the school cover attainment and progress (4.1); attitudes, behaviour and personal development (4.2) and attendance (4.3). Quality of education provided concerns teaching (5.1); the curriculum and assessment (5.2); pupils' spiritual, moral, social and cultural development (5.3); support, guidance and pupils' welfare (5.4); and partnership with parents and the community (5.5). The management and efficiency of the school covers leadership and management (6.1); staffing, accommodation and learning resources (6.2); and the efficiency of the school (6.3). The curriculum areas and subjects are areas of learning for children under 5; English, mathematics and science; and other subjects.

It is helpful for a school to consider each section of the schedule and see what inspectors will look at, what criteria they will use and what evidence they will collect. It follows from this that the school will then appreciate what evidence will need to be available to inspectors and what that evidence will tell the inspectors about the provision. Working back from this the school will realise what action needs to be taken to assure good quality provision in the school and to demonstrate it.

Under section 4.1, for example, inspectors look at the attainment and progress of pupils. One criteria is to consider the question, 'Do high, average and low attaining pupils, including those with special educational needs, progress as well or better than expected?'

The school will want to anticipate the inspectors in asking and answering this question. It implies that the school has assessed the attainment of its pupils on entry and at key points in the school career of the children. These assessments will of course draw on national tests but will also use other forms of assessment such as standardised psychometric tests.

Having established who the high, average and low attaining pupils are, the school will track the progress of these pupils to satisfy themselves that each is making commensurate progress. Where such progress was not being made, the school would recognise this early on and use the information to review provision to rectify matters.

Was the lack of progress due to poor teaching, high absenteeism, insufficient resources or some other reason? Once a hypothesis has been made as to the cause, the school will seek to rectify it.

A particular issue arises with pupils with special educational needs. These pupils on the register of special educational needs may be below national standards in, say, English. Targets will be set for pupils at stage 2 or above on the *Code of Practice on the Identification and Assessment of Special Educational Needs* (Department for Education, 1994). The targets which are set for them need to be sufficiently challenging but may not always assume that the pupil will reach national averages.

Using this approach the progress of pupils is likely to be improved so that the school can answer affirmatively the question: 'Do high, average and low attaining pupils, including those with special educational needs, progress as well or better than expected?'

In asking questions like this, long before the inspection the school will be moving into the sort of consideration and review of policy and practice which is so important if provision is to be improved.

A similar approach can be taken with other sections of the inspection schedule, for example, teaching and the curriculum and assessment.

When the inspection takes place, discussions with the staff and others will help inspectors determine certain issues. For example, such discussion is one of the ways (but only one) in which inspectors assess the strengths and weaknesses of the school's provision for spiritual, moral, social and cultural development of all pupils. Teachers and other staff should therefore be ready to discuss the moral values promoted by the school.

This implies that a set of moral values has been agreed by staff, parents, pupils and others and that these have been discussed and are understood. Time for discussion and for staff training will be necessary to secure this.

A similar approach can be taken to other matters for discussion. The staff or governors will be aware of the sort of questions which the inspector will need to ask to form a judgement and will be prepared to give information and evidence relating to these questions. Reflecting on the issues, they will realise, before an inspection is pending, the actions which need to be taken so that positive evidence will be available reflecting good provision.

The school will find that the Handbook provides a most useful tool for reviewing policy and practice. The implication in all this, of course, is that the school accepts the issues which are examined by inspectors as central ones to the success of a school. Given that this is accepted, it then becomes legitimate in preparing for inspection to use the OFSTED Handbook as a school development manual.

The long term preparation then becomes not an exercise in seeking a good report but a way of moving the school forward in a way which makes sense whether an inspection was to take place or not.

Once the inspection has taken place the school becomes involved in preparing an action plan to develop the school from the key issues for action that came out of the inspection. This is a further powerful tool to move the school forward having, as it does, time limitations.

The use of the OFSTED Handbook will still be relevant and the action plan will be integrated into the existing school development plan although it may replace or change some of the school's previous priorities.

Central to the inspection and to the use of the inspection approach to school improvement are the quality of teaching, leadership and management, and efficiency and these should be kept in clear focus throughout.

As the regime of re-inspection of schools moves forward, the requirement that each school should have improved sufficiently since its previous inspection will be felt. From September 1998, when a primary or nursery school is inspected for the second time (Office for Standards in Education, 1997), inspectors must assess the progress which the school has made since its last inspection or over the last four years, whichever is the longer period. Inspectors must also assess whether the school has the capacity to secure improvement or maintain high standards.

Schools should:

- be familiar with the use of *The OFSTED Handbook: Guidance on the Inspection of Nursery and Primary School* (Office for Standards in Education, 1996) as a school development tool
- be ready in this context to use the key issues for action and the school's subsequent action plan as a further development opportunity.

References

Department for Education (1994) *Code of Practice on the Identification and Assessment of Special Educational Needs*, London, DfE.

Office for Standards in Education (1996) *The OFSTED Handbook: Guidance on the Inspection of Nursery and Primary Schools*, London, HMSO.

—— (1997) *Inspection and Re-inspection of Schools from September 1997: New Requirements and Guidance on their Implementation* (August), London, OFSTED.

Address

Office for Standards in Education (OFSTED), Alexandra House, 29–33 Kingsway, London WC2B 6SE, tel: 0171 421 6800, fax: 0171 421 6707.

OFSTED Publications Centre, tel: 0171 510 0180.

Learning resources and their full use

Limited resources can engender ingenuity. This does not have to be the fraud that led an Anglophile on the *New York Times* to refer to the padding of expenses by a White House aide in the tradition of Watergate as 'double Billingsgate'. Nor does it have to be centred on the cynicism that leads to the view of jewellery as an insurance policy as in 'Diamonds are a Girl's Best Friend'. Rather it can stimulate the creativity which led script writers Denis Norden and Frank Muir to respond to a request for the return of a cheque mistakenly sent to them by the BBC. Seeking the exact language of dead officialdom which would quell any further requests, they successfully responded with, 'We regret we have no machinery for the returning of cheques'.

Schools are unlikely ever be in a position where they can say they have too many resources, so ingenuity in their use is essential. Resources can be widely defined. Physical resources will include such items as books, calculators, camcorders, computers, information and communication technology, overhead projectors, tape recorders and video recorders. Teacher journals are a different form of resource, and buildings, displays and even teachers themselves can be included in the definition.

The use which a school makes of its physical resources to achieve the best outcomes for pupils is an aspect of school efficiency in the Office for Standards in Education (OFSTED) model (1995). Learning resources are expected to be adequate for the school's curriculum and range of pupils.

A way of ensuring that resources reflect the school's curriculum needs is for the head teacher to allocate funds to curriculum subject co-ordinators and require them to prioritise requirements and cost them. Where there is a positive whole-school approach, each co-ordinator will do this in consultation with other colleagues to ensure that the resources requested reflect the greatest needs of staff and children.

As increasingly detailed schemes of work are developed, these will not only indicate the resources required but also the time of the year when they will be needed. Consequently, the purchasing or otherwise acquiring of resources is made more efficient.

This does not preclude the difficult decision, usually made by the head teacher, that some reasonable requests from subject co-ordinators will have to be turned down or at least postponed. This decision will be informed by the school development plan which will prioritise resources as it prioritises other aspects of the school.

Where a head teacher has to turn down a reasonable request from a teacher for resources, at least this decision ought to be transparently supported by the school development plan. The more that staff are involved in developing and agreeing the priorities of the school development plan, the more likely they are to understand the need for the acquisition of some resources to be deferred. Ideally they would recognise the need for resources in another area and understand that, say, this particular year was not the one for their own requirements.

A further useful approach is to have a system in which the whole staff assesses value for money, reviews the school's purchases, and seeks to assess how they have contributed to pupil achievement.

The quality of resources depends on the ability of subject co-ordinators to know the range that is available and to recognise which resources offer the best quality at the most reasonable price. Attendance at a national resources exhibition can help the co-ordinator to see the wide range of what is available and compare prices and quality, after-sales service, reliability and other factors. Bulk purchases by clusters of schools can reduce costs. An example of this is the annual education show held at the National Exhibition Centre in Birmingham.

The range, quantity and quality of learning resources should be appropriate to curricular requirements and to the particular learning needs of the children, and the resources should be well deployed. Where statements of special educational needs specify that a pupil requires particular items of equipment or other resources, in order to comply with the requirements of the statement the school should ensure that these are provided. School accommodation, furniture and technological support may have to be adapted to meet the needs of pupils with physical or sensory disabilities (Office for Standards in Education, 1995).

This raises the particular issues of agreeing on resources for a co-ordinator who does not have a curriculum subject specialism, such as the special educational needs co-ordinator (SENCO). Here it is particularly important that all staff are consulted and that the expertise of the SENCO informs the decision of what to purchase.

Books, materials and equipment may be held centrally in the school, for example in a resources room or library, or may be dispersed in classrooms. If resources are held centrally, there should be a simple and efficient system to ensure that they are equitably available to all staff. Weekly planning will indicate the resources needed by staff and a check one week ahead will indicate if more than one member of staff needs a single resource at the same time so that alternative arrangements can be made.

If the materials are in the classroom the teacher will ensure that there is a correct balance between the resources being available and their being kept securely and safely. Pupils should be shown how to care for resources and treat them with respect. This in itself will reduce the cost to the school of resources as fewer go missing or are damaged.

The level of provision, deployment and condition of these resources should enhance the quality of work in subjects or areas of learning. The range of resources should be appropriate to the needs and the age of pupils. Due attention should be given to the choice of materials to ensure that they reflect a positive attitude to boys and girls, different cultures and individual interests and individual differences among people, such as disability.

What steps can be taken to maximise a school's existing resources and plan to get the best value from future resources? An audit of resources which the school already possesses is a first step. Next, it is necessary to develop systems that ensure the maximum use of those resources, usually the optimum use for each class. If there is a limited number of televisions, are there arrangements for recording programmes so that all classes can see necessary programmes at convenient times? Are computers optimally used? If the movement of items between classes is necessary perhaps the equipment needs to be more strategically placed or mobile stands for equipment purchased.

It is possible that existing resources can be shared with other schools in exchange for some resources which another school has. If such a system is adopted, it tends to work best if the exchange is rather formal with written agreements as to what happens if an item is lost or damaged. The friendlier the relationships between the sharing schools, the more important it is to have such agreements so that friendships are kept!

Such a sharing approach can be used with new equipment. Three schools for example may wish for three items of equipment such as a video, camera or a computer. Each school could buy each item and arrange a 'carousel' system to have each item one term per year. Work could be planned so that maximum use is gained from the item for the period which each school possesses it. Again, written agreements to cover damage, loss and other issues would be necessary.

Teachers should make full use of free or low cost materials from libraries, museums, teachers' centres, companies, parents, friends, local shops, industry and businesses, and other sources. At the same time it should be ensured that resources are of the highest quality and match the learning needs of pupils. Cheapness should be no substitute for good quality.

The library should be sufficiently resourced to play a central role in supporting learning. Material should be supplemented as appropriate from other sources such as the local authority library services.

There should be good provision of information and communications technology resources across the curriculum and their use to support learning should be effective. Where technological communication aids are provided for pupils they should be in good condition, be well maintained and effectively and appropriately used.

Visits to outside venues should contribute effectively to learning. Such venues may include libraries, museums, art galleries, field centres, theatres, exhibitions and others.

The provision of adequate resources tends to reflect good decisions being made by the management team over a period of years, acquiring and using to the best possible effect the funds available to the school.

Schools should:

- use a whole-school approach to allocating resources
- link the acquisition of resources closely to the curriculum and the school development plan
- develop systems to ensure the fullest and equitable use of resources
- review the contribution which resources have made to raising standards.

References

British Educational Suppliers Association (annually) *The Complete Guide to British Educational Supply*, London, BESA.

Office for Standards in Education (1995) *The OFSTED Handbook: Guidelines on the Inspection of Nursery and Primary Schools*, London, HMSO.

Address

British Educational Suppliers Association (BESA), 20 Beaufort Court, Admirals Way, London E14 9XL, tel: 0171 537 4997, fax: 0171 537 4846, www page: http://www.besanet.org.uk.

Literacy

A national strategy

Jack Warner of Warner Brothers had a low opinion if not of literacy certainly of writers, whom he described as, 'Schmucks with typewriters'. But fortunately the ability to read and write, if you are not a film magnate, is prized and has been the subject of a series of government initiatives since the 1997 General Election.

Literate primary children read and write confidently, fluently and with understanding. Being interested in books, they read with pleasure and evaluate and justify their preferences. Such children know and understand various fiction and poetry genres. They understand and are familiar with some ways in which narrative is structured through character, setting and plot. Literate primary children understand and can use a range of non-fiction texts. They can bring together a full range of reading cues to monitor and self-correct their reading from book and screen. Able to plan, draft, revise and edit their writing on paper and screen these children have fluent, legible handwriting. They are interested in words and their meanings and understand the sound and spelling system and use this to read and spell accurately.

Literacy (and numeracy) is recognised as a key to learning and excites the interest of politicians, teachers, researchers, parents and others. In a review of reports on educational standards, the 'three wise men' considered that they had found evidence of downward trends in literacy and numeracy. This led to their suggestion that primary schools must ensure that their policies and practices for teaching literacy and numeracy were correct (Alexander, Rose and Woodhead, 1992).

The National Literacy Project, a pilot project for some schools, was set up by the Department for Education and Employment (DfEE) in 1996. Other partners were the Office for Standards in Education, the Qualifications and Curriculum Authority, the Teacher Training Agency and the Basic Skills Agency. The project was co-ordinated from the National Centre for Literacy and Numeracy in the town of Reading. Linked to the national centre are local centres serving local education authorities.

Further to this, the government set up pilot literacy Summer Schools in

1997 as a short term measure to try to raise standards in literacy. These supported 11-year-olds with difficulties in reading and writing skills by offering 50 hours of tuition during the Summer holidays – that is, before their transition to secondary school. About 900 children joined the Summer Schools in 1997. In 1998 there were several thousand because the project was substantially expanded and specifically targeted at those pupils just under the level 4 expected attainment at age 11.

After the Labour government was elected in 1997, earlier research projects were manifested in the National Literacy Strategy. The National Literacy Strategy is described in a DfEE document (Department for Education and Employment, 1997) produced by the Literacy Task Force. The measures aim to improve literacy standards so that 80 per cent of 11-year-olds will reach level 4 of the National Curriculum by the year 2002. The strategy includes several elements: school target setting, training for head teachers, school literacy co-ordinators and literacy governors, distance learning materials for training in schools, a dedicated hour for literacy from September 1998, and a framework from which to plan the teaching of literacy. Thus, there is a programme of professional development in literacy for all primary school teachers. Where schools are far behind the proposed minimum target, they are given intensive support and training. Two hundred literacy consultants were appointed to deliver literacy training and aid professional development especially in the above mentioned schools which, for a variety of reasons, are well below government targets.

The Framework provides a detailed scheme of term-by-term teaching objectives and a common approach to curricular planning. The framework of teaching objectives helps teachers to be rigorous as to interpreting the National Curriculum programmes of study for reading and writing, and aspects of the speaking and listening programmes of study are involved.

The programme of teaching objectives for each term is set out in three related strands: text level work (comprehension and composition), sentence level work (grammar and punctuation) and word level work (phonics, spelling and vocabulary). All classes must teach literacy for one hour a day of continuous dedicated time. The hour is structured so that whole-class and differentiated group teaching is balanced and includes shared reading (teacher to class) and guided reading (small groups) and writing tasks (class and group).

The National Literacy Strategy seeks to improve the project schools' management of literacy through target setting which is linked to planning, monitoring and evaluation by head teachers and others. This involves not only percentage level of achievement targets but also curriculum targets such as reading inference skills. The overall aim is to improve the quality of teaching through focused literacy instruction and effective classroom management.

By September 1998, all primary schools were required to produce school literacy action plans for the period Autumn 1998 to Summer 1999. The Office for Standards in Education (OFSTED) is inspecting the implementation of literacy strategy in schools and local education authorities (LEAs). Registered inspectors were trained in the inspection of literacy in the Summer term 1998. In the year 1998–99, primary schools were asked to allocate three of their training days or the equivalent time in staff meetings to improve their own literacy skills, using the distance learning materials. In Spring 1998, each LEA was required to draw up a plan of their schools' targets to meet the LEA literacy targets for 2002. These targets would contribute to the National Literacy Target of 80 per cent of 11-year-old pupils achieving level 4. Various projects have encouraged parents to help their children with reading at home, one such project being the Family Literacy Project.

Literacy is also promoted though the Basic Skills Agency, an independent national development agency for basic skills in England and Wales, funded by government. Its aims are to:

- promote the importance, and increase the knowledge of, basic skills and encourage an increase in the take up of provision
- initiate and support the development of basic skills provision
- improve the effectiveness of basic skills programmes and teaching
- improve the efficiency of our central services and support and make the most effective use of staff expertise.

The agency's Basic Skills Quality Mark for primary schools mirrors many of the aspects of good practice associated with the National Literacy Project. Applications for schools to be considered for the Quality Mark are made by local education authorities (LEAs) on behalf of primary schools. The Basic Skills Agency defines basic skills as: 'the ability to read, write and speak in English and to use mathematics at a level necessary to function and progress at work and in society in general'.

There are ten elements of the Quality Mark and these are outlined in the publication *Basic Skills Quality Mark for Primary Schools* (Basic Skills Agency, 1997). These are summarised in this volume's later section on 'Numeracy'.

The Teacher Training Agency National Standards for Subject Leaders (Teacher Training Agency, July, 1998) are not specifically related to literacy but include reference to subject leaders having a knowledge and understanding of how to develop pupils' literacy skills through the subject.

Drawing on advice from the Teacher Training Agency, the Department for Education and Employment announced measures designed to boost literacy (and numeracy). From September 1998, all trainee teachers had to reach new standards to achieve qualified teacher status. Consequently, initial teacher training courses had to comply with these standards from 1 September 1997.

The measures aim to ensure that new teachers teach the three Rs effectively. A new national curriculum for primary teacher training courses in English (and mathematics) was introduced. Trainee teachers are now taught about using phonics for teaching reading, the literacy hour, whole-class interactive teaching (and mental arithmetic for mathematics).

The school should ensure:

- a whole-school commitment to careful planning
- regular, consistent and intensive practice in literacy work
- the use of varied proven teaching techniques
- assessment of pupil progress
- monitoring of teaching
- the close involvement of parents.

References

Alexander, R., Rose, J. and Woodhead, C. (1992) *Curriculum Organisation and Classroom Practice in Primary Schools*, London, Department for Education and Science.

Basic Skills Agency (1997) *Basic Skills Quality Mark for Primary Schools*, London, BSA.

Department for Education and Employment (1997) *The Implementation of the National Literacy Strategy*, London, DfEE.

Teacher Training Agency (1998) *National Standards for Subject Leaders*, London, TTA.

Further reading

Qualifications and Curriculum Authority (1998) *Sharper Focus on Literacy*, London, QCA.

Addresses

The Basic Skills Agency, Commonwealth House, 1–19 New Oxford Street, London WC1A 1NU, tel: 0171 405 4017, fax: 0171 440 6626.

The National Literacy Project, The National Centre for Literacy and Numeracy, London House, 59–65 London Street, Reading RG1 4EW, tel: 0118 952 7500, fax: 0118 952 7507.

Teacher Training Agency, Portland House, Stag Place, London SE1E 5TT, tel: 0171 925 3700, fax: 0171 925 3792, e-mail: TTA@GTNET.GOV.UK.

Marketing the primary school

George Bernard Shaw said that there was a crucial difference between an Englishman and an Irishman. An Englishman sees a difficult situation and maintains that it is serious but not hopeless. An Irishman regards a similar situation as hopeless but not serious. A marketing expert would no doubt present the situation as neither serious nor hopeless.

Business marketing is a process through which an organisation meets the needs of its customers while making a satisfactory profit. Preparatory schools, pre-preparatory schools and private nurseries have long been aware of the importance of marketing. In state primary schools factors such as open enrolment, local management of schools and grant maintained status have in recent years raised the profile of marketing, particularly for head teachers and governors.

Changes in the structure of schools to community, foundation and voluntary schools still mean that schools retain an element of control over admissions. This will ensure that market forces continue to act and therefore that marketing remains important. As local education authorities have looked critically at the high cost of provision outside their local boundaries, non-maintained primary special schools have had to market themselves to survive and develop.

Marketing is integral to school management. This reflects a situation nationally that education is increasingly a buyer's market as parents exercise their right, however circumscribed, to choose their child's school.

Marketing can offer other benefits from harnessing local support to developing a school's corporate identity. It involves giving information in a suitable style to help parents and others recognise how the school is meeting and can continue to meet the educational needs of the children.

A school creates an image in everything it does: every time a telephone is answered at the school; every time a visitor enters the building and every time a child in the school's uniform is seen outside school behaving badly or well, an image is projected. Even when staff from the school attend courses and conferences or when the school is host to a visiting provider of in-service education and training, the school is projecting an image.

Recognising this, and seeking to ensure that these signals are positive, is a feature of good management.

Deciding on an image is a matter of finding which aspect of the school's identity is central and attractive and recognising how that image is or is not projected. If the school prides itself on openness, how is this shown? Are there any aspects of school life which run counter to this approach?

Like other areas of school life, marketing needs to be strategically planned. A designated person should be responsible for the marketing effort and for co-ordinating publicity. This person might be the head teacher, deputy, a senior teacher, an administrator or even a parent. There should be clear links between the aims of the school and its public relations and marketing. Marketing involves a cycle of market research, product development, promotion and evaluation.

Market research may involve finding out in detail what parents think about the school and what they want from it. This can be done through a questionnaire and through an analysis of information which comes from parents in the normal course of school life, such as complaints, telephone calls, letters and exchanges at open evenings. Such information gathering addresses fundamental questions such as, 'What do you think of the school as it is now?', 'What improvements and additions would you like to see?' and 'What do you need for your child's education which is not at present being provided?'

Product development includes determining what would benefit the pupils and then researching and planning it. This forms part of the school's overall development plan but marketing elements should infuse the planning. As a whole-school issue marketing cannot be an optional bolted-on activity. The school will identify its strengths and sustain and develop them while at the same time working on weaknesses which could become tomorrow's strengths. However, it is current strengths which are marketed.

Information is passed from the school to others in many ways, all of which should convey the identity and aspirations of the school. Promotion involves the selecting and presentation of information either to the 'media' or through school publications. These publications include the school brochure, the way assessments are presented, press releases such as that after an Office for Standards in Education inspection, posters, advertising, letters, reports and many others. Clarity of organisation and expression, attractiveness, and interest are key aspects of good promotion. Carefully chosen type, illustration, design and colour can be used to enhance the profile of the school. The school can be promoted through direct advertising, open days, via the Internet, and in many other innovative ways.

Evaluation completes the marketing cycle. This phase involves monitoring and assessing the whole marketing effort and learning from the information gleaned to refine and improve future efforts. Targets can be set for marketing efforts, and the contribution of the various strategies used in meeting those targets will be evaluated. Then research, development, promotion and quality control continue as the developmental cycle.

Budgeting needs to be built in for such items as printing the school brochure, mailings to interested organisations, advertisements and so on. Sponsorship can be helpful for both sponsor and school and might involve the sponsoring of the school brochure for a year, or the purchase of equipment. It is important to agree details of any sponsorship with the potential sponsor, to set parameters such as time limits to the sponsorship and to be clear about what is expected on both sides. All agreements should be in writing and it may be fitting to have a formal contract drawn up to avoid any misunderstandings.

The scheduling of time is important, as marketing results do not accrue without commensurate work to produce them. This reflects the fact that marketing is not a gloss but an integral part of the school's work.

Corporate identity is a part of marketing and is important as it projects to the media and the public the standards and values of the school. It is supported by such features as the school's house style and its logo. An important promoting force for the school is the school building and grounds themselves for they send out clear messages about the school's values and priorities. Naturally, they must be clean and attractive but should also show the distinctive identity of the school through the style and displays of what the school holds dear.

The school entrance is particularly important for visitors. It should be welcoming, have clear signs and should display pupils' work and evidence of their achievements attractively. Some schools have a rolling programme of single subject displays in the entrance so that over a year, each area of the curriculum is celebrated. This may become particularly important to state schools which wish to convey the message that a range of subjects is still valued, not just the core subjects of English, mathematics, science, information and communications technology, and religious education. Photographs of staff and governors in the entrance complemented by photographs of the pupils elsewhere are used by some schools. Clear signs to main areas of the school can be presented in an attractive house style.

It is difficult for the school to be as open and welcoming as it would like when it must also address the issue of school security. But even the way which a security door speaker is used can be welcoming or forbidding. This is important as it is one of the first impressions the new visitor gets of those inside the school. The school may decide on a standard welcoming phrase which is used by all staff who may respond to the door speaker.

Particular subjects seem to lend themselves better to marketing the school than others. Performance subjects such as drama, dance and music can be taken out of the school to publicise it or can be the source of impressive performances for prospective parents in the school. Art and design and technology lend themselves to portable and interesting displays within the school and elsewhere. Sporting achievements reported in the press bring welcome publicity. But all subjects, given sufficient flair, can contribute to the marketing drive of the whole school. These might include a science fair, a geography display and video of a recent visit or mathematics displays, including three-dimensional work.

For schools developing their links with business, contacts made with companies can offer an opportunity for senior staff and others to learn from the marketing approach adopted by the business. This may be particularly useful where head teachers and senior staff have not worked in business or industry before entering teaching.

Marketing is particularly important in the special school, not least to raise the esteem of pupils and parents for the school. Parents may need help over a long period in coming to terms with the realisation that their child has special educational needs which require attendance at a special school. To have their child attend a special school which markets its achievements well and shows a justifiable pride in its service to children can help to support parents in their acceptance of their child's difficulties.

All schools should:

- develop a planned, coherent marketing strategy
- ensure that an element of marketing infuses the school improvement plan
- use the cycle of market research, product development, promotion and evaluation.

References

Marland, M. and Rogers, R. (1991) *Marketing the School*, London, Heinemann Educational.

Address

Education Department, Chartered Institute of Marketing, Moor Hall, Cookham, Maidenhead, Berkshire SL6 9QH, tel: 01628 427 500, fax: 01628 427 499. (The Chartered Institute of Marketing can put head teachers and others in touch with marketing consultants who advise on marketing approaches and related matters, for a fee.)

Media management for the school

Members of the media have not always been held in high esteem. Humbert Woolfe wrote in *The Celestial City*:

You cannot hope
To bribe or twist
Thank God! The British journalist
But seeing what that man will do
Unbribed, there's no occasion to.

However, an ability to work closely with members of the media is important to schools.

Media management relates to the marketing of the school (see 'Marketing the primary school') but encompasses other issues. It is part of the partnership between a school which has information and a media which is hungry for information. Information is passed in many ways, all of which should convey the identity and aspirations of the school.

Promotion in part involves selecting and presenting information to the 'media'. Contacts with members of the media require careful thought and planning to present the best picture of the school.

A succinct press release provided at the right time to the right person can give powerful publicity. These include press releases such as those after an Office for Standards in Education inspection. Articles written by staff about the school could appear in general or professional publications.

Radio and television interviews can be helpful but it is worth taking the time to get to know the perspective of the reporter and also how news can best be presented to make it attractive to the media.

Difficult media contacts include unsolicited media attention which may result from an unwelcome or unsavoury piece of information about the school. In such cases the school should present its own view but should remember that the journalist will inevitably be speaking to someone who will give the other side of the picture. The school can appear more in touch and more open by showing that it knows of and perhaps understands the views of others, but that it has its own perspective.

For example, 'We are aware that there are rumours about the future of the school but we are confident that the best way forward is to consider each option carefully before reaching a conclusion', would be better than. 'Closure? What closure?'

In such situations, particularly, it is imperative that one person is the media contact for the school. If anyone else is approached they should refer all enquiries to this person. This avoids a reporter accidentally or maliciously hearing several different, possibly conflicting, stories from different members of staff.

Taciturnity can be an attractive quality, as illustrated by many accounts of the restraint of the Duke of Gloucester. In Baghdad in May 1953 at the coronation of King Faisal II the Duke had to attend a succession of parades and processions. These took place in the blistering heat of the morning sun day after day. It was only on the third day that the Duke spoke, saying, 'That was not only the longest and the hottest but also the cheapest Turkish bath that I have ever had'. But taciturnity is not appreciated by journalists being pressured by their editors for a story.

If a journalist contacts the school for information which may give a negative picture of the school, the head teacher should normally take the call. It is important to be prepared, so if the call is out of the blue, it is quite legitimate to take the caller's number and agree to call them back once you have the information you need to hand.

It is not good to say 'No comment' if you need time to respond because such a response included by the journalist as part of a negative story about the school can make the head teacher appear to be out of touch or even evasive. It is much better to say something like, 'Thank you for calling. I would like to help you with your query, but this is something that I am still looking into and I do not want to respond until I have the facts in front of me'.

Once a promise has been made to call back, it is important to keep it, even if it has not been possible to gather all the information needed. In such a situation, the head teacher might simply say that the matter is being looked into and further information is needed.

Head teachers may decide never to say anything which is off the record to a representative of the media in case, by misunderstanding or design, their words appear explicitly attributed to them in a damaging news story.

Schools are sometimes anxious that the media is only seeking bad news but this is generally an over-exaggeration. Bad news is news but some branches of the media, particularly local newspapers, are interested in good news too. Previous bad publicity about the school can be used as a news incentive for the media.

Because news is about change, a local paper which criticised a school after, say, an unfavourable OFSTED report will often be interested in a subsequent news angle which shows how the school is beginning to turn the corner to improvement. This good publicity can in itself boost staff confidence and help parents recognise that things are getting better.

Also, good human interest stories are appealing to the media and can be angled to show the school in a good light. Newsworthy human interest items might concern, for example, a pupil who has achieved well against the odds; a teacher who has raised money for charity by doing a parachute jump; or a parent who started as a helper at the school and has now trained as a teacher and works at the school. These are just a few examples of newsworthy stories.

Anniversaries are also part of the staple diet of journalism. If a school activity coincides with a national or local anniversary, it is likely to be included in the wider coverage that such an event commands. For example, during the week of Remembrance Sunday, what is the school doing to commemorate the war dead? Is it innovative and original? Is the school for example inviting disabled war veterans to a concert put on by the children? Or a special tea prepared by pupils?

The displaying of positive news stories in the entrance of the school adds to the good impressions that a visitor should receive. If a school get multiple copies of favourable press publicity, the displayed copies can be replaced each year when they become discoloured or worn. In that way even the pristine cuttings will reflect a school which cherishes its good image.

Opportunities for interesting or attractive photographs will improve the chances of a newspaper being interested in a school event. Sports events, drama presentations and outdoor pursuits lend themselves to good action shots. Ceremonies attended by local dignitaries or celebrities can attract news attention. This may be a school anniversary, say ten years after opening. It may be the opening of a new wing of the school. It could be the receipt of a photogenic piece of equipment such as a new playground climbing frame.

If the school itself can take really professional photographs, these could be offered as part of the news story. It is best to check first on the exact requirements of the newspaper. For instance, the school may have a member of staff, a parent, a governor or even better a pupil who is a skilled photographer. The school might be able to supply photographs to go with a press release about the school, again increasing the likelihood that a newspaper will accept the story.

Good publicity can be generated for two parties at once. The media would have a double reason to attend an event which combined a local business representative presenting an educational gift and the school receiving it. There is the story of why the business decided to give the gift, along with the story of how the school intends to use it to benefit children.

Stories which may not originate with the school but which reflect well on it can be particularly helpful. A successful local person may be interviewed and speak warmly of his or her time as an old pupil of the school. A company speaking of its links with the community may speak highly of its links with the school and how it values them.

The school could make high quality tapes, for example of a concert, for the local radio station. The head teacher could offer to be interviewed about a new project in the school or local people could be asked to give their favourite memories of the school. Pre-recorded tapes of suitably high quality may be accepted by a local station.

It is important to be as honest as possible with the media. Where there are problems in the school these can be presented in the least damaging way possible. Genuine mitigating reasons for any shortcoming may be given if appropriate.

Educational correspondents of national and provincial newspapers are listed in the *Education Year Book* (Collier, Farrell, Langtry, Mann and Nolan, annually).

The school should:

- ensure that one named person (usually the head teacher) carries the responsibility for all contact with the media
- cultivate good relations through this person with contacts in the media especially the local newspaper
- develop an understanding of what makes a good media story and use this to project positive images of the school.

References

Collier, A., Farrell, M., Langtry, J. I., Mann, J. and Nolan, T. (Editorial Advisory Panel) *Education Year Book*, London, Pitman.

Address

Press Complaints Commission, 1 Salisbury Square, London EC4Y 8AE, tel: 0171 353 1248, helpline 0171 353 3732, fax: 0171 353 8355, e-mail: pcc@pcc.org.uk.

Numeracy

Numbers can be mysterious. James Thurber was puzzled that 'If I called the wrong number, why did you answer the phone?'

The issue of numeracy, along with literacy, is high on the political agenda and at the forefront of issues in teaching. The importance of numeracy is being recognised both as an essential aspect of core learning and as a means of access to subjects of the curriculum.

The National Numeracy Project was set up by the Department for Education and Employment (DfEE) in 1996 as a five-year developmental project but became a national project in 1998. Other partners are the Office for Standards in Education, the Qualifications and Curriculum Authority, the Teacher Training Agency and the Basic Skills Agency. The project is co-ordinated from the National Centre for Literacy and Numeracy in the town of Reading. There are twelve local centres serving local education authorities. Each individual school which participates in the project is directly involved for two years.

The National Numeracy Project definition of numeracy was adopted by the Numeracy Task Force in 1997. Numeracy was seen as more than merely knowing about numbers and number operations. It includes the 'ability and inclination to solve numerical problems, including those involving money or measures'. It requires familiarity 'with the ways in which numerical information is gathered by counting and measuring' and the way in which such information is presented in tables, charts and graphs (National Numeracy Project, 1997a).

The project aims to raise standards in numeracy in the participating schools in line with the national expectations for primary schools. Each local centre has two full time consultants to work with local groups of schools and the consultants meet frequently at the national centre in Reading. The consultant carries out an audit of numeracy in the school, working closely with the head teacher and the mathematics co-ordinator. At about the same time the school itself administers numeracy tests to establish a baseline and aid monitoring progress. Both the audit findings and the test results are used to set targets for improvement and to set up an action plan and a training programme.

The new Labour government set up a Numeracy Task Force in 1997 chaired by Professor David Reynolds. The Task Force produced a preliminary report (Department for Education and Employment, 1998). Among its recommendations were the training of head teachers, governors and mathematics co-ordinators, and a daily mathematics lesson of between three-quarters of an hour and an hour. It recommended that primary teachers should have training on: particular methods including spoken and mental work, spending more time talking with and listening to pupils, understanding different types of classroom organisation, developing lesson plans and assessing the progress of pupils. Each school should develop an action plan to raise the standards of numeracy, which should include targets for improvement and staff development. Oral and mental work should be emphasised more. There should be summer numeracy schools for children and homework guidelines for parents.

The mathematics co-ordinator and another teacher from each school attend training courses provided by the local consultants. The head teacher attends part of the course. Twilight sessions on planning and teaching certain aspects of numeracy are held for co-ordinators and other teachers at the local centre.

In each school, the consultant supports training days and provides school-based consultancy. The school-based support includes demonstration lessons and partnership teaching. In each school, the mathematics co-ordinator is given extra release days each year to provide classroom support and coaching to staff. Also, teacher assistants have the opportunity for special training in numeracy and literacy.

The report recommends the time and structure of lessons. Each class has daily lessons in mathematics. These last from 45 to 60 minutes. Between three and five of these lessons concentrate on numeracy. The beginning of each lesson usually comprises ten minutes of oral work/mental calculation and includes the rehearsal of number bonds and times tables. This is followed by the main teaching activity and then a plenary session. Head teachers and senior staff in each school frequently monitor planning and teaching.

Various materials are developed by the National Numeracy Project, such as a booklet giving the mathematical vocabulary to be emphasised each year (National Numeracy Project, 1997b).

A framework is provided by the project which covers: numbers and the number system; calculations; making sense of number problems; and shape and space. The framework aims to help teachers interpret the National Curriculum programmes of study and to plan and pace their work. It provides teaching objectives for each year and gives a template for deriving termly plans from them. Examples are given of what most pupils in each year should achieve.

Another influence on the teaching of mathematics was the work of Barking and Dagenham LEA on numeracy, the 'Improving Primary School Mathematics Initiative'. This work, funded by the Gatsby Foundation and the National Institute of Economic and Social Research, was influenced by the teaching of mathematics found in Bavaria and the Zurich Canton of Switzerland. Among the key features of this approach were: the 'horse-shoe' layout of the classroom, the extensive use of oral work for teacher and pupils, and the opportunity for pupils to show their workings to the whole class on a white-board or over-head projector.

The Basic Skills Agency Basic Skills Quality Mark for primary schools reflects many of the aspects of good practice in the National Numeracy Project. Applications for schools to be considered for the Quality Mark are made by local education authorities (LEAs) on behalf of primary schools. Basic skills are defined by the Agency as, 'the ability to read, write and speak in English and to use mathematics at a level necessary to function and progress at work and in society in general'.

The ten elements of the Quality Mark are set out in the publication *Basic Skills Quality Mark for Primary Schools* (Basic Skills Agency, 1997). All apply to basic skills and can of course be related directly to numeracy. There must be a whole-school policy including an action plan, to improve pupil performance. An assessment of pupil performance should be carried out in the school. A target must be set for the improvement of the school's performance. There must be improvement plans for pupils who are under-attaining. Regular reviews of the progress of each pupil under-attaining must be made. The school should make a commitment to improving staff skills to teach and extend basic skills. A range of teaching styles should be used to improve basic skills. Appropriate teaching and learning resources must be used to improve basic skills. Parents should be involved in developing their children's skills. There must be an effective procedure for monitoring the action plan and assessing improvement in performance.

Schools should:

- ensure all staff are familiar with the developments by the Numeracy Task Force, the Numeracy Project, the Teacher Training Agency and the Basic Skills Agency which are described above
- keep up to date with future developments from these bodies
- note the common themes which emerge from these bodies and use these to inform the school's provision for numeracy.

References

Basic Skills Agency (1997) *Basic Skills Quality Mark for Primary Schools*, London, BSA.

Department for Education and Employment (1998) *Numeracy Matters: The Preliminary Report of the Numeracy Task Force* (January), London, DfEE.

National Numeracy Project (1997a) *Framework for Numeracy Draft, November, 1997*, London, NNP.

—— (1997b) *Mathematical Vocabulary*, London, NNP/BEAM (BE A Mathematician).

National Numeracy Project/BEAM/The Hamilton Trust (1997) *Numeracy Lessons*, London, NNP/BEAM/HT.

National Numeracy Project and Hamilton Mathematics Project (1998) *Numeracy in Action*, London, NNP/HMP.

Office for Standards in Education (1997) *Teachers Count Video*, London, OFSTED.

Qualifications and Curriculum Authority (1998) *Sharper Focus on Numeracy*, London, QCA.

School Curriculum and Assessment Authority (1997) *Mathematics and the Use of Language: Key Stage 1 and 2*, London, SCAA.

Teacher Training Agency (1998) *Assessing Needs in Mathematics (Diagnostic feedback/Diagnostic tasks)*, London, TTA.

Addresses

The Basic Skills Agency, Commonwealth House, 1–19 New Oxford Street, London WC1A 1NU, tel: 0171 405 4017, fax: 0171 440 6626.

National Numeracy Project, National Centre for Literacy and Numeracy, London House, 59–65 London Street, Reading RG1 4EW, tel: 0118 952 7500, fax: 0118 952 7507.

Organisation of pupils in school (including class size)

When Bertolt Brecht wrote, in *Mother Courage*, 'You know the trouble with peace? No organisation', he was intimating that national organisation is improved in wartime. This is probably true but schools undoubtedly benefit from good organisation whatever the state of the nation. Here we are concerned with the whole-school issues of class size, setting, streaming and vertical grouping.

In organising pupils into groups within the school, decisions about the relative sizes of classes are important. It seems self-evident that effective teaching is more easily achieved in smaller classes than in larger ones. It also seems reasonable to assign a degree of the success of some independent schools to their smaller classes. Other contributory factors may be the level of achievement of the pupils on entry and the parental support which may be associated with paying directly for education over and above what is paid from taxes. But class size seems a plausible contributory factor to pupil achievement.

It is relatively easy to be persuaded that wide differences in class size influence standards. Classes of six are likely to produce better pupil achievement than classes of 36, all other things being equal. A more difficult challenge is to determine the effect of narrower ranges of class size in state schools. The more realistic question here is whether classes of 28 make a difference to achievement compared with, for example, classes of 32. If larger differences in class size make a difference in achievement then class size is related to achievement. Consequently, smaller differences in class size would be expected to make at least a small difference in achievement.

Class size is seen as an important determinant of successful teaching by head teachers, chairs of governors, teachers and parents who are unanimous in their perceptions on this point (Bennett, 1994). Some research evidence also points in the same direction. Perhaps the strongest evidence comes from the Project STAR (Student/Teacher Achievement Ratio) funded by Tennessee's state legislature. It examined achievement and progress in three types of classes to which the children were randomly assigned. The longitudinal study focused on classes of 13 to 17 pupils per teacher, classes of 22 to

25 pupils per teacher and classes of 22 to 25 pupils, but with a teacher and a classroom assistant. Children were followed from kindergarten in 1985–86 to third grade in 1988–89. The study involved children attending inner city, urban, suburban and rural schools. Pupils in the smallest classes scored the highest on achievement tests in all four years and in all locations (Pate-Bain et al. 1992).

The matter, however, is not completely straightforward. The Centre for the Assessment of Educational Progress in the United States of America analyses annual tests of school children in 20 countries. Several subjects and different age rages are covered. In 1992, younger children in England tested in science were behind Taiwan, South Korea, Italy and the United States of America. Yet the average class size in South Korea for 13-year-olds is 49 while in England it is around 27. In English primary schools class sizes may be around 30 to 35, but rarely at South Korean levels. Class size within certain parameters may therefore not be the most significant factor determining pupil achievement.

Other issues are likely to be influential, such as the ethos of the school, effective management and leadership, and the quality of teaching. These may, however, interact with the factor of class size. Clearly the teacher of a very large class may not be successful using techniques which might work quite well with smaller classes. In particular it is important that the teaching method used is adapted to suit the size of class.

In its White Paper *Excellence in Schools* (1997) the new Labour government restated its election pledge to reduce primary class sizes. The intention is to reduce class sizes for children aged 5, 6 and 7 years old to 30 or below by the September 2001 at the latest. It is thought that smaller class sizes will enable teachers to spend more time in the early stages of children's education catering for their individual needs and helping them master the basics.

The government plans to work with local education authorities (LEAs) and schools to try to ensure that the reduction in class size is well managed, cost effective and carried out at an appropriate pace. LEAs will be required to produce action plans to meet the government's targets.

The cost of reducing class size was planned to be met in part by phasing out the assisted places scheme which helped pay the fees of pupils who would otherwise not have the opportunity to attend independent schools. The relatively small amount of funds saved would be redistributed. A bill to phase out the assisted places scheme gained Royal Assent in July 1997, which will release funds from 1998 onwards. An unintended outcome of this well intentioned initiative was that vertical grouping is being forced on some schools at Key Stage 1.

Streaming (involving permanent groups based on ability), setting (temporary re-grouping) and vertical grouping are aspects of organisation which can have a powerful effect on achievement.

Decisions about setting and streaming are not made in isolation from vital aspects of the school. They are influenced by the skills of teachers in using differentiation as a tool for matching tasks to pupils' prior learning. The composition and spread of prior learning in a particular year group or class is important. The curriculum subject plays a part. The philosophy of the head teacher, staff, governors and others is also highly influential.

In favour of streaming it is claimed that it is a type of organisation which matches pupils of similar overall prior learning in a single group. Against streaming it is argued that it creates 'sink' groups which are sometimes taught by the least able teachers.

Setting is no more than a system of streaming by subject with the built-in flexibility that a particular pupil may be in one set (for instance top) for one subject but in another set (for example bottom) for another. In recent years, primary schools have been encouraged to consider carefully the advantages of subject specialist teaching. It follows from this that where schools have moved to subject specialist teaching with pupils moving from class to class for different subjects, there is the opportunity also to adopt streaming or setting.

Vertical grouping (for example, children of 5 to 7 or 7 to 9 grouped together in one class) may be used in a small primary school where entry numbers are insufficient to justify two forms but too large to be realistic for one form. Also in primary special schools, a similar organisation may be used. Vertical grouping may be the form of organisation in some primary schools. Among the advantages are that older children have the opportunity to help younger ones. Children can develop responsibility. Children are in their classes for several years, perhaps with the same teacher and with many of the same children, which can increase the security of children and can enable the teacher to get to know the children very well. The potential for a deeper knowledge of the children by the teacher can lead to more effective matching of the provision to the child.

Conversely, the mixture of ages may lead to the younger children feeling that they are in the shadow of older ones. Whole-class activities such as physical education may be more difficult but imaginative flexible timetabling can enable the school to separate groups sometimes for certain lessons where this is a difficulty. The wider range of ability and interests makes it more of a challenge than otherwise to ensure that the tasks are matched to the child. This can be off-set by the fact that the teacher can get to know the children better over the longer than normal period that the class is together, but careful monitoring is necessary to assure suitable matching (Pollard, 1997). While continuity is aided by the National Curriculum in which the course of learning is set out, vertical grouping can make the organising of continuity of learning more difficult to achieve.

Schools should:

- review the effects on pupil achievement of organisational decisions such as class size, setting, streaming and vertical grouping
- ensure that the various aspects of school organisation are adjusted and refined to contribute optimally to raising standards of pupil achievement.

References

Bennett, N. (1994) *Class Size in Primary Schools: Perceptions of Head teachers, Chairs of Governors, Teachers and Parents*, Birmingham, National Association of Schoolmasters/Union of Women Teachers.

Department for Education and Employment (1997) *Excellence in Schools*, London, DfEE.

Pate-Bain, H., Achilles, C., Boyd-Zaharius, J. and McKenna, B. (1992) 'Class size does make a difference', *Phi Delta Kappan* November, 253–55.

Pollard, A. (1997) *Reflective Teaching in the Primary School: A Handbook for the Classroom Third Edition*, London, Cassell.

Address

Class Size and Teacher Supply Team, Department for Education and Employment, Sanctuary Buildings, Great Smith Street, Westminster, London SW1P 3BT, tel: 0171 925 5470, fax: 0171 925 6073.

Parents and the community
Improving partnership

Philip Larkin's view of parents was bleak. The bowdlerised version of one of his poems begins 'They mess you up your mum and dad'. His view of the community could be equally chilling. But a school has to be more optimistic.

The notion that a school should have a shared vision and goals in order to function most effectively extends not just to the school community of staff and children. It also encompasses the parents of children attending the school and the wider local community.

An Organisation for Economic Co-operation and Development (OECD) report (1997) looked at parental involvement in the following countries: Canada, Denmark, England, Wales, France, Germany, Ireland, Japan, Spain and the United States of America. Three factors were found to combine to make it more recognisable that the roles of the family, school and the community were interrelated. These three factors were:

- pupil support and parental involvement often being associated with higher achievement
- a general trend of offering parents more choice in determining their child's school (within reasonable logistical boundaries)
- the increasing accountability of schools through such means as supplying more information.

At a national level in England and Wales, the government consults parents' associations, including the National Confederation of Parent–Teacher Associations, on matters of policy. Similarly, the White Paper *Excellence in Schools* (1997) proposed that a parent should be co-opted to the education committee of each local education authority.

The OECD report indicated that an approach widely developed in Denmark, France, Germany and Spain is the class parent council. Parents of all the pupils in a particular school class periodically meet each other and the class teacher to discuss issues, developments and problems.

A school's partnerships with parents and the community are considered together in the Office for Standards in Education Handbook *Guidance on the Inspection of Nursery and Primary Schools* (Office for Standards in Education, 1995). There is a logic in this as parents are part of the community and the school's involvement with the community is likely to percolate back to parents and affect their opinion of the school. Two important aspects of the partnership with parents are communication and support, and these should be clarified by a school policy.

The importance of clear and concise communication with parents can hardly be over-emphasised. It is easy to spot the muddy communication of others. We may smile at the euphemisms so loved by Americans which lead to terms like 'correctional facility' for prison, or those of business which have 'cleaning the clocks' as an antiseptic way of saying closing down a business. Even Shakespeare has Lady Macbeth speak of murder as the 'great quell' and 'the enterprise'. But poor communication, whether through euphemism, jargon, loquatiousness or confusion, is harder to spot when it is our own. For written material, involving potential readers in criticising drafts is one way of improving potentially murky communications.

Communication with parents involves the provision of clear and good quality information about the school and about pupils' progress. This is achieved through such publications as the school prospectus, annual reports, other reports and through parents' evenings. It is a statutory requirement that parents are given regular information about pupils' attainment and opportunities to discuss their child's progress.

For pupils with special educational needs, the *Code of Practice on the Identification and Assessment of Special Educational Needs* (Department for Education, 1994) indicates the involvement of parents in each stage of special educational need. For pupils with statements of special educational needs, reviews must be held at least annually in which parents are involved.

Particular care in matters such as translations will need to be taken in communications with the parents for whom English is an additional language. Other important forms of communications are home–school books or reading diaries, newsletters, and reports of governors' meetings.

Imaginative forms of communication are used by some schools in particular circumstances. A video tape showing the activities of the school can be shown at parents' evenings for existing or prospective parents. An audio tape of recent developments can be borrowed by parents to listen to at home or in the car. Twenty-four hour helplines are sometimes set up on a dedicated school line to provide information to parents who may not have been able to attend a particular school function but are interested to hear the outcome.

Communication and support work hand in hand. If parents are provided with good information about the curriculum and teaching, they are more likely to be willing and able to support their child's learning at home.

Support for the school is shown in the parents' involvement with the school and with their child's work at home. This might be encouraged through staff making home visits before a child enters school, by parents working in the classroom or helping on school visits or on extra curricular activities, by sending books or work home, by having a lending library for books or toys and by holding regular meetings and activities. Home–school contracts could formalise such arrangements.

An important role is played by parent governors of the school and parent members of any parent teacher association. By straddling the role of being formally involved in the school and also being a parent, such people can form a most helpful channel of communication between other parents and school. Their ability to be tactful and discreet at times is most important.

Perhaps inevitably, there are parents who are reluctant to become involved and they are often the parents which the school might feel most need to be involved for the sake of their child's education. Such parents may be disaffected and may have had unproductive experiences of school when they were children. Other parents seem to make contact with the school only to complain vigorously. In some instances, parents may be abusive and physically threatening. If there is an easy way to build relationships with such parents, the secret is being kept very well hidden. Most schools simply try their best in difficult circumstances and hope for a gradual improvement in relationships over time.

For parent–school relationships to flourish, the respective roles should be clear. What the school expects of parents and what parents expect of school should be spelt out prior to pupils going on the school roll. The mutual responsibilities that complement expectations should be equally clear. The support of parents for their child's education can be one particular advantage of an independent school. To pay for a child's education over and above taxes for state education often indicates a commitment to high expectations.

Turning to the local community, the way in which it is involved with school is important because of its effect on the attainment, progi. personal development of pupils. The school's work benefits from enriched by a variety of links with the community.

Some community links directly enhance the curriculum. For example, a school might have contacts with a local farm which contributes to the study of geography. Other links aid the personal development of pupils. These might include relationships with an old people's home or a local charity. Such bonds enable pupils to understand society better and to develop a notion of citizenship.

Like other aspects of school life, links with parents and the community benefit from being monitored. It is not too difficult to establish which aspects of partnership with parents are yielding the most impact on parental involvement with the school and involvement with the child's work at home. Similarly, it is manageable to judge the relative impact on the curriculum, and on pupil achievement and personal development of various community links. Such monitoring and assessment will help weed out the less productive ventures and will raise teacher and pupil motivation for those activities which are shown to be assisting the pupils' education.

The school should aim to improve its links with parents and the community through:

- clear communications
- a clear policy of nurturing support and involvement
- making roles and expectations clear
- making systematic and full use of the community
- monitoring the effects of all this on the school, particularly in relation to pupil standards.

References

Department for Education (1994) *Code of Practice on the Identification and Assessment of Special Educational Needs*, London, DfE.

Department for Education and Employment (1997) *Excellence in Schools*, London, DfEE.

Office for Standards in Education (1995) *Guidance on the Inspection of Nursery and Primary Schools*, London, HMSO.

Organisation for Economic Co-operation and Development (1997) *Parents as Partners in Schooling*, London, OECD.

Addresses

National Confederation of Parent–Teacher Associations (NCPTA), 2 Ebsfleet Estate, Stonebridge Road, Gravesend, Kent DA11 9DZ, tel: 01474 560 618, fax: 01474 564 418. (NCPTA is a registered charity which promotes home–school co-operation and seeks to develop the interest of parents in education policy and what happens at school. NCPTA publish the magazine *Home and School*.)

The National Association of Parents (NAP), e-mail: NAPARENTS@aol.com.

Planning for teaching and learning

A. E. Houseman wrote of people sitting in taverns, 'while the tempest hurled their hopeful plans to emptiness'. Many a beginning teacher, and some seasoned ones as well, may identify with those words.

Planning helps ensure progression and continuity in pupils' learning and breadth, balance and differentiation in the curriculum experience of pupils. It involves work at all levels, and schools need to decide when developing planning and when reviewing it the sequence of activities which will deliver coherent planning for the school. Generally, the task will begin at the level of the whole school and then each area of planning and the involvement of particular members of staff will be determined.

It is well known that teaching involves a constant stream of information flowing from pupils about how they are learning or not learning and that much of this cannot be anticipated. But this is a reason for careful planing, not a justification for avoiding it. The more that can be anticipated and set out before the lesson, the more successful the teacher is likely to be in responding to the unexpected from a secure planned basis.

A report by the Office for Standards in Education (1991) involved case studies of six teachers and outlined features which contributed to well managed classes. Among these features was effective planning for teaching and learning.

The factors which make planning effective were identified as follows. A considerable amount of time is spent on planning and preparing personal teaching materials. It is detailed and thorough but flexible. It specifies the content to be taught at different levels: to the whole class, to specified groups and to some individual pupils. The teacher's planning is part of a whole-school system. This system aims to ensure full coverage of the National Curriculum attainment targets and programmes of study. It seeks to provide consistency, progression and continuity in learning. Collaborative planning is carried out where there is more than one class in a year group. The planning occurs over several time scales: yearly, termly, half-termly, weekly, and daily. The planning model complements the school's own curriculum model: which involves topics, themes, subjects, and so on. The planning identifies how aspects of the work will be assessed and the evidence that will be gathered to judge attainment. It also considers how the coverage of National Curriculum subjects will be checked. The assessment of pupil's previous learning informs planning. The planning uses the Programmes of Study and teachers specify the attainment targets to be aimed for and the levels at which the work will be pitched.

As well as topics, subject specific work is planned. Links with other subjects are included when the content of planned activities is considered. The planning includes classroom organisation, resources, tasks allocated to other adults, organisational strategies and teaching techniques. Classroom displays and their educational purposes are planned before the work starts. The amount of teaching time to be given to particular groups or individuals is specified in the planning of specific lessons. Planning and teaching are especially effective when the class teacher has a particular subject expertise. Planning includes deciding beforehand the method of recording the outcomes of each activity so pupils can present their results in different ways and therefore show a variety of competencies.

Turning from the cases studies, more generally, where planning is effective teachers own planning is set in a framework provided by planning at the whole-school level and at key stage level where appropriate. The challenge of the comparatively new approach of whole-school curriculum planning for teachers includes learning how to plan with colleagues (Burgess, Southworth and Webb, 1994).Whole-school planning comprises aims, curriculum policy statement and subject policy statements. This leads to key stage planning. The key stage planning may involve subject schemes of work and topic plans if appropriate which could be done at year group level. Key stage planning in turn leads to termly or half-termly plans, weekly plans, and daily plans. Weekly plans may be seen as strategic and daily plans as tactical and flexible.

A format for weekly planning could comprise:

- the activity or task to be undertaken by the children
- learning intention/outcomes, that is, what it is intended the children will learn as a result of the activity
- assessment methods to be used to determine whether the learning outcome was achieved
- resources to be used, including human resources such as teaching associates
- differentiation strategies, which will also indicate how the class is to be organised.

Given a sufficient degree of detail at the level of weekly planning, daily planning could be reduced. It might comprise an outline of the activities and organisation throughout the day, such as groupings and the use of classroom support. A time schedule would be included and assessment notes would be made to contribute to the planning cycle. Assessment notes feed into the outline plans for the following day and some key assessment observations may be used to contribute to summative assessments, perhaps for end of year reports to parents. In parallel with daily planning, it is important that the teacher knows exactly what she/he intends to teach in each lesson. The teacher may tell the class what they are going to study and learn at the start of the lesson and may summarise at the end of the lesson what has been covered.

In the *Guidance on the Inspection of Nursery and Primary Schools* (Office for Standards in Education, 1995), the criteria for good planning are that lessons have clear objectives for what pupils are to learn and how these will be achieved. Good planning will take into account the different learning needs of the pupils.

Inspectors will look for evidence of teaching intentions and how they will be met. Inspectors will seek evidence that planning covers the areas of learning for pupils under five; incorporates National Curriculum programmes of study and the requirements of the agreed syllabus for religious education, where appropriate; sets clear objectives; summarises what pupils will do and the resources they will need; and shows how knowledge and understanding can be extended and the work adapted to suite pupils who learn at different rates.

Assessment information should inform curriculum planning. Inspection guidance (Office for Standards in Education, 1995) states that planning is at its best when certain features are present. These include whole-school agreement on subject coverage and the balance between subjects and topics. Also, outcomes are monitored by senior staff. Between classes, the work is consistent. In planning, teachers make explicit the knowledge, understanding and skills which they anticipate pupils will develop. But also, very importantly, planning sets out the teaching methods and organisational strategies to be used so that the educational goals are reached.

As staff are involved in varying ways in the more general planning, so the role of their own termly, weekly and daily lesson plans will be informed by the whole-school structure. Like any team effort, good planning involves an eye for the detail of every day while not losing sight of the overall scheme of things.

Schools should:

- encourage careful planning by all staff for teaching and learning
- develop an integrated whole-school balance of long term, medium term, short term (weekly and daily) planning
- ensure that assessment information informs planning.

References

Burgess, H. Southworth, G. and Webb, R. (1994) 'Whole school curriculum planning in the primary school' in A. Pollard (ed.) *Look Before you Leap? Research Evidence for the Curriculum at Key Stage Two*, London, Tufnell Press.

Office for Standards in Education (1991) *Well Managed Classes in Primary Schools: Case Studies of Six Teachers*, London, OFSTED.

—— (1995) *Guidance on the Inspection of Nursery and Primary Schools*, London, OFSTED.

Project management in primary education

While the importance of leadership and general management in the primary school is widely recognised, the growing importance of project management at all levels is not always perceived. In community and voluntary (controlled) schools, the delegation of funding by local education authorities to school level has made the management of discrete funded projects a necessary part of the school's overall management. In foundation and independent schools, project management is similarly important.

Some ventures are very obviously projects. Among particularly impressive examples are the Olympic games and the channel tunnel. There are numerous less dramatic examples of projects: from putting on a play or completing a school mural to organising a sports week or raising standards in reading.

A project is a task which needs to be managed and which has a starting and finishing point. Some tasks are clearly discrete, and present themselves as appropriate for a project approach. Others are to do with general management but can on closer examination be broken down into specific projects. The discrete nature of projects is highly motivating because it gives the satisfaction that a particular job is completed, whereas with general management there is a sense in which it is never finished.

Project management has three basic principles. These are:

- identifying the objectives and ensuring that everyone is working to them and reaching them
- forward looking control which is flexible and quick to respond
- high quality decision making.

Three components of the project approach may be identified:

- quality which is reflected in measurable targets
- cost, which includes financial cost directly and other resources
- time (which is of course also money).

Let us consider an example of a project to improve standards of achievement in reading in a school. The quality of the reading to be reached would be specified, for example, that 90 per cent of Year 4 (present Year 2) will reach level 4 of the National Curriculum tests in reading comprehension within two years of the start of the project.

The project team could note down all the activities involved in the project on separate pieces of card. They would then add to each activity a note of the resources needed and the time it would take to complete each task. Next, the team would organise the activities in a logical sequence.

In our example, the tasks might include arranging and carrying out staff training, carrying out an audit of resources currently used, purchasing new books, monitoring the teaching of reading, and so on.

For each activity, it is important to decide the following:

1   what do you want to do now?
2   what must you do before that?
3   what can be done at the same time (parallel tasks)?
4   what must follow what you do now?

In our reading example, one of the things which might be done 'now' could be to carry out an audit of materials presently used. A task which would have to be done 'before that' would be deciding who would carry out the audit and how they would do it. A task which might be done at the 'same time' as this is to plan to monitor the teaching of reading, perhaps through lesson observations. A task which might 'follow what you do now' could be the consideration of what new resources might be needed following the audit.

As a result of the discussions to make the decisions above, the team would determine which activities depend on others being completed before they can be tackled. In major projects this may be approached through sophisticated computer software. More appropriately for small projects, it can be managed by using pieces of card on which are written the discrete activities. These cards are pinned to a board so that they can be moved around as discussion takes place about the possible alternative ordering of tasks. The cards form a 'network' which is arranged to show how the activities depend on each other.

The length of time each activity will take (the earliest start date/time of the activity and the latest finish time) is added to this. The earliest start time for each activity is calculated by adding together the duration of prior activities and working from left to right on the board. So, in the reading example, the time at which staff training is to be started might depend on the outcome of the monitoring of the teaching of reading because the content of the training would be influenced by the outcome of the monitoring. So the earliest starting time for staff training would be worked out by adding the time it would take to monitor the teaching of reading to, say, the starting time of the project.

As the 'network' develops it will be seen that many tasks can run in parallel with others, thus saving time. Some tasks will depend on others being completed. The duration of the project is worked out by calculating the time from the start of the project through the longest line of tasks which have to follow one another in sequence to the finishing time of the final task in that sequence. For example, in the reading project, the longest sequence of tasks may be those relating to monitoring staff teaching of reading, arranging and carrying out training, monitoring the effects of the training on the quality of the teaching and arranging further, perhaps individual, staff training if necessary. Clearly these have to happen in order.

In all this, the concept of the 'critical path' is important. This involves establishing what activities need to be done, which ones depend on each other, how long they will take, when they have to be done and who has to do them. The critical path is the path where there is no opportunity for parallel activities. This also suggests the milestones of the project which it is vital to reach. A simple way of recognising the importance of the critical path is to recognise that it represents the activities which are essential to be completed on time if the total project is to be completed on time. In the reading example, it would be essential for the initial monitoring of the teaching of reading to take place on time if the training were subsequently to occur on time. For such milestones, it would be appropriate to have contingency plans.

The characteristics of good project management are good communications, accurate budgeting and cost control mechanisms, effective team building and good relationships, and problem solving and decision making skills. Essential, should things begin to unravel, is good contingency planning.

The project manager must be a good communicator, both as a listener and as a speaker. (S)he must be able to delegate and to think ahead and think clearly. The project manager must involve people with the right expertise and establish what is to be done, when, where and by whom.

It will be seen that our reading example has the three components of a project: quality, cost and time. There is a quality element reflected in a target to be reached, the specified improvement in reading. There is a cost in terms of staff time and probably resources such as books and equipment. There is a specified time in which to achieve the results.

Quality would be assured not just by the single quality test of improvement or lack of it in subsequent achievement tests but also by interim measures of the quality of the project. This might include quality assessments of any new materials acquired or assessments of the quality of the training received. These would all feed back into judging the degree to which the final target is reached. In other words, if the achievement expected in reading was not as high as predicted, the previous quality points could be examined to see if they could be improved upon for similar future projects. Cost controls will be provided through the monitoring of the budget for the project. Time controls are provided through the time schedule which includes the critical path.

The ongoing monitoring should ensure, however, that the project is successful, that is that the end of the project is reached on time, within budget and to the quality specified.

Similar approaches can be taken to many aspects of school life, including improving the behaviour of pupils to a specified target, improving attendance, reducing staff absence, and so on. Project management fits in well with a rigorous approach to school development planning where the targets in the plan are measurable, time constrained and indicate a level of quality.

The school should:

- identify aspects of school development which lend themselves to project management
- focus on the interrelated aspects of quality, cost and time
- plan a critical path for the project.

Address

Association of Project Managers, Westbourne Street, High Wycombe, Buckinghamshire HP11 2PZ, tel: 01494 440 090, fax: 01494 528 937, e-mail: secretariat@apm-uk.demon.co.uk.

Research

Action research in the school

Research is not always well regarded. Wilson Mizner said of the subject, 'If you steal from one author it's plagiarism. If you steal from many it's research'.

The White Paper *Excellence in Schools* (Department for Education and Employment, 1997a) promised research and development into 'schools of the future'. The government also undertook to 'learn the lessons of international research projects' and to promote 'imaginative research and development in schooling'.

The Green Paper *Excellence for all Children: Meeting Special Educational Needs* (Department for Education and Employment, 1997b) promises to fund research to 'assess the relative costs, benefits and practical implications of educating children in mainstream and special schools'. Research will be commissioned on 'aspects of special educational needs or including a special educational needs dimension in other commissioned research'. The government will 'promote research designed to establish good practice, and disseminate the results'.

Too often research confirms notions which could have been established by a moment's reflection, or it is unrelated to the main issues as seen by those working in the classroom. Where research has merit it is not always disseminated to those whom it would interest or benefit. Yet good educational research can assist schools.

Educational research is an activity which involves gathering and analysing data to provide worthwhile information about, and insights into, teaching and learning and the educational settings in which they take place. On a broader front, it may be concerned with evaluating educational policy. It may involve examining the relationships between the education institution and the wider community, for example the relationships between parent and school. There is an increasing expectation from schools that research should be valid and relevant, if not immediately useful.

As with all research, the very choice of activity and area for research, the methods used and the way in which the information is presented are all influenced by the people conducting the research or those commissioning it.

To this extent, educational research is influenced by the social and political context in which it takes place.

Where educational research strives for objectivity its methods are typified by quantitative research. It involves hypotheses to be tested, samples reflecting the whole population about which generalisations are to be made, experimental and matched control groups, rigorous statistical models and analysis and other scientific structures. A more subjective element may be introduced by qualitative information such as personal accounts and case studies.

Both quantitative and qualitative research are important. Quantitative research has subjective elements in its context. Therefore, the use by schools of the more subjective research tools such as action research should not be overlooked simply because they may be mis-perceived as inferior to quantitative research.

Action research is a potentially powerful agent of change. The notion of research into education usually creates images of a researcher, perhaps in the classroom, being scrupulously careful not to influence what is being observed. Action research turns this notion on its head and makes a virtue of being involved as a participant observer. An obvious candidate to be a participant observer is the teacher. An example of a piece of action research is a teacher trying a new approach, say, to the teaching of reading, monitoring the results and comparing it with the previously used approach.

On a larger scale, action research may involve a team of researchers co-operating closely with teachers who are, for example, introducing new strategies to improve pupil behaviour. The various outcomes would be monitored but there would be a continuing opportunity to adapt and develop approaches to behaviour as the action research indicated ways which were working well and ways which were not. This can prevent an approach with various imperfections and inconsistencies in application being used throughout a period of research simply to maintain supposed objectiveness. The research itself continually feeds in to the activity being examined and acts to improve it.

Action research should be systematic and have timelines and objectives for its different phases. Within the school, it should be functional. The researcher ought to be able to record what he is doing and why and should document all the evidence. Research implies finding out new facts which can be used to inform something else.

Some aspects of research inform the teacher's role as a 'reflective practitioner'. A reflective practitioner teacher seeks to continuously refine the skill of teaching through systematically feeding the effects of the teaching into an assessment of how it can be made better. The reflective teacher reviews his/her practice systematically. Using skills of analysis, the teacher experiments with teaching skills to extend professional development. Such a reflective practitioner is constantly engaged in self appraisal through various means. These include concern with aims and consequences; ongoing self monitoring and evaluation; and awareness of different techniques and of classroom research. Other features are willingness to discuss practice with others and to learn from them, and a general openness to change.

In action research, the teacher is not constrained throughout the period of the research to pursue a particular aspect of an approach that professional training and instinct soon tells him or her is unhelpful. Participants are more in control, making this type of research attractive.

In adapting to the findings of the research as they emerge to their own responses and views, teachers are undergoing a form of intense professional development at the same time as developing an approach which is tested in practice. This potentially powerful combination of finding out and thinking about what has been found can lead to useful findings. The Nobel Prize-winning biochemist, Albert Szent-Gyorgi saw discovery as seeing what everybody has seen and thinking what nobody else has thought. If this is true, then the reflection part of the process is particularly important.

This stands in contrast to the more traditional in-service education in which an 'expert' often coveys knowledge and skills from outside the school. However, the better type of in-service education does draw on staff expertise and knowledge and skills. The emphasis is on problem solving. The approach encourages flexibility, which is another valuable quality to develop in all staff.

Criticisms of action research focus on experimental rigour being traded in for adaptability. However, it is difficult to transfer even the most rigorously tested approach to a new school setting simply because so many influences and factors may be different. Given this, action research is effective because it encourages the tailoring of any new approach to the particular circumstances of the school in a quickly evolving way.

Another criticism of action research is that the observer is not objective. But it can be a useful way to observe while being involved, and insights can be revealed in this way which may not emerge when observers are more detached.

The school should:

- recognise the respective benefits of objective and subjective research
- encourage staff to develop action research skills as part of their role as reflective practitioners.

References

Department for Education and Employment (1997a) *Excellence in Schools*, London, DfEE.

Department for Education and Employment (1997b) *Excellence for all Children: Meeting Special Educational Needs*, London, DfEE.

Further reading

Dadds, M. (1995) *Passionate Enquiry and School Development: A Story About Teacher Action Research*, London, Falmer.
Webb, R. (ed.) (1991) *Practitioner Research in the Primary School*, London, Falmer.

Address

National Foundation for Education Research, The Mere, Upton Park, Slough, Berkshire SL1 2DQ, tel: 01753 574 123, fax: 01753 691 632, e-mail: http://www.nfer.ac.uk.

School improvement plans within strategic planning

When Mrs Einstein was being shown round the Mount Wilson Observatory in California, the principal astronomer gave a lengthy explanation of the great telescope. He concluded that one of the main purposes of the instrument was to establish the shape of the universe. His guest replied, quite unimpressed, 'My husband does that on the back of an envelope'.

The school needs its own way of simplifying the complexities of school life. With so many developments to initiate and monitor, the use of a school improvement plan has become an essential part of the school's repertoire. The term, 'school development plan' has traditionally been used but 'school improvement plan' is becoming more preferred. This is because it emphasises the purpose of the plan, which is to encourage improvements, often specifically raising standards of achievement.

The school improvement plan is essentially a business tool which has been adapted to meet educational needs. Yet without a wider strategic context, the plan can become a rather sterile way of getting from A to B without ever considering whether B is a place worth getting to. There can be too much emphasis on measures of school improvement and not enough on outcomes.

Certainly, as part of school improvement, the plan has a pivotal role. The view of the planning cycle is typified as audit, making the plan, making the plan work, and evaluating the outcomes. Looking at the same issues in a different way, school improvement planning involves asking basic planning questions such as, 'Where is the school at present?', 'What needs to be changed?', 'How are the changes to be brought about?' 'Do changes represent value for money?' and 'What evaluation of the success or otherwise of the changes will take place?'.

Improvement planning is both a planning procedure and a management tool. As a planning procedure, it encompasses creating improvement and change, and is concerned with the present position of the school and what can be changed. As a management tool, improvement planning involves providing a purpose to planning and ensuring that apparently disparate developments are coherent. Like other forms of planning, it begins with aims or long term goals which need to be clear and agreed and reflect the school's values.

These lead to an assessment of the school situation at present (audit) which may include an analysis of the internal strengths and weaknesses and the external opportunities and threats – a so-called 'SWOT' analysis. The audit enables the school to describe, record and understand the current situation and may involve the scrutiny of documents, discussions with staff, pupils and parents, and the analysis of test results and other assessment data. It may further include the observation of lessons, an inventory of resources, an examination of procedures and many other techniques.

The audit may cover various issues. These range from developing a policy to enhancing the curricular provision for a subject. They encompass a range from improving procedures for financial planning to raising the level of attendance. The procedure may involve an audit of curricular provision, resources, assessment, relationships with parents, or many other areas.

National and local policies will need to be taken into account and built into the audit and the plan. Where it is not clear how national government policies will be interpreted in a local setting this requires careful judgement. Sometimes it is not even clear whether government aspirations will see the light of day as legislation as the political development of a policy unfolds.

For a school, this points towards the setting of priorities according to urgency, importance and cost. In turn, this leads to the framing of objectives which may be expressed in terms of the output required or as the changes expected. They need to be SMART targets, that is, specific, measurable, achievable, realistic and time limited.

Next in line come the action plans which include targets, tasks and resources, and provision for review according to specified criteria for success. Targets need to be attainable, appropriate and have an appropriate time scale. Tasks need to help the school reach the targets. Resources will include people and time as well as materials and equipment. The criteria for success should be appropriate and yield the evidence that is required.

At the heart of all this is regular monitoring. If the progress or otherwise of the school improvement plan is not monitored, then it will not be recognised sufficiently early that plans are slipping, and remedial action will not be possible. This is the progress chasing aspect of school improvement planning which is often carried out by members of the school senior management team. The levers of project management are important, that is the monitoring of time, quality and cost. Time is monitored through a time schedule, perhaps visited monthly to see that progress is being made at the required rate. Quality is monitored through statements of standards to be reached and this implies that these are clear and widely agreed. Cost is monitored through budget procedures.

Another way of looking at the essentials of school improvement planning is to recognise the cyclical components of audit, plan construction, implementation and evaluation. School improvement plans pull together the levels of planning in different areas for the whole school. Normally the plan is detailed for one year with the plan for subsequent years sketched in less detail up to five years ahead. As the plan is reviewed, so the level of detail is rolled forward so that at all times the school has detailed plans for a year ahead.

It is important that all who contribute to the success of the plan and its targets being achieved feel a part of the plan development. The head teacher, governors, staff, parents (and in community and voluntary controlled schools local education authority staff) may all play a part in its development.

Action plans would include a setting out of the school's current position, perhaps in relation to practice and provision and how effective they presently are. Targets would be included with success criteria. Particular tasks would be identified, the time allocated to completing them and the people involved. The resources needed, including financial resources, would be indicated. Staff development needs would be set out in terms of such provision as in-service education and training. There would be built into the plan ways of monitoring and checking progress.

A limitation of school improvement planning is that it focuses on the more immediate requirements of the school which are apparent and perhaps pressing. Longer term thinking brings in another dimension and can feed back into more effective school improvement planning.

This could begin with an attempt to envisage what might be developing in, say, ten years time. What might be the impact of modern technologies? How might the roles of various members of school staff have changed? How might government aspirations work out in practice? These and many other questions will pose themselves. This is an attempt to read current trends and to project from them.

The need for strategic planning then arises. Strategic analysis will involve identifying which factors are likely to influence development. It will take into account the views of a wide range of people involved in the school and how they see the future direction of the school. A range of choices can then be considered which will meet the challenges and the future direction which is seen. The best options will be decided upon. Taken together these form the strategic plan. Acting on these choices will feed into the school improvement plan. The plan will then have vision as well as having necessary maintenance elements. It will give a greater sense of long term direction to the school.

Such approaches need not be seen as too speculative. Rather they are an extension of the three-year development plan which is increasingly detailed as the time scale becomes closer. In strategic planning the time scale is far in advance and so the options are more general and are likely to be more flexible.

Even a strategic plan which proves to be far from the mark can give a basis for later judgements which is stronger than simply starting from scratch. Also, the habit of looking critically to the future refers back to more recent planning and tends to make it more informed. A useful analogy is that of a team player who continues to keep an eye on the ball but is always aware of what is happening with the rest of the team and the wider implications of winning or losing the current game.

Schools should devise improvement plans which:

- involve audit, action planning, implementation, and evaluation
- fit within the context of wider strategic planning.

Further reading

Rogers, R. (1994) *How to Write a School Development Plan: Whole School Issues Project*, Oxford, Heinemann.

Address

School Improvement Research Centre, National Foundation of Educational Research, The Mere, Upton Park, Slough, Berkshire SL1 2DQ, tel: 01753 574 123, e-mail: eval@nfer.ac.uk www page: http://www.nfer.ac.uk.

Security of the school

'The only real danger that exists is man himself', said Carl Jung. The terrible truth of this dictum has been sadly evident in recent years. School security has been highlighted by such tragedies as the murder by stabbing of the London head teacher Philip Lawrence in 1995 and by the fatal shooting of children in a school gymnasium in Dunblane Primary School, Scotland in 1996. Arson, vandalism and theft cost British schools tens of millions of pounds each year.

A Working Group on School Security, involving education professionals, police, governors, parents and local government officers, reported to the then Secretary of State for Education and Employment Gillian Shepherd in 1996 (Department for Education and Employment, 1996a). Its recommendations were accepted and received cross-party support. Among the stipulations was the development of clearer and more detailed guidance on school security. Schools should regularly review their security measures paying particular attention to the control of access to the premises. Training in personal safety is important for those working on the school premises, that is, teachers and non-teaching staff.

Lord Cullen's report on the Dunblane tragedy includes a chapter on security which emphasises the importance of controlling access to schools. Security may centre on unauthorised visitors entering school premises which are often easy targets for criminals to rob or vandalise. In 1996, legislation came into force to make it an arrestable offence for anyone to carry a knife or other offensive weapon while on school premises. Police were given greater powers of search on school sites.

Following the Working Group Report, a guide, *Improving Security in Schools*, was produced in September 1996 (Department for Education and Employment, 1996b). This publication covers the roles and responsibilities of various parties: the local education authority, the governing body and the head teacher. The involvement of staff, pupils and parents is stressed. The importance of a security strategy is explained and the matters of identifying and assessing risks. The guide concerns different security measures including visitor access control systems, fire and burglar alarms, property marking and personal safety equipment. Security lighting, secure storage and security fencing are further topics covered. Parents should be informed of the school security policy and encouraged to help. Parents should be involved. Governors have to include school security in their annual report to parents.

The Working Group on School Security recommended in its report of May 1996 that the government should give guidance to schools, the police and others about the powers of the police and the criminal justice system to deal with 'trouble makers' in and near schools. It was also recommended that guidance should be given on good practice in local liaison between the school, police and other pertinent agencies. The result was the publication, *School Security: Dealing with Troublemakers* (Department for Education and Employment/ Home Office, 1997). This covers the issues of trespass, offences not involving assault, assault, offensive weapons and other criminal matters not involving the threat of violence or the use of violence. It also concerns co-operation between police and schools, and the role of the Crown Prosecution Service, magistrates and the judiciary.

School security can be approached as a dimension of risk assessment (see also *Health and Safety in Schools*). While physical modifications to a school building and its site may be effective, it is important that staff and pupils act in ways to minimise risks stemming from school security. This involves a realistic understanding of the potential hazards (in the case of pupils commensurate with their age and maturity), a knowledge of why rules and procedures are necessary, and a commitment to following them.

To improve school security it is necessary to review the security problems that the school has experienced. This implies that all breaches of security are recorded. Priority measures should be based on this. Most local education authorities employ risk managers or crime prevention officers who advise schools. A security audit carried out with the help of experts will yield a risk assessment, which can then lead to steps to fill security gaps.

Adequate funding is crucial for such developments to be fully effective. There was a £22 million programme in 1997–98 through Grants for Education Support and Training (GEST) funding, and through equivalent grants for grant maintained schools, specifically for school security. That money was allocated by formula to all local education authorities which had to pass it on directly to schools. The more recent Standards Fund Grant (and the grant maintained schools equivalent) is also £22 million and works on exactly the same principle. Under the previous Conservative government, there was also extra funding through the Schools Renewal Challenge Fund. The Labour government made extra funding for security available through the New Deal for Schools initiative and there has been some extra funding through the government's School Challenge Fund with many local authorities bidding for money earmarked for school security. The Standards Fund categories for 1998–99 included a grant for school security.

One approach to security is to have closed circuit television cameras installed to act as a deterrent and for observation. Access may be restricted to one main entrance protected by a combination lock known only to staff. Cameras may be used to vet visitors before they enter. Signing in and signing out procedures may be followed, coupled with a visitor's badge. Equally important are the routines of security used in the school. Clear guidance for visitors to the school should take them through a system in which they wear identification badges and/or are escorted round the school by the head teacher or a member of senior staff.

All staff should be routinely informed of expected visitors through the staff notice board or day book so that unexpected visitors are easier to identify. Electronic identification cards can help provide secure areas for valuables.

Poorly maintained buildings invite vandalism. Fencing and gates are important and new ones may need to be erected or existing ones repaired or improved. Also potentially helpful are intruder-proof windows operated by multi-point non-key operated locks, solid doors and frames, anti-scaling obstacles and security lighting linked to passive infra red detectors. Intruder alarm systems should conform to British Standards 4737 specifications. Alarms which call the police must be installed and maintained by a company which belongs to a nationally recognised inspectorate body. Intruder alarms with external boxes can be an effective deterrent, as can dummy closed circuit television cameras.

Other potentially useful measures are personal panic alarms or mobile telephones for staff on potentially vulnerable sites. Classroom doors may be fitted with locks which can only be opened from the inside. Full time site managers could be responsible for school security and visitor access.

As part of a national conference on school security in 1996, a directory was produced and was subsequently expanded. The revised directory (Department for Education and Employment, 1997) comprises details of local authority initiatives and a contact person in each authority from whom further information can be obtained. Examples of initiatives are: governor training seminars, a risk management manual, an initiative in which schools are supplied with information on the 'Indsol Tracer' property marking solution, a school watch scheme, safe school accreditation, coded locks, closed circuit television, guidance on protection from personal attack, police liaison, safety glazing, trespass guidance notes and many other ideas.

It would be impossible to stop any unstable irrational person harming those in a school if they were determined to do harm, except by taking such stringent security measures that the quality of school life would be greatly diminished. What schools must achieve is a reasonable level of security conversant with a happy and unrestricted life in the school. Much can be done to achieve this.

The school should:

- control access of visitors to the school site
- manage the movement of visitors around the school
- train all members of the school community in personal safety
- liaise effectively with the police and others to improve school security.

References

Department for Education and Employment (1996a) *Report of the Working Group on School Security*, London, DfEE.

—— (1996b) *Managing School Facilities, Guide 4: Improving Security in Schools*, London, HMSO.

Department for Education and Employment/Welsh Office (1997) *Directory of Local Education Authority Practice on School Security*, London, DfEE.

Department for Education and Employment/Home Office (1997) *School Security: Dealing with Troublemakers*, London, DfEE.

Address

School Security and Behaviour Support Team, Room 2 R 8, Department for Education and Employment, Sanctuary Buildings, Great Smith Street, Westminster, London SW1 P 3BT, tel: 0171 925 6322 (team direct line), fax: 0171 925 6986.

Sex education

Steering a steady course

The need for balance in sex education is illustrated by the story of the boy who returned from school one day and asked his father, 'Where did I come from?' The father had prepared for such a day and lost no time in taking out the facts of life books and explaining the answer to the boy's question. It suddenly dawned on the father that his son was looking rather confused and he asked what had prompted his question. 'I was just curious dad,' replied the lad 'because we had a new boy in class today and he said he came from Liverpool.'

Sex education poses particular challenges for a primary school. The most effective approach is one of balancing the interests of those who have a say in the schools approach and at the same time having channels in which dissident views can be expressed and through which, ultimately, parents can withdraw pupils from the provision offered.

The Education Act 1996 requires all maintained schools to offer a curriculum which prepares children for the opportunities, responsibilities and experiences of adult life. The definition of sex education given by the Act is that it should include education about Human Immunodeficiency Virus (HIV) and Acquired Immune Deficiency Syndrome (AIDS) and any other sexually transmitted disease.

Under the Act, all county, controlled and maintained special schools (except those established in a hospital) have a duty relating to sex education. This is that the articles of government for these schools must make it a duty of the governing body to:

- consider whether sex education should be part of the secular curriculum of the school
- make and keep up to date a separate written statement of whatever policy they adopt on sex education.

The statement must state the governing body's policy on the content and organisation of the relevant part of the curriculum. Where the governing body concludes that sex education should not form part of the secular curriculum, the statement must say this.

The governing body must make the statement available to parents on request. School governors are responsible for this. The decision about what the policy is has to be taken by the whole governing body, not a sub-committee or an individual governor. The booklet *School Governors: A Guide to the Law County and Controlled Schools* (DfEE, 1997) offers information in section 4:18 and section 7: 21–24.

In a primary school, the governing body should consider sex education in consultation with the head teacher. They should have regard to any representations made to them:

• by anyone connected with the community served by the school
• by the chief officer of police in connection with his responsibilities (Education Act 1996).

The articles of government for a grant maintained, county, controlled or maintained special school must provide that in discharging duties regarding sex education the head teacher ensures certain things. He or she must ensure that the secular curriculum as it relates to sex education is compatible with the policy of the governing body. The exception to this is where any policy is incompatible with any part of the syllabus for a course which is part of that curriculum and leads to public examination. The head teacher must ensure that the secular curriculum is compatible with enactments relating to education, including the Education Act 1996. Provisions relating to children with special educational needs must be heeded.

Under the Education Act 1996, children with disabilities have an equal right to school sex education. The governing body of a primary school can decide not to offer sex education which lies outside the National Curriculum.

Parents have the right to withdraw their child from all or any aspect of sex education which comes outside the National Curriculum (Education Act 1996). The LEA, the governing body and the head teacher must take any reasonably practicable steps to ensure that sex education encourages the pupils involved to have due regard to moral considerations and the value of family life.

The Department for Education (DfE) Circular 5/94 concerns sex education. While the legal references in the Circular have been superseded, the Circular contains some useful points. The Circular provides advice on the appropriate content and purpose of sex education. It offers guidance on the development of policies (and programmes) of sex education and their implementation. The Circular outlines the roles of governors, head teachers and other staff and of parents. It indicates the action which is expected of those concerned.

Sections of the Circular deal with:

- statutory provisions
- the role of parents
- a moral framework for sex education
- the content of sex education
- developing a school policy on sex education (covering the roles of governors, head teacher and other teachers and the role of the local education authority)
- implementing sex education policies and programmes (concerning information for parents, the right of parents to withdraw their child from some sex education, advice to individual pupils and teacher in service training)
- action to be taken by schools.

Annexes to the Circular cover schools' legal obligations; a summary of the law on sexual behaviour; and guidance on good practice in developing a school sex education policy. In developing a policy, a school might follow eight steps:

- reviewing the current policy and practice
- identifying the pupils' needs
- identifying staff needs and community needs
- drafting the policy (or changes where there is an existing policy)
- consultation
- communication
- implementing the policy
- monitoring the implementation of the policy.

The Circular gives guidance and sets out the moral framework for sex education. Pupils should, 'be encouraged to appreciate the value of stable family life, marriage and the responsibilities of parenthood'.

The document advises that in primary schools, sex education should prepare pupils to cope with the physical and emotional challenges of growing up. It should give pupils an elementary understanding of human reproduction. Due consideration should be given to the wishes of parents and to cultural or religious factors.

There has been some confusion about whether issues around homosexuality can be addressed in schools. The Local Government Act 1988, section 28 prohibits local authorities from:

- intentionally promoting homosexuality
- publishing material that intends to promote homosexuality

- promoting teaching in any maintained school of the acceptability of homosexuality as a 'pretended family relationship'.

However, it is the governing body which decides the content, approach and organisation of sex education. The guidance in Circular 5/94 indicates that the prohibitions mentioned above apply to the activities of local authorities 'as distinct from' the governing bodies and staff of schools on their own behalf.

If a pupils reveals to a teacher that he or she is having sex under the age of consent, Circular 5/94 indicates that the teacher must inform the head teacher who should arrange that the parents are 'made aware'. This is, however, guidance and not law, which places schools in a difficult position. The Sex Education Forum (address below) suggests agreeing a policy in which teachers can make decisions using their professional judgement while always maintaining the best interests of the child. If child protection issues arise where the teacher believes that the child is at risk of physical or sexual harm then the teacher is obliged to inform a named member of staff and follow child protection procedures.

A policy on sex education will involve a wide range of people who are consulted: parents, staff, governors, pupils and advisors from outside the school. The draft policy will again involve wide consultation and will lead into the formation of a scheme of work, the purchase of resources and decisions about teaching approaches, all of which can involve consultation.

The Sex Education Forum is an umbrella body comprising around 40 organisations representing education, child care, health, parents and religious groups. It seeks to improve sex education for children and young people. The Forum organises seminars and projects and produces a termly newsletter 'Sex Education Matters', and resources.

Schools should:

- be familiar with the legislation relating to sex education
- consult widely and seek advice on the issues around sex education
- be aware of bodies such as the Sex Education Forum which organise seminars, projects and provide information.

References

Department for Education (1994) *Circular 5/94: Education Act 1993: Sex Education in Schools*, London, DfE.

Department for Education and Employment (1997) *School Governors: A Guide to the Law County and Controlled Schools, June 1997 edition*, London, DfEE.

Addresses

Sex Education Forum, 8 Wakley Street, London EC1V 7QE, tel: 0171 843 6000, fax: 0171 843 6053.

Personal, Social and Health Education Team, Department for Education and Employment, Sanctuary Buildings, Great Smith Street, Westminster, London SW1P 3BT, tel: 0171 925 5498, fax: 0171 925 6954.

Spiritual, moral, social and cultural development

Complex interrelationships

Although the spiritual, the moral, the social and the cultural have each come under scrutiny from humorists over the years, the concentration has been on the spiritual and the moral. For example, in the spiritual sphere, Ambrose Bierce defined heaven as a place where the wicked cease from troubling you with their personal affairs and the good listen with attention while you expound your own. Of morality, the writer and satirist Hector Munro – 'Saki' – commented, 'In my day men were content with ten commandments and one wife. Now the situation is reversed'.

But such jibes no doubt arise from the gulf that often comes between, on the one hand, our desires and aspirations, and on the other hand, our conduct and achievements. We still lay a huge responsibility on schools to help us make our children better people than perhaps we are ourselves.

In comparatively recent legislation, the Education Reform Act 1988 required schools to promote the 'spiritual, moral, cultural, mental and physical development of pupils'. This terminology did not match that of the notion of spiritual, moral, social and cultural development (SMSC) which arose from the onset of Office for Standards in Education (OFSTED) inspections. This has caused much confusion for schools and educationalists generally. The *OFSTED Handbook: Guidance on the Inspection of Nursery and Primary Schools* (Office for Standards in Education, 1995) regards SMSC development as aspects of personal development (*OFSTED Handbook*, p. 43).

Under the OFSTED criteria, schools are judged on the extent to which they are successful in promoting pupils' SMSC development. The provision is reflected in the curriculum and life of the school, the example which adults set for pupils and the quality of the act of collective worship. The *Handbook* intimates that opportunities should be given for pupils to learn about and explore different values, beliefs and views and to develop and express their own.

The *Handbook* acknowledges links with the pupils' attitudes, behaviour and personal development; teaching; the curriculum and assessment; support, guidance and pupil welfare and the relationships established in the school; and the partnership with parents and the community. In short, SMSC, as much as any other feature of school life, permeates the whole school and beyond. It should reach all pupils irrespective of their background, although some pupils, for example pupils with special educational needs, may need support to fully benefit.

Regarding spiritual development, the school is expected to give pupils a knowledge of and insight into values and religious beliefs. It should also enable pupils to think about their experiences so as to develop self knowledge and spiritual awareness. Acts of worship have a particular role and religious education can make a significant contribution to spiritual development. Spiritual insights imply in some degree an awareness of how pupils relate to others and this links these insights to moral and social development.

In the area of moral development, it is important that the school teaches principles which separate right from wrong. Moral development involves building a framework of values which regulate personal behaviour through principles. Moral and social education are related and depend on the school encouraging positive values such as honesty. The school should provide a moral code as a basis for behaviour which is promoted through the life of the school.

Turning to social development, the school should encourage pupils to relate effectively to others, take responsibility, take part fully in the local community and develop an understanding of citizenship.

Schools take on a wide range of cultural responsibilities. They should teach pupils to appreciate and develop their own cultural traditions. Pupils should also be taught to appreciate the variety and complexity of other cultures.

It will be clear from the above that the *Handbook* recognises the interrelationships between spiritual, moral, social and cultural development and education. Perhaps the strongest bonds of interrelationship are between spiritual, moral and social elements.

Various issues emerge from the centrality of SMSC to the life of the school and the way it permeates so much of the other aspects of the school. One of these is the importance of understanding spiritual, moral, social and cultural development in children at different ages. What level might be typical of a child under 5 and what might be typical of a child at 7 and 11? While teachers are able to give accurate judgements about academic attainment according to National Curriculum levels, some find it more difficult to make similar judgements on SMSC development.

Neither is it necessary that spiritual, moral, social and cultural development progress at similar rates. A child may have a good grasp of moral behaviour based on reason but not have much spiritual awareness. A child may be socially well developed yet understand little of other cultures. It would be necessary to make judgements on the development of children on each aspect of SMSC development. Provision may be interrelated but progress may be uneven.

Such judgements are difficult, but if they are not formed it is impossible to know whether any progress is being made because of the school's provision. Like any other area in which the school is striving to promote progress, it is necessary to know the starting point and the progress or lack of it, in order to develop and refine provision.

In a school which promotes religious values, say a church school, it would be surprising if there was not a greater coherence than in other schools in the spiritual and religious life of the school and the moral and social aspects. If this is so it could be taken as an indication that the pupils had a more developed sense of spiritual, moral and social issues. Yet this coherence may be a reflection of an emphasis on a single coherent view taught by the school rather than a reasoned unity on the part of the child. This could further complicate any judgements made within the school or by anyone else concerning the level of SMSC development and what school factors were contributing to it.

In a religious school, say a church school, it may be difficult to determine the level of moral development if this draws on religious precepts. A child may believe that it is wrong to steal because God says it is. This raises the question of whether this child is less or more morally aware than a child who considers stealing wrong because the thief has not worked for the thing which was stolen (or some other explanation based on reason).

One way forward could be to make a clearer distinction between faith and reason in this context. If religious faith is valued by a school, the degree to which this permeates the life and conduct of the school community could be judged. At the same time the school could assess SMSC development based on reason as to some degree separate. This is not to say that faith should not and would not infuse SMSC in religious schools but that such schools would encourage a parallel development of SMSC aspects based on reason. Such a reasoned approach would be appropriate to schools in which staff and pupils and parents did not have religious faith.

An attempt to provide a reason-based set of moral values was made by the School Curriculum and Assessment Authority (1996). A moral values statement was prepared by the National Forum for Value in Education and the Community. The values identified concerned society, relationships, the self, and the environment and each area was linked with principles for action. Consultation followed involving organisations, a survey of the general public, a postal survey of schools, and research among school governors, teachers and parents. The School Curriculum and Assessment Authority (SCAA) submitted advice to the Secretary of State in February 1997. In 1998, the Qualifications and Curriculum Authority (QCA) into which the work of the former SCAA was subsumed, worked on guidance for schools.

In independent schools, religious education is a compulsory subject at common entrance but not for all scholarship examinations.

Schools should:

* recognise the interrelationships between the strands of SMSC
* for teaching purposes assess the development of pupils in each strand.

Reference

Office for Standards in Education (1995) *OFSTED Handbook: Guidance on the Inspection of Nursery and Primary Schools*, London, HMSO.

School Curriculum and Assessment Authority (1996) *Education for Adult Life: The Spiritual and Moral Development of Young People (SCAA Discussion Papers No. 6)*, London, SCAA,

Address

Personal, Social and Health Education Team, Department for Education and Employment, Sanctuary Buildings, Great Smith Street, Westminster, London SW1P 3BT, tel: 0171 925 5498, fax: 0171 925 6954.

Staff development including newly qualified teachers

Charles Burgess Fry was in need of no development at all, excelling in everything he tried. An Oxford scholar and a triple blue, he also became a superb sportsman after college. A first division footballer and for a time the world long jump holder, Fry was also an expert tennis player and represented England at athletics and cricket. When in his seventies, the all rounder was chided by a friend for being such a one man band. Fry had announced his intention to open a racing stables and become involved in the sport when his friend enquired, 'In what capacity, trainer, jockey or horse?'

For less talented people, continuing development is necessary in order to achieve well. For teachers, staff development is one important way of assisting high levels of performance. Essential to successful staff development are a clear policy and a school development plan complementing this. The professional development of all staff, including ancillary staff, should be encompassed by the policy.

A co-ordinator with specific responsibility for staff development can assess staff and whole-school development needs and ensure that there is a balance between what is required by the school and what is appropriate for the professional and personal development of individual staff. This is a two-way needs analysis. Class teachers, school midday supervisory assistants (SMSAs), school administrative staff and others are all included in planning. Another source of identifying in-service education and training needs is through the process of appraisal which is itself most efficient when it is integrated into other school processes (see also the chapter 'Appraisal: towards an integrated system').

The practicalities of people attending courses and the use of supply cover need to be carefully planned and budgeted for. Such long term planning does not exclude the possibility of a school responding to the unforeseen. It makes it easier to do so if necessary because the school will be able to make adjustments to its plans rather than respond in an ad hoc way.

Sources of income for staff development include the Standards Fund, which reflects government shaping of the training agenda for teachers. The government channels funds to local education authorities (LEAs) and consequently to community and voluntary controlled schools on an annual basis to use on the in-service education of teachers and similar initiatives. This money is allocated by bid following an annual Circular which advises in which areas of training money is available. LEAs might provide, say, 40 per cent of the cost while government provides the remaining 60 per cent, usually up to a predetermined upper limit. Through controlling the categories of money available and through audit, the government controls the development of in-service training and the activities in schools which result from it.

In the case of foundation schools, funds for training come from the Standard Grant. This represents a larger amount than that allocated to community schools because the LEA is not involved. However, LEAs have to provide some forms of training such as that on health and drug awareness.

Given this element of control, what flexibility does a primary school have to use the system to suit its own needs? First, the school needs to make an audit of the skills and knowledge which staff already possess and consider the gaps in knowledge and skills which need to be filled. Often such gaps will relate to newly introduced procedures and practices which government has introduced and which Standards Fund money may well support. In this case there is no discrepancy between what the school would wish to do for staff education and the direction in which the Standards Fund points them.

Where there is a discrepancy, the school has two options. It can undertake training without the support of funds such as the Standards Fund money, or it can look at any flexibility there may be in addressing training needs with Standards Fund money which at first sight they do not appear to match.

An economical way to maximise training is to develop a cascade system in which staff attending a course of general interest make careful notes of the proceedings, collect any printed information and other resources from the course and use these to update other staff in meetings or on training days, or more briefly at a staff meeting soon after the course. A systematic file of courses attended, handouts received and feedback given will help in the monitoring of the process. Each member of staff may have a portfolio of professional development. The National Literacy Strategy training is one such example of cascade training.

Like all policies and school development this will benefit from being monitored and the evidence of improvements, for example in pupil achievement, should be related as far as practicable to the staff training. This is difficult to achieve in practice because there is no control group against which to measure improvement. However, some broad links may be made which appear to relate staff training to better provision and consequently to improved achievement.

The professional development of newly qualified teachers is of particular importance. From June 1998, all providers of initial teacher training were required to give newly qualified teachers (NQTs) a Teacher Training Agency

(TTA) Career Entry Profile. Only those successful in gaining Qualified Teacher Status (QTS) can receive a TTA Career Entry Profile.

The profile gives a basis for support and monitoring during induction. It summarises information about the new teacher's strengths and priorities for further professional development, in relation to the standards for the award of QTS, from initial teacher training to their first teaching post.

The profile has four sections:

- a summary of the NQTs' initial teacher training including any distinctive features of their training
- the NQTs' strengths and priorities for further professional development during induction (agreed between the provider and the NQT)
- the NQTs' own targets for the induction period
- targets and action plan for the induction period (agreed between the school and the NQT).

NQTs bring fresh ideas to a school and can make a valuable contribution. However, if things go wrong the NQTs can find themselves under great stress and can create difficulties for other staff and for the school as a whole. Perhaps these issues arise to a degree with any new member of staff but there is an added dimension of the unknown in that a NQT does not have a long track record in other schools with which a school can partly reassure itself when recruiting an NQT who is new to the school.

For a school, the management of NQTs begins with recruitment. Care is normally taken when recruiting any member of staff. But schools will wish to take particular care when recruiting an NQT to ensure that the match between school and new staff member is as close as possible. This takes on a different complexion when schools have themselves been the part trainers of an NQT in such a scheme as primary partnership.

When visiting a school for a post an NQT may not be as skilled as a more seasoned member of staff in picking up the signals about the ethos and other important factors about the school. These may be made clear and time should be allowed for questions to be asked and for discussion when prospective staff visit the school. Opportunities may be given for interaction with the pupils and this may range from sitting with pupils over lunch to taking a small group or a class for a lesson. For a school that is in the fortunate position of being able to pick and choose its staff all this is easier than for a school which is struggling with recruitment and retention.

When an NQT is recruited, this will initially be for an induction period of (usually) a year. Government consulted in 1998 about induction for new teachers (Department for Education and Employment, 1998). The aim of the proposals is to ensure that structured support and training is provided to secure and develop the skill acquired in initial teacher training. It is intended that a national framework will give new teachers a statement of what is expected from them; a guarantee that the support needed to help meet the expectations is provided; the chance to learn from observing good teaching; opportunities to reflect on their performance and develop it; and chances to share experiences with other teachers. Subject to the passing of legislation, all newly qualified teachers who complete their initial teacher training will have to complete the induction period successfully in order to remain eligible to be employed in a maintained school (or in a non-maintained special school).

Although problems will still have to be faced, a comprehensive staff development policy will help ensure that all staff, including NQTs, progress and contribute to the school with increasing effectiveness.

Schools should:

- have a whole-school development policy linked with the school development plan
- ensure that the staff development co-ordinator balances staff and school development needs
- audit staff skills and knowledge
- link staff training to the raising of pupils' standards
- take particular care to support newly qualified teachers.

References

Department for Education and Employment (1998) *Induction for New Teachers: A Consultation Document*, London, DfEE.

Teacher Training Agency (1997) *Career Entry Profile for Newly Qualified Teachers*, London, TTA.

Address

Teacher Training Agency, Portland House, Stag Place, London SE1E 5TT, tel: 0171 925 3700, fax: 0171 925 3792, e-mail: TTA@GTNET.GOV.UK.

Standards

The new watchword

Standards are sometimes insufficiently explicit. A local Labour council is said to have been disappointed with a Barbara Hepworth sculpture which they had commissioned. This was not so much because the piece lacked originality as because there were rather too many holes in it and some members felt they were not getting their money's worth. This is a case of some confusion between the standards of artistic merit and the cost per pound of the artefact.

But in education, until recently, it was difficult to talk about standards in any meaningful way at all because of the lack of firm data. Now it is possible to talk about and measure standards of academic achievement. With the bedding in of the National Curriculum and its associated assessment procedures, standards have become one of the prime issues in education. Office for Standards in Education (OFSTED) inspections incorporate attainment, progress, pupils' attitudes, behaviour and personal development and attendance under the broad definition of 'educational standards achieved'.

The Education Bill 1996 included measures to raise standards in schools. It required primary schools to assess children on entry to provide a baseline against which their education could be planned and progress measured. The Act also required schools to set targets for improving their performance, and gave the Office for Standards in Education (OFSTED powers to inspect the effectiveness of local education authorities in raising standards in schools.

A Standards Task Force was established under the chairmanship of the Secretary of State for Education and Employment. Vice chairmen were Chris Woodhead (Her Majesty's Chief Inspector for Schools) and Tim Brighouse (Director of Education for Birmingham). Other members were representatives of the education service, including successful classroom practitioners and representatives from industry and commerce.

The Task Force introduced an annual award for the most outstanding example of school improvement. It meets four times a year. The Task Force was set up to:

- unite the various educational interests to raise standards
- act as an advocate for raising standards
- advise the Secretary of State on the development and implementation of policies to improve school standards and meet the national targets for literacy and numeracy
- keep the Secretary of State abreast of good practice nationally and internationally.

The Standards and Effectiveness Unit at the Department for Education and Employment is the responsibility of the School Standards Minister and is headed by Professor Michael Barber.

The first remit of the unit included a range of tasks. It was to spearhead government policy to raise school standards particularly with regard to schools achieving targets for primary literacy and numeracy. It would support the Secretary of State in establishing a mechanism for consulting teachers and others. The unit would advise the Secretary of State on the school improvement role of local education authorities (LEAs) and advise him on individual LEA development plans. It would co-ordinate the contribution of the Office for Standards in Education (OFSTED), the Teacher Training Agency (TTA) and the Qualifications and Curriculum Authority (QCA) to school improvement.

Through keeping abreast of developments in schools and elsewhere it would enable the department to contribute to and take cognisance of best practice in schools and LEAs building on the Improving Schools Programme. The unit would implement the literacy strategy outlined in the Literacy Task Force report and oversee similar work arising from the Numeracy Task Force.

It would ensure coherent systems for collecting, analysing and using performance data to measure pupil progress, compare performance and encourage improved performance. The unit would make sure that schools used the data to set targets for measurable improvement.

The unit would advise the Secretary of State on the improvement of schools judged by OFSTED to be failing or seriously weak, in order to raise the performance of these schools and disseminate the lessons learned to benefit all schools. The unit would co-ordinate research activities in school improvement and ensure that relevant research informed government policy. It would promote effective relationships on standards and effectiveness with others, including business. It would develop and implement where fitting the concept of education action zones. The unit would develop a national data base of best practice to be accessible to all schools.

A further indication of the tight concentration on standards is the renaming and revamping of the previous Grants for Education Support and Training (GEST) funding. Government Circular 13/97 invites local education authorities in England to apply for grant support on their expenditure in the financial year 1998–99. The source of money is now known as the Standards Fund.

The range of grants mirrors the government's priority of raising standards in schools as set out in the White Paper *Excellence in Schools*. The main focus is on school self improvement through targets agreed with the LEA and embodied in the school and LEA development plans.

A new grant supports the implementation of the National Literacy Strategy in all primary schools. From September 1998 all schools will be expected to introduce a daily literacy hour. The Standards Fund is also intended to support the baseline assessment of pupils entering compulsory schooling and training those who educate the under-5s.

Most of the Standards Fund is allocated to schools with LEAs supporting schools in raising standards. From 1998 it is expected by government that LEA targets and priorities will be reflected in Education Development Plans (EDPs). Activities funded through the Standards Fund should not replicate activities funded through LEA resources or other government grants such as the Single Regeneration Budget or projects involving the Training and Enterprise Councils.

The programme reflects the national priorities for teacher professional development as seen by the Teacher Training Agency. Schools and LEAs should follow certain principles to underpin professional development.

Development opportunities should be targeted through needs assessment and appraisal. Professional development activities should address needs through quality assurance of the provision. It should be ensured that professional development has the maximum impact on classroom practice through monitoring and evaluating development activities and setting improvement targets. The five non-contact days should be used as part of schools' planned programmes of professional development. School governors should be accountable for the professional development of staff and its impact. Schools and LEAs are expected to ensure all this.

The Circular concerns 20 grants, and 15 of these attract a rate of 50 per cent of the expenditure. LEAs submit bids competitively. For most grants, allocations are formula based, for example according to the number of schools or pupils.

LEAs cannot delegate the Standards Fund supported expenditure to schools via the Aggregated Schools Budget. This is precluded by the Education (Financial Delegation to Schools) (Mandatory Exceptions) Regulations 1995 (Statutory Instrument 1995/178). LEAs are asked to confirm that all expenditure supported by the devolved Standards Fund grants will be met from resources held centrally by the LEA within its General Schools Budget. This expenditure includes the LEA's own required contribution. The LEA cannot draw on schools' own delegated budget shares.

The individual entries indicate the expenditure eligible for support within the devolved grants, although schools are allowed to determine their own pattern of expenditure. Schools should keep clear records of expenditure available for audit.

LEAs should involve schools closely in developing and implementing school related grants under the Standards Fund. The grants involved are as follows:

- school effectiveness
- school leadership
- induction of newly qualified teachers
- early years training and development
- reduction of infant class sizes
- assessment
- national literacy strategy – primary
- national literacy project – Key Stage 3
- Summer literacy schools
- family literacy
- premier league club study sports centres
- special educational needs
- qualifications
- work related learning
- improving attendance and behaviour
- drug prevention and schools
- youth service
- school security
- specialist schools
- specialist teacher assistants.

Schools will increasingly need to consider their provision in terms of the effect on standards. A review of standards can be the starting point for a closer examination of provision where standards are lower than expected. An improvement in standards will be the measure of success of any new initiative aimed at improving provision. As national and local benchmarks become more accepted, schools will be able to use standards as a tool of management, both as an indicator of concern and as a sign of progress.

The school should:

- so far as is practicable, relate its work to the raising of pupil standards
- be aware of the remit of Standards Fund grants and be familiar with the role of the grants in raising standards
- be aware of the work of the Standards Task Force and the Standards and Effectiveness Unit.

Reference

Department for Education and Employment (1997) *Circular 13/ 97: The Standards Fund 1998–99*, London, DfEE.

Address

Local Education Authority Finance Division, Department for Education and Employment, Sanctuary Buildings, Great Smith Street, London SW1P 3BT, tel: 0171 925 6086, fax: 0171 925 6986.

Support for children
Maximising outside help

Shakespeare, in *Timon of Athens*, writes,

> 'Tis not enough to help the feeble up
> But to support them after.

As schools look at the support that they themselves offer to their children, ensuring that it is as effective as possible, they must also look to the way that support from other sources is used and co-ordinated. The degree of this outside support will not always be under the school's control but it is within every school's grasp to maximise what support is available.

When inspecting schools, inspectors have to evaluate and report on various aspects of support, guidance and pupil welfare (Office for Standards in Education, 1995). Specifically, the inspectors evaluate the school's provision for pupils' educational and personal support and guidance. They consider the contribution of this provision to the educational standards achieved. In looking at this, inspectors take note of individual needs and action taken to ensure the welfare of pupils. The school's arrangements for child protection and anything posing a threat to health and safety are also evaluated.

The judgements are founded on the degree to which the school:

- gives pupils effective support and advice
- has effective ways of encouraging discipline and good behaviour and getting rid of oppressive behaviour
- has effective child protection procedures
- promotes pupils' health, safety and general well being.

The school's support and guidance should enable pupils to benefit from the educational opportunities offered and should help ensure that pupils have high yet realistic self expectations. The school is expected to monitor pupils' progress and personal development, offer individual support and advice, and create an ethos in which the pupils' well being has the highest priority.

While support that takes place using staff within the school requires careful co-ordination, external support offers particular challenges.

The school will have contact with agencies such as the police, social services, the health service, the education services, voluntary bodies and others. Local education authority support may include visiting support teachers, education inspectors, advisory teachers, psychologists and many others. The use of such services has always depended on availability and continues to do so. Consequently the school may have to prioritise its needs.

It might look first at the suitability of the pupils at Stage 3 on its register of special educational needs. Given that the placement of pupils on the special educational needs register in part reflects the capability of the school to meet the needs of pupils, it could be that the training of teachers in, say, behaviour management could reduce the number of pupils which the school considers need outside intervention, reducing those at Stage 3.

The school would then prioritise the remaining pupils in terms of time and agree with, say, external behavioural support staff when the visits would be made. The reduction of pupils at Stage 3 may create some time in which the behavioural support staff could visit to carry out preventative work. This preventative work may in the longer term mean that fewer pupils would be considered as requiring the longer term intervention which may have been necessary later.

Another approach indicated by government in its SEN Green Paper is the possibility that Special Educational Needs Co-ordinators (SENCOs) would undertake some of the work previously carried out by psychologists (Department for Education and Employment, 1997). The Green Paper envisages that as the skills of SENCOs and other SEN staff develop, they could, given the necessary training carry out some aspects of statutory assessment which would release educational psychologist time to enable the latter to perform other tasks.

An important aspect of support to a school is that it is co-ordinated. At the local education authority level, it is important that various teams work together to ensure that a school is able to receive the support that it needs. Funding issues should not encourage different teams to compete to fulfil the same task for the school. For example, education inspectors should not be in competition with advisory teachers.

A key feature of good support from outside the school is that it should be co-ordinated as far as possible by those offering the support. This implies an understanding of the work of other colleagues. Education specialists, social services staff and health staff, to take only three examples, may see issues in different ways. This may be partly due to training, the perspective developed from the work that each carries out, and differing personal and service-wide views of priorities.

At the very least it is necessary that structures are in place to minimise misunderstandings brought about by differing perspectives. These structures may include meetings to discuss and decide jointly issues of common concern, occasional but regular joint conferences which allow time not just to listen to speakers but for focused discussion to take place in small multi-disciplinary groups. Where staff are jointly qualified, they can play a key role in bridging professional perspectives.

Again the SEN Green Paper touches on these issues. It states that the contribution of the government, local agencies and business need to be developed, improved and co-ordinated. One of the aims of doing this is to raise standards of achievement of pupils. The Green Paper recognises that the fragmentation of services between various statutory agencies, competition, and tight budgets has meant that parents have had to take responsibility for co-ordinating provision for their child. What can happen in fact is that the school seeks to co-ordinate provision for the pupil, sometimes feeling that it has to manage the co-ordination of services that ideally ought to happen at the level of service co-ordination and delivery.

One example of collaboration which takes place in some authorities is that between the education, health and social services with regard to children 'in need' under the terms of the Children Act 1989. These include children who are 'looked after' by local authorities. The joint planning and funding of placements in residential education or packages of care for children in need are two examples of working together, although much more needs to be done about monitoring the subsequent placements. Voluntary services could be used much more. Regional planning may encourage such joint working.

An area where the lack of joint working at the services level has posed difficulties for schools and parents is that of speech therapy for children with communication difficulties. The effective delivery of speech and language therapy has been hindered by the misfitting duties and powers of the heath and education services. There has also been confusion about who pays for what. Some schools have taken matters into their own hands and directly bought in the services of speech therapists.

At the school level, the head teacher should ensure that the support received by the school complements the school's aims. The school development plan should indicate the key priorities for the year ahead. Targets should further refine the focus. All support should be assessed to the degree to which it meets the priorities.

For instance, the training programme for the staff should be informed by the school priorities. This is not to say that the staff should not pursue a training session which does not relate directly to the school aims. The member of staff may be new and may need training in a subject specific issue which is not directly related to the aims for that year. Staff development may include their future aspirations and perhaps a future job move. However, generally, the training of staff should be related tightly to the needs of the school.

To take another example, if improving reading is the priority, the support of an English advisor may be sought. Where possible some assessment of the effectiveness of the outside intervention should be made. If support relating to mathematics is used, what is the effect on the standards of pupils? Where a member of staff attends a course, the fullest use should be made of the new learning of that member of staff. The new expertise needs to be shared and steps taken to ensure that it has a positive effect on the school.

Schools should:

- expect of support agencies that they are working to co-ordinate the services which they provide
- co-ordinate the provision of services at the school level
- prioritise needs to gain a realistic match between school needs and available services.

References

Department for Education and Employment (1994) *The Code of Practice on the Identification and Assessment of Special Educational Needs*, London, DfEE.

—— (1997) *Excellence for All Children*, London, DfEE.

Office for Standards in Education (1995) *The OFSTED Handbook: Guidance on the Inspection of Nursery and Primary Schools*, London, HMSO.

Address

Special Educational Needs Policy Division, Department for Education and Employment, Sanctuary Buildings, Great Smith Street, Westminster, London SW1P 3BT, tel: 0171 925 5498, fax: 0171 925 6954.

Target setting

Goals can be reached in many ways. To realise his ambition of making a healthy profit, estate agent Roy Brookes turned to the expedient, unheard of in such circles, of telling the unvarnished truth about the properties he put up for sale. 'Tiny flat suitable for dwarf' and 'Georgian slum would suit social climber' were the sort of advertisements that attracted property seekers scenting a bargain.

Target setting in schools aims to raise educational standards by establishing specific, measurable goals for pupil performance. It uses assessment and other performance data to predict potential, focus effort on raising attainment, and support school improvement initiatives. The government having set national targets for literacy and numeracy at age 11 and for General Certificate of Secondary Education examination results at age 16, local education authorities (LEAs) and schools are expected to follow suit.

The White Paper, *Excellence in Schools* (Department for Education and Employment, 1997a) indicated the government's intention to act in partnership with LEAs, schools and others involved in raising standards. The Department of Education and Employment (DfEE) sought to develop target setting and school improvement. This included publishing additional information, data and guidance to help LEAs and schools.

Schools were required to set targets for raising their pupils' levels of attainment in National Curriculum assessments and tests. Government regulations were introduced which required schools to set targets and to publish them from September 1998. The government targets for achievement for 2002 were that 80 per cent of 11-year-olds will reach level 4 of the National Curriculum in English and 75 per cent of 11-year-olds will reach level 4 for mathematics. This does not of course imply that the targets set by all schools will be the same as the national targets.

From September 1998, each school had to have 'challenging' targets for improvement and take direct responsibility for them. Governing bodies would consider all the available information and discuss their school's targets, together with proposals from the head teacher on the necessary improvement plans to achieve them, and agree them with the LEA.

School targets should be based on: benchmark information on the performance of similar schools, at national and local level; information on the rate of progress needed to achieve national targets; and, where available, the most recent inspection evidence. The government sets national targets and publishes national performance and benchmark data. Each LEA may provide benchmarking data and guidance to all its schools to help them set targets. Each school sets draft targets, taking account of the comparative data and their own previous best performance, for discussion with its LEA.

Schools and LEAs agree targets covering a three-year period and reviewed annually. Where the LEA cannot agree with a school on its targets, it may invoke an early warning system (where the LEA has specific concerns, it may intervene directly and ultimately can withdraw budget delegation from the school). The individual school targets are included in the Education Development Plan of each LEA. The accumulation of the targets ideally would be intended to total the LEA targets, which in turn would be intended to reflect national targets. The DfEE and OFSTED exercise a monitoring function to ensure targets are ambitious enough.

The LEA advises and, as necessary, challenges schools to set their sights 'at the right level'. This applies especially to schools which have average performance but higher potential. OFSTED inspection reports comment on whether the school's targets are appropriate and on the progress towards them.

Within a school, the use of performance analysis enables teachers to assess progress by their pupils and to change their teaching strategies accordingly. Comparisons of performance by different subjects, classes, year groups and other features help schools to set targets for individual pupils which take account of each pupil's starting point. These comparisons also help head teachers to monitor the performance of classroom teachers.

To ensure that all schools deliver high standards, there are two external checks. OFSTED inspects the school at least once every six years. Also, LEAs regularly monitor performance on the basis of objective performance information and the LEA discusses annual targets for each school.

A SCAA consultation document (School Curriculum and Assessment Authority, 1997) indicated the relationship between 'value added' and target setting. By showing pupil progress as well as raw attainment data can both encourage and challenge complacency in schools. The paper sets out SCAA's proposals for a national system of value added feedback for schools based on National Curriculum test results and public examination results. This aims to help schools look at the progress of their own pupils in relation to the national picture so that they can use this information to set targets for improvement. Value added information provides a starting point for schools considering targets for future attainment. It does not indicate exactly what targets schools should set. Schools recognise that children's real attainment 'influences their future progress and life chances, not measures of their progress'.

Writing to Chief Education Officers in 1997, Michael Barber outlined how the work on target setting and school improvement would be taken forward, specifying the additional information, data and guidance the DfEE planned to publish to help LEAs and schools. All schools would be required to set and publish targets for raising their pupils' levels of achievement in National Curriculum tests and in public examinations and qualifications at age 16.

The LEA would support/challenge schools to ensure that targets were 'realistic and challenging'. Each LEA would report on these targets in its Education Development Plan. The Secretary of State would then satisfy himself that the schools in the LEA were aiming high enough to contribute fully towards the attainment of national targets. The DfEE, the Qualifications and Curriculum Authority (QCA) and OFSTED would provide analysis at national level. LEAs and others could provide local supplementary data.

From 1997, several sources of information were available: summary results, national benchmark analysis, national value added information, school performance tables, and school performance and assessment analysis.

From 1997, summary national test results data were published in September from the National Curriculum Assessments at Key Stage 1, 2 and 3 carried out earlier in the same year. This allows schools, early in the Autumn term, to compare their results with the national picture. In November, QCA published reports on pupil performance in the 1997 tests for 7-, 11- and 14-year-olds which spotlighted strengths and weaknesses and set out some implications for teaching and learning. Summaries of results in public examinations are published in August and the government published further analyses of these in the Autumn of 1997.

Regarding national benchmark analyses, in November each year QCA publishes further analyses of national results at 7, 11, 14 and 16 which show schools' intake grouped by certain factors. These include free school meals, English as an additional language, gender and selection. The analyses include benchmarks showing the performance of the most successful schools to help all schools raise expectations and set appropriate targets.

Turning to national value added information, in November 1997, QCA published analyses comparing the performance of a sample of students at Key Stage 4 against their attainment at the previous Key Stage 3. This enabled schools to compare the progress of their own pupils with the national averages at these key stages. Once the national value added system is in place, schools will be able to compare their pupils' progress in English, mathematics and science with the average progress made by pupils nationally.

In 1997, primary performance tables showing 1997 Key Stage 2 data were published locally and LEAs were able to include extra information and analysis.

From February 1998, OFSTED sent all schools Performance and Assessment Reports (PANDAs) which included some of the benchmark and value added analyses which were published in the Autumn of 1997.

To help schools reach the targets for literacy and numeracy, the Secretary of State lifted the statutory requirement for schools to follow the KS 1 and 2 programmes of study in the non-core National Curriculum subjects of design technology, history, geography, art, music and physical education. This applies for two years from September 1998 until a revised National Curriculum is brought in from September 2000. Some preliminary guidance on target setting was provided by the government (Department for Education and Employment, 1997b).

In order to reach targets schools may resort to a range of strategies, some of which are less acceptable than others.

These include:

- making more explicit the literacy and numeracy aspects of other subjects
- analysing national test results question by question and teaching to reduce weaknesses and build on strengths
- teaching test success strategies such as attempting all questions or at least part of a question
- avoiding gender bias by encouraging pupils not to be put off by the way a question is phrased
- making it clear that family holidays are unacceptable in the week of national tests
- focusing efforts on pupils at the cusp of level 3 nearing 4 (and 1 nearing 2) possibly at the expense of pupils with SEN and the more able
- using all the training available and all literacy and numeracy support structures.

Schools should:

- use, with discrimination, a range of relevant information in setting targets
- take charge of target setting and as far as possible set their own agenda
- try to ensure that targets are reached using the more acceptable approaches available.

References

Department for Education and Employment (1997a) *Excellence in Schools*, London, DfEE.

—— (1997b) *From Targets to Action: Guidance to Support Effective Target Setting in Schools*, London, DfEE.

School Curriculum and Assessment Authority (1997) *Value Added Indicators for Schools: A Consultative Paper by the School Curriculum and Assessment Authority*, London, SCAA.

Address

Standards and Effectiveness Unit, Department for Education and Employment, Sanctuary Buildings, Great Smith Street, Westminster, London SW1P 3BT, tel: 0171 925 5119, fax: 0171 925 6001, e-mail: improving schools.dfee@gtnet.gov.uk.

Teaching assistants and associates

'Nothing is so dangerous as being too modern,' warned Oscar Wilde. 'One is apt to grow old fashioned quite suddenly.' The use of classroom assistants, while not entirely modern, has certainly increased in recent years. They are used for various reasons including to provide for children with special educational needs. Although classroom assistants do not work as substitute whole-class teachers their use in the school as a whole tends to save money because the school may not employ as many teachers as they might if classroom assistants were not used. As long ago as 1967, the Plowden Report (Central Advisory Council for Education, 1967) suggested the recruitment of 'teacher aides' which raised similar concerns about teachers' jobs.

To ensure that the modern phenomenon does not become old fashioned, schools need to continue to be innovative in their use of classroom assistants. Assistants also need to be better trained. To stay in the forefront, schools have to keep moving forward and provide even better value for money.

The White Paper *Excellence in Schools* (Department for Education and Employment, 1997) recognised the importance of teaching assistants and teaching associates in schools. Such staff can contribute to the raising of standards by working directly with pupils or by freeing the teacher to work more effectively.

The terminology needs to be agreed because so many different terms are used. A teaching assistant may be called a teaching auxiliary, a member of the non-teaching staff, a classroom support assistant or a classroom assistant. In a nursery or primary school the member of staff may be a nursery nurse or a special needs assistant. It would be clearer to parents and others if at least the term teaching assistant was used and if necessary any other title in brackets afterwards.

Teaching associates are visiting speakers such as police officers, religious leaders, artists and others. Artists and craftsmen or women may be 'resident' with the school for a time, perhaps funded from an outside source. People from industry, business, commerce and the service sector may contribute as teaching associates.

The school should develop clear guidelines for teaching associates so that they and other members of the school community are clear about their role and what exactly they are doing in the school. The contribution of teacher associates to raising standards should be assessed to make sure that they are making a genuine contribution to the school.

A teaching assistant works with pupils but the pupils remain the responsibility of the teacher. The teaching assistant works under the overall direction of the class teacher with small groups of pupils or individuals. For example, a teaching assistant may teach small groups within the classroom in a particular subject, enabling the teacher also to teach a smaller group on focused work.

Because many teaching assistants have little or no training, the government in its White Paper proposed to consult local education authorities regarding developing a programme of courses and qualifications which are flexible enough to have regard to the knowledge, skills and role of individual teaching assistants.

If such an approach followed the direction of the training and qualifications developed for other staff such as head teachers and subject leaders by the Teacher Training Agency (Teacher Training Agency, 1998) it might comprise standards and qualifications. The standards could comprise: the core purpose of teaching assistants' work; the key outcomes; the professional knowledge and understanding required; the skills and attributes; and the key areas of the work.

The school wishing to prepare the ground for any future developments could begin to draft a set of standards which it would require of teaching assistants. The possible headings for these and the general framework could be judiciously informed by the structure of the National Standards for Qualified Teacher Status (Teacher Training Agency, 1998).

In many schools, teaching assistants work well to contribute to the education of pupils. There is a worry though that such staff may be used to deal excessively with some of the most needy pupils and yet are less well qualified to do so than the teacher.

The worst case scenario is that the teacher, when faced with demanding pupils, purposely or unconsciously uses the teaching assistant as a coping strategy. If the teacher is not aware of this possibility, then when teaching pupils who exhibit challenging behaviour or who have difficulties with learning, he or she may not learn the skills to work with these pupils. If the teacher has the rudimentary skills to work with such pupils and she or he does not develop them, the skills may become eroded.

The pupil thus becomes dependent on individual adult attention and finds it difficult to cope without it setting up a vicious cycle. The school begins to feel that it cannot cope with these pupils and requires more and more teaching assistants, rather than questioning the approach it is using.

Reality is less stark than this extreme caricature, but the concern nevertheless needs to be addressed. A positive approach is to develop careful protocols for the work of teaching assistants. There should certainly be joint planning between the teacher and the teaching assistant to ensure that the latter is clear about her or his role in the overall lesson. The practicalities of this are not always easy and require the whole school and particularly the senior management team, to be behind the joint planning approach. At the very least there needs to be a sharing of the planning with the teaching assistants in a regular and structured way.

In order to address directly the concern that teaching assistants may effectively block the pupil from the skills of the teacher, the possibility needs to be recognised. The teacher needs to ensure in planning that (s)he spends time with the pupils with whom the teaching assistants also work. The teaching assistants should not be too strictly deployed to one or two pupils but should also circulate to help the teacher as appropriate. The teacher should monitor the effectiveness of learning programmes taught by teaching assistants. There should be regular sessions where the teacher has sole responsibility for the whole class to keep the skills of teaching the more reluctant pupils well honed. This should be encouraged by the emphasis on direct teaching, including whole-class teaching, implicit in the national literacy and numeracy hour.

Care needs to be taken that teaching assistants are used effectively and not left sitting without a clear educational task while a teacher uses whole-class teaching. There are legitimate tasks to fulfil while the class teacher teaches the whole class, such as acting as a model of good listening for pupils who may find it difficult to concentrate; discreetly encouraging more reluctant pupils to contribute or encouraging the concentration of pupils with behaviour difficulties. But this needs to be planned and agreed and should not simply happen by default.

Teaching assistants should have a clear and agreed job description which reflects their place in the whole-school structure and approach. This should build in time, with the expectation of joint working and planning with the teacher so far as this is appropriate within the skills and experience of the teaching assistant. The teacher's job description should complement that of teaching assistants by making it clear that sharing planning and conveying clearly the purpose of the lesson is part of the teacher's role.

It is also important that the teaching assistant passes back to the teacher information about the progress of the pupil(s) with whom he or she has been working. This may be a verbal report which the teacher notes down, or a brief note. The teacher will then use this information to inform subsequent planning. By drawing in such information, the teacher can help ensure that he or she does not neglect pupils supported by a teaching assistant in the whole-class planning of subsequent lessons.

A particularly important aspect of lesson planning to convey to the teaching assistant is the learning outcomes expected of the pupil or pupils with whom the assistant is working. Sometimes only the tasks to be done are conveyed by the teacher and it is not clear to the assistant or the child what behaviour is required of the child to demonstrate that he or she has learned what they are supposed to have learned.

Schools should:

- make accurate and consistent use the terms teaching assistant and teaching associate and ensure that all members of the school community including parents understand the terms
- systematically develop a range of teacher associates, paying due regard to the safety and protection of children
- establish standards for teaching assistants, perhaps drawing on the core purposes of their work, the key outcomes, the professional knowledge and understanding required, the skills and attributes and the key areas of their work
- ensure that the teaching assistant and teacher work closely in planning and monitoring pupils' progress;
- make sure that a pupil is not deprived of a teacher's skills and that a teacher is not de-skilled by the inappropriate use of teaching assistants
- draft clear job descriptions for teacher assistants and clear guidance for teacher associates.

References

Central Advisory Council for Education (1967) *Children and their Primary Schools* (Plowden Report), London, HMSO.

Department for Education and Employment (1997) *Excellence in Schools*, London, DfEE.

Teacher Training Agency (1998) *National Standards for Qualified Teacher Status*, London, TTA.

Address

Teacher Training Agency, Portland House, Stag Place, London SE1E 5TT, tel: 0171 925 3700, fax: 0171 925 3800, e-mail: TTA@GTNET.GOV.UK.

Topic work as an approach to the curriculum

'Just as the twig is bent, the tree's inclined' said Alexander Pope in relation to the importance of education in forming 'the common mind'. This importance extends to aspects of whole-school curricular planning including 'topic work' approaches and 'subject' approaches.

Among the areas addressed by school schemes of work is that of how teaching takes place in the school. The organisation of the curriculum includes consideration of the extent to which subject-oriented or topic work-oriented approaches are used. A related continuum is that between a predominantly subject-based curriculum and a more 'integrated' curriculum. Topic work and especially the 'integrated' curriculum have been increasingly squeezed out of primary schools by factors such as the subject-based National Curriculum and the apparent opposition to the approach in annual reports of Her Majesty's Chief Inspector of Schools.

A distinction has been made between the 'basics' of reading, writing and mathematics and other subjects in that the basic subjects have tended to be taught relatively discretely while attempts to establish integration have applied largely to other subjects (e.g. Alexander, 1992). This implies that the integrated curriculum is concerned mainly with the subjects other than the 'basics'.

There are several potential advantages of an integrated curriculum. It can build from the experience of the child who at an early age lacks the understanding of subjects which would make them meaningful. However, an alternative view is that a more subject-based emphasis would provide opportunities for the child to be gradually initiated into the ways of thinking associated with the subject. Another possible advantage of the integrated curriculum (Pollard, 1997) is that it allows greater emphasis to be placed on process, skills and attitudes which have a general, transferable application than would be the case if there was too much of a subject focus. However, it should not be overlooked that subject-focused studies also allow the transfer of processes, skills and attitudes and are not confined simply to facts which may become out of date.

Topic work is associated with an integrated curriculum. Topic work may be variously called themes, projects, integrated work or multi-disciplinary modules. 'Themes' is a somewhat misleading term because topic work tends to be not simply thematic but interdisciplinary. Whereas projects are sometimes individual, topic work tends to use work in pairs or small groups, less use being made of whole-class teaching. (This group working can be used to encourage co-operation and collaborative learning.) 'Integrated work' at least conveys the notion of interdisciplinary approaches. The term 'multi-disciplinary modules' very specifically highlights the interdisciplinary approach.

So what essentially is the topic work approach? Active learning is involved in the sense that pupils may go on visits and will be encouraged to use reference material and develop research skills. Visits and other aspects of topic work can encourage pupils to be aware of and learn from the environment outside school. This implies that the teacher will be more occupied as a helper in the enquiries of pupils than in more direct teaching and this facilitating role requires considerable skill. The approach can encourage curiosity and creativity because it allows pupils some choice in what they study and allows individual and group motivation to enhance learning.

This encourages children to learn from other children as well as learning from the teacher. Also, the focus of different pupils on different aspects of the topic work allows differentiation according to pupil prior learning to be planned into the process.

While topic work allows pupils to practise skills such as reading, writing, speaking and listening, numeracy, experimental skills, speculation, hypothesis, research, and others, it gives a context in which these skills are exercised in a real way. Similarly, while topic work allows knowledge to be gained it also offers opportunities for that knowledge to be applied. At the end of the topic work (and during it) it is usual to have displays of work and pupils may give a presentation to the class about a particular aspect of the topic work on which they have focused.

Research summarised by Kerry (in Farrell, Kerry and Kerry, 1995) suggests that teachers judge the success of topic work according to criteria relating to the topic work itself and to the pupils involved.

The topic work uses the knowledge, skills and understanding to meet National Curriculum requirements, leads to good display material being produced; and expands in scope spontaneously. The work is of a high quality and an acceptable or large quantity.

The pupils are interested, enthusiastic and have enjoyed the work; bring items of work from home; talk informally about the work; have gained knowledge and information; sustain interest at a high level for a long time; can remember the work months afterwards; follow the interest outside school/timetabled time; have acquired and developed skills; offer ideas and ask questions; have gained experience and understanding; have produced creative work; and look forward to topic work lessons.

Parents comment favourably while the teacher has a feeling of job satis-faction and has fulfilled the original aims of the topic work.

This gives some notion of how topic work can be judged. Clearly the qualities of topic work are not restricted to this approach only, but the combination of qualities indicates the distinctive nature of topic work. One of the most difficult aspects of topic work to manage is its interdisciplinary nature. This creates challenges in planning topic work to ensure that in the subject areas that comprise it, progress is made and areas of learning are covered.

Topic work may be tracked back from its multi-disciplinary aspects to the subjects of the National Curriculum and other aspects of the curriculum. This can help ensure that progress is assured in these curriculum threads and that measurement of progress in the topic work can be recognised and recorded in the curriculum components. The relationships between the National Curriculum and topic work planning can strengthen topic work (Arnold, 1991).

Within the framework of the National Curriculum, a survey by Her Majesty's Inspectors (1993) sought to identify some features associated with successful topic work. In order to ensure continuity and progression, there was an agreed system of consistent, structured planning. Planning was co-operative to enable teachers to share their expertise and the workload. It referred to learning outcomes, activities and assessment. National Curriculum requirements were given due regard and topic work was usually chosen to fit National Curriculum attainment targets and programmes of study. Attainment targets which did not fit within the topic work framework were taught separately. Topic work was biased towards one particular subject. There was whole-school agreement about the coverage of subjects and the relative balance of subjects and topic work, and the outcomes of teaching were monitored by the senior management team.

In some quarters a moving away from the interdisciplinary aspect of the topic work and a move towards a more subject-based approach to a theme seems to be favoured. This is thought to use more fully the subject expertise of primary school teachers The 'one teacher one class' approach is seen as under-using the subject expertise of, say, a graduate in theology who uses his or her expertise mainly to teach their own class the subject while other colleagues may be struggling with religious education (Office for Standards in Education, 1997). Schools would need more staff to cover a range of subjects in this way and yet still retain the important pastoral role of the class teacher. If projects become more subject focused, the benefits of a multi-disciplinary approach may be reduced but assessment, recording and reporting may be easier.

Another approach is to use specialist subject expertise by having the subject specialists teach several classes specifically in their subject. This keeps accountability tight because if results in a particular subject area are poor compared with other subjects, the responsibility for this can be more confidently related to the subject specialist who directly taught the subject.

Schools should:

- be aware of the benefits of topic work
- be aware of the criteria by which topic work can be judged successful
- ensure that continuity and progression is assured.

References

Alexander, R. J. (1992) *Policy and Practice in Primary Education*, London, Rout-ledge.

Arnold, R. (ed.) (1991) *Topic Planning and the National Curriculum*, London, Longman.

Farrell, M., Kerry, T. and Kerry, C. (1995) *The Blackwell Handbook of Education*, Oxford, Blackwell.

Her Majesty's Inspectors (1993) *Curriculum Organisation and Classroom Practice in Primary Schools*, London, OFSTED.

Office for Standards in Education (1997) *Using Subject Specialists to Promote High Standards at Key Stage 2: an Illustrative Survey*, London, OFSTED.

Pollard, A. (1997) *Reflective Teaching in the Primary School: A Handbook for the Classroom, Third Edition*, London, Cassell.

Further reading

Kerry, T. (1996) in M. Farrell (ed.) *The Classroom: Organisation, Effectiveness and Resources*, London, Centre for British Teachers.

Value added measures and their relation to league tables

Marcus Aurelius Antoninus may almost have been foreseeing twentieth-century education when he wrote more than 1,800 years ago, 'there is a proper value and proportion to be observed in the performance of every act'. For today not only is this the perspective that every school is encouraged to take, but they need to ensure that there is added value in the performance of every act.

A series of propositions were set out in a consultative document by the School Curriculum and Assessment Authority (1997). These included the view that value added allows schools to determine the extent to which pupils have made the progress expected of them over a specified period. Value added analysis can help schools evaluate their effectiveness by providing information about the relative progress of pupils in the school relative to others.

SCAA proposed that a national value added system should be set up so that a national analysis for Key Stages 2, 3 and 4 is available from the 1998 results. For 7-year-olds, the data from baseline assessment matched to Key Stage 1 results will be analysed as soon as it becomes available from the 1999 results. All schools should be sent the national value added data to enable them to analyse their own performance in the light of it. As schools' results can fluctuate from year to year, published value added data should cover a minimum of three years.

Against a background of interest in value added, schools which come out on top of 'absolute' league tables take them in their stride. They may see league tables as a way of presenting an assessment of how a school has succeeded in terms of the measure of assessment used, usually test or examination results. Schools which perform in absolute terms less well than others, as indicated by test results, regard this as one of the reasons to be worried about league tables. They are keen to explain why they might be being unfairly relegated to the lower reaches of these tables. This concern over league tables, and the worry that they over-simplify the relative success or otherwise of a school has led to an interest in one aspect of value added analyses.

This approach seeks to enable fairer comparisons of schools to be made. It gives estimates of the average progress of each school. One has to adjust for certain factors and for prior attainment by the individual child. It is important to develop appropriate measures to analyse educational outcomes. These range from the aggregation of academic results and attendance figures to multi-level modelling techniques. An important aspect of the technique is that it looks at the value which is added by the school over and above that which would be expected if only anticipated progress was made.

Currently, league tables and some value added analyses concentrate on national test results and on attendance. Less work has been done on pupil attitudes which relate to pupil attainment. Similarly, less work has been carried out on aspects of performance which are important in schools, such as problem solving, flexibility, creativity and co-operation.

The most important indicator of future achievement is pupil prior attainment and this has led to the introduction of baseline assessments and on-entry assessment. Information from the Office for Standards in Education (OFSTED) is also important in relation to value added analyses, for example the Pre-Inspection Context and School Indicator (PICSI).

More recently Performance and Assessment Reports (PANDAs) have been issued to schools drawing on data held by the Department for Education and Employment, OFSTED and the Qualifications and Curriculum Authority (QCA). This comprises basic information about a particular school and the characteristics of the area around it. Further information covers key performance data about the particular school's effectiveness. This includes recent inspection evidence and the National Curriculum tests and teacher assessments. The school performance data is shown in comparison with national averages and with other like schools. One of the purposes of the PANDA is to help schools to set targets for improvement. Such measures may not have the capacity to reflect the complex factors in the community that may affect educational performance. For example, unstable family relationships are unlikely to be shown in such raw data.

Value added analyses do not entirely solve the problems of league tables by providing adjusted league tables. Results still need to be interpreted with care. The effects which a school has cannot easily be separated statistically from the differences between schools that would be expected by chance. Only where there are great differences in schools can the effect of what a particular school is doing be considered with sufficient confidence to be influential in contributing to that difference.

Also, the power of the newspaper headline or the top story on the television and radio news cannot be underestimated. Any head teacher who faces a headline which places his or her school at the bottom of a league table has a difficult task in persuading parents and others to read the fine print of a value added analysis which indicates that if all background factors and pupil prior attainment is taken into account, the school made better progress than the school at the top of the table. People tend not to listen to the success stories of runners who come second, never mind those who come last.

Ambitious parents are more interested in overall academic achievement and the opportunities that are offered by a school from which pupils move onto secondary schools with high academic results in the national tests, rather than a school which offers 'better' progress for the lower performing pupil. Parents whose children attend preparatory school also know the power of the Common Entrance Examination and will require a good deal of convincing that value added in attitudes, co-operation and creativity can count as much for practical purposes as high academic achievement.

This is a difficult message to get across at a time when a veritable industry is developing to 'help' the anxious head teacher concerned that his or her school is in the lower reaches of the academic league. Research organisations and others offer advice on how to develop value added measures. Local education authorities are keen to devise models of value added to help measure the 'real' progress which schools are making. When we look at which schools are at the front of the queue for help from such services, how many schools do we see who are at the top of the crudest league tables?

But value added measures are not only applied to whole-school measures. They have a role as a management tool to compare individual teachers, departments and aspects of school life. These can be used to explore any differences, let us say, in the relative progress of mathematics groups, pupils with special educational needs, girls compared with boys, and a variety of other measures. What is important is the way in which results are used, the quality of the professional dialogue and action which they generate, and the effect on improving standards within the school.

In this respect, value added analyses contribute to measures of school effectiveness and can potentially lead to school improvement. They may increase the accountability of teachers and others and, if professionally followed through, may raise standards.

Unique pupil reference numbers would enable value added to be measured in various interesting ways. For example, comparisons could be made between schools as pupils transfer from one school to another. Comparison could be made between teachers as pupils move from class to class.

Other important developments in this field are benchmarking and target setting. Through benchmarking, schools of similar characteristics are grouped so that they can learn from each other how to improve. A school is able to plot its own performance against similar schools and set itself challenging but realistic targets. Local education authorities (LEAs) may receive from the QCA more detailed data than goes directly to schools. LEAs are expected to produce local comparative data which would cover more than the national test information.

If we are to answer the question, 'Are value added measures the answer to the problems created by school examination league tables?', the answer would probably be 'No'. But the other potential uses of value added should not be forgotten.

Schools should:

- be aware of the difficulties of promoting value added progress rather than absolute achievement
- recognise the use of value added measures as a management tool.

References

School Curriculum and Assessment Authority (1997) *Value Added Indicators for Schools Consultative Paper Primary* June 1997, London, SCAA.

Address

School Improvement and Support Team, Qualifications and Curriculum Authority (QCA), 29 Bolton Street, London W1Y 7PD, tel: 0171 243 9348, fax: 0171 243 9434.

Very able pupils

If we accept Karl Marx's principle, 'From each according to his abilities, to each according to his needs', the very able have a large responsibility.

Opinions vary about the terminology used to refer to very able pupils and consequently about the percentage of pupils involved. One credible approach is to consider about 20 per cent of children as more able, about 5 per cent of all children as very able (Her Majesty's Inspectorate, 1992) and about 2 per cent of all children as exceptionally able (Department for Education, 1994). These figures refer of course to the same 20 per cent of children who are more able, within which there are those who would be very able and within these in turn there are children who are 'exceptionally able'. When consulting literature on the subject, it is helpful to establish the terminology used and the percentage of children the identified group is supposed to represent.

Very able pupils in preparatory schools may take scholarship examinations at age 13 rather than common entrance. This would tend to affect their teaching from Year 7 if not before. The methods used vary from school to school according to the numbers involved.

Provision for very able children in state schools (HMI, 1992) was found to be most effective when certain conditions were fulfilled. One of these is that local education authorities offer well planned and co-ordinated support to schools, provided by inspectors and advisory teachers such as in-service training and support groups. Another condition is that schools nominate a member of staff to co-ordinate work with very able pupils.

Also it is important that the co-ordinator has a role which is integral to curriculum development in the school and schools have a policy for very able pupils (and more widely for more able pupils). Other factors are that schools seek to encourage individual effort and develop independence and that teachers intervene as appropriate to spur pupils on to a higher level of knowledge, skill, understanding and thinking.

The identification of very able (and more able) children may involve assessment of the child, classroom observation and interviews with parents. Indicators include: verbal fluency, creativity, superior reasoning and a good memory, entrepreneurial skills, leadership qualities (and many others). Some very able (and more able) pupils may try to cover their ability by such means as lack of co-operation, inattentiveness and scepticism. This may stem from a wish to seem average because of peer pressure, boredom with tasks which they find simple, alienation and many other factors.

A whole-school policy could include the following sections (Ayre, 1994): general rationale; aims; definitions; general approach; identification and monitoring; organisational responses; classroom approaches; out-of-class activities; personal, health and social education considerations; responsibility for co-ordinating and monitoring; review and development; and the use of outside agencies.

At the whole-school level, decisions are made about whether to accelerate a very able pupil out of their chronological year group and into one of older children. It is important that strategies are developed in the pupil's chronological age group before acceleration is considered and the pupil's social, emotional and psychological well being must be considered as well as intellectual needs. Some accelerated learning may be arranged through team teaching of two year groups together. The prospect of a very able child being moved out of his or her year group may lead the child to mask their ability in order to stay with friends of his or her own age.

Among classroom strategies which can be particularly important with very able pupils (and more able pupils) are the provision of some open ended tasks, the opportunity for the pupil to work at greater speed, enrichment (the opportunity to deepen and extend knowledge and understanding through supplementary tasks) and the general high quality differentiation. The teaching of independent study skills, research skills and access to resources at the appropriate level are important. Some schools have developed a form of individual education plan for very able pupils to help ensure that their particular needs are met.

Whole-school targets, perhaps informed by external assessments, could be set for very able pupils and processes agreed to plan and monitor them. However, planning for the very able involves effective planning for all. Schools should consider whether the tracking of National Curriculum programmes of study sections, attainment targets and levels of attainment to planning (medium term and weekly) would help ensure coverage and balance of subjects and also indicate levels of very able pupils and their progress. If medium term planning satisfactorily covers the programmes of study by tracking them into planning, then assessment sheets could be used effectively to record levels of achievement and help ensure that these influence subsequent planning. This would naturally benefit all pupils.

The pros and cons of grouping very able pupils together and of dispersing them among others or pairing them with less able pupils need to be carefully thought through. Teachers need to be aware of the factors which influence the decision, such as providing a variety of approaches, enhancing the self esteem of the very able, enabling children of similar levels of ability to interact and so on.

Even where pupils are 'set', approaches need to be worked out for pupils who are very able at mathematics but may not be good at English. Language is an integral part of mathematics achievement so cannot be ignored and consequently key words for mathematics could be explicitly taught and the language of mathematics could be given particular focus.

Special care could be given to maximising the use of information and communication technology for very able pupils, particularly of course if this is an area in which they excel. Collaboration with other schools may enable after-school clubs to be set up and expensive equipment and software might be jointly bought and shared under some form of written agreement.

Strategies can be framed to ensure that the learning outcomes expected of very able pupils be made clear and the extent to which these would be shared with the very able pupils, and how. A classroom ethos in which the contributions of all are valued is conducive to the valuing of very able pupils and can contribute to raising their achievement. At worse, an ethos in which very able pupils are regarded by other pupils with jealousy or otherwise negatively is counter-productive for all.

Care needs to be taken that expectations of greater and deeper knowledge, higher level of skills and more mature attitudes are conveyed to very able pupils without alienating them. Homework for very able pupils may be different from that of others pupils in that it requires more depth of thought or is more open ended.

The progression and continuity of such things as research skills and study techniques need to be ensured for all children and perhaps particularly for the very able who may extend the upper reaches of any existing school programme. Problem solving can be built into lessons, in group activities for example, and such activities when well structured can be highly motivating for a very able child. Approaches are needed to ensure that initiative is encouraged and developed.

The role of questioning to improve the achievement of very able pupils is important, and sufficient open ended questions with time to answer them are helpful. Also, the teacher may sometimes need a little extra time to grasp the angle from which a very able child is perceiving an issue when the child's response seems at first odd or simply wrong.

If behaviour difficulties get in the way of the achievement of very able pupils, then strategies are necessary to manage the behaviour just as is the case with other pupils. This is not necessarily at the level of behaviour difficulty which would constitute a special educational need but at less severe levels also.

Among organisations which represent the very able are the National Association for Gifted Children (NAGC) and the National Association for Able Children in Education (NACE). The NAGC is a national charity aiming to support the ablest children. It provides direct help to gifted children and their families and provides a consultancy service to teachers and others concerned with the education and welfare of gifted children. The NACE assists teachers to help able and talented children. It produces publications, runs conferences, provides in-service education and training for schools, and produces newsletters and a journal.

Schools should:

- have clear definition of very able (and more able) pupils and an effective procedure for identifying them
- have a co-ordinator for very able (and more able) pupils
- fully use external support and ensure that it is co-ordinated
- develop and regularly review the whole-school policy on very able (and more able) pupils
- ensure that the ethos, planning, assessment, teaching techniques, resources and staff training take proper account of the needs of very able (and more able) pupils.

References

Department for Education (1994) *Exceptionally Able Children: Conference Report*, London, DfE.

Her Majesty's Inspectorate (1992) *The Education of Very Able Children in Maintained Schools*, London, HMSO.

Office for Standards in Education (1995) *The OFSTED Handbook: Guidance on the Inspection of Nursery and Primary Schools*, London, HMSO.

Addresses

National Association for Gifted Children (NAGC), Elder House, Elder Gate, Milton Keynes MK9 1LR, tel: 01908 673 677, fax: 01908 673 679.

National Association for Able Children in Education (NACE), Westminster College, Harcourt Hill, Oxford OX2 9AT, tel: 01865 245 657, fax: 01865 245 658, e-mail: nace@ox-west.ac.uk.

Bibliography

Alexander, R. (1992) *Policy and Practice in Primary Education*, London, Routledge.

Alexander, R., Rose, J. and Woodhead, C. (1992) *Curriculum Organisation and Classroom Practice in Primary Schools*, London, Department for Education and Science.

Arnold, R. (ed.) (1991) *Topic Planning and the National Curriculum*, London, Longman.

Association of Assessment Inspectors and Advisers (1997) *Baseline Assessment*, London, AAIA.

Audit Commission (1996) *Trading Places*, London, Audit Commission.

Ball, Sir C. (1994) *Start Right: The Importance of Early Learning*, London, The Royal Society for the Encouragement of Arts, Manufacture and Commerce.

Basic Skills Agency (1997) *Basic Skills Quality Mark for Primary Schools*, London, BSA.

Bearne, E. (ed.) (1996) *Differentiation and Diversity in the Primary School*, London, Routledge.

Bennett, N. (1994) *Class Size in Primary School: Perceptions of Head Teachers, Chairs of Governors, Teachers and Parents*, Birmingham, National Association of Schoolmasters/Union of Women Teachers.

Bennett, N. and Dunne, E. (1992) *Managing Classroom Groups*, London, Simon and Schuster.

British Educational Suppliers Association (annually) *The Complete Guide to British Educational Supply*, London, BESA.

Bruner, J. (1986) *Actual Minds: Possible Worlds*, Cambridge, Mass.: Harvard University Press.

Burgess, H., Southworth, G. and Webb, R. (1994) 'Whole school curriculum planning in the primary school' in A. Pollard (ed.) *Look Before You Leap? Research Evidence for the Curriculum at Key Stage Two*, London, Tufnell Press.

Byrne, B. (1994) *Coping with Bullying in Schools*, London, Cassell.

Campbell, J. (1993) 'A dream at conception: A nightmare at delivery' in J. Campbell (ed.) *Breadth and Balance in the Primary Curriculum*, London, Falmer.

Campbell, J. and Neill, S. R. St J. (1992) *Teacher Time and Curriculum Manageability at Key Stage 1*, London, Assistant Masters and Mistresses Association.

Central Advisory Council for Education (1967) *Children and their Primary Schools (Plowden Report)*, London, HMSO.

Clay, M. (1984) *The Early Detection of Reading Difficulties* (third edition), London, Heinemann.

Clegg, D. and Billington, S. (1994) *The Effective Primary Classroom: Management and Organisation of Teaching and Learning*, London, David Fulton.

Collier, A., Farrell, M., Langtry, J. I., Mann, J. and Nolan, T. (Editorial Advisory Panel) *Education Year Book*, London, Pitman.

Dadds, M. (1995) *Passionate Enquiry and School Development: A Story About Teacher Action Research*, London, Falmer.

Dearing, Sir R. (1993) *The National Curriculum and its Assessment: A Final Report*, London, School Curriculum and Assessment Authority.

Department for Education (1994) *Circular 5/94: Education Act 1993: Sex Education in Schools*, London, DfE.

—— (1994) *Circular 8/94: Pupil Behaviour and Discipline*, London, DfE.

—— (1994) *Circular 9/94: The Education of Children with Emotional and Behavioural Difficulties*, London, DfE.

—— (1994) *Exceptionally Able Children: Conference Report*, London, DfE.

—— (1994) *School Attendance Policy and Practice in Categorisation of Attendance* (May), London, DfE.

—— (1996) *Improving Schools: Teamwork for School Improvement*, London, DfE.

—— (1996) *Raising Standards for All: Report on the DfEE Conference on Systematic School Self Improvement* (20 November), Westminster Central Hall, London.

Department for Education, Home Office, Department for Health (1991) *Working Together Under the Children Act 1989: a Guide to Arrangements for Interagency Co-operation for the Protection of Children from Abuse*, London, HMSO.

Department for Education and Employment (1994) *The Code of Practice on the Identification and Assessment of Special Educational Needs*, London, DfEE.

—— (1995) *The Education (Pupil Registration) Regulations 1995, Statutory Instrument 2089*, London, DfEE.

—— (1996) *Circular 14/96: Supporting Pupils with Medical Needs in School*, London, DfEE.

—— (1996) *Guidance on Good Governance*, London, DfEE.

—— (1996) *Supporting Children with Medical Needs*, London, DfEE.

—— (1996) *Report of the Working Group on School Security*, London, DfEE.

—— (1996) *Managing School Facilities, Guide 4: Improving Security in Schools*, London, HMSO.

—— (1996) *Nursery Education: Desirable Outcomes for Children's Learning on Entering Compulsory Education*, London, DfEE.

—— (1997) *School Governors: A Guide to the Law (June edition) County and Controlled Schools*, London, DfEE.

—— (1997) *The Education (Pupil Registration) (Amendment) Regulations 1997, Statutory Instrument 2624*, London, DfEE.

—— (1997) *Excellence in Schools*, London, DfEE.

—— (1997) *Excellence for All Children: Meeting Special Educational Needs*, London, DfEE.

—— (1997) *Connecting the Learning Society*, London, DfEE.

—— (1997) *The Implementation of the National Literacy Strategy*, London, DfEE.

—— (1997) *School Performance and Extra Curricular Provision*, London, DfEE.

—— (1997) *From Targets to Action: Guidance to Support Effective Target Setting in Schools*, London, DfEE.

—— (1997) *Circular 13/97: The Standards Fund 1998–99*, London, DfEE.

—— (1998) *Circular 4/98 Teaching: High Status, High Standards: Requirements for Courses of Initial Teacher Training*, London, DfEE.

—— (1998) *Numeracy Matters: The Preliminary Report of the Numeracy Task Force* (January), London, DfEE.

—— (1998) *Homework: Guidelines for Primary Schools (Draft for Consultation)*, London, DfEE.

—— (1998) *Induction for New Teachers: A Consultation Document*, London, DfEE.

Department for Education and Employment/Home Office (1997) *School Security: Dealing with Troublemakers*, London, DfEE.

Department for Education and Employment/Welsh Office (1997) *Directory of Local Education Authority Practice on School Security*, DfEE.

Department of Education and Science (1991) *Circular 11/91: The Education (Pupils Attendance Records) Regulations 1991*, London, DES.

—— (1991) *The Education (Pupils Attendance Records) Regulations 1991, Statutory Instrument 1582*, London, DES.

Department of Education and Science/Welsh Office (1989) *Discipline in Schools: Report of the Committee of Enquiry Chaired by Lord Elton* (The Elton Report), London, HMSO.

Equal Opportunities Commission (1991) *Sex Discrimination in Schools: A Guide for Governors*, London, EOC.

—— (1994) *An Equal Start: Guidelines on Equal Treatment for the Under-eights*, London, EOC.

Farrell, M. (1998) *The Special Education Handbook*, London, David Fulton.

Farrell, M., Kerry, T. and Kerry, C. (1995) *The Blackwell Handbook of Education*, Oxford, Blackwell.

Galton, M. and Williamson, J. (1992) *Group Work in the Primary Classroom*, London, Routledge.

Griffin, M. and Woolley, A. (1997) 'Risk Assessment for Pupils and Schools', *The Head Teachers' Legal Guide Bulletin*, Issue 29, July.

Her Majesty's Inspectorate (1992) *The Education of Very Able Children in Maintained Schools*, London, HMSO.

Kerry, T. (1996) in M. Farrell (ed.) *The Classroom: Organisation, Effectiveness and Resources*, London, Centre for British Teachers.

Marland, M. and Rogers, R. (1991) *Marketing the School*, Oxford, Heinemann Educational.

Merlin Publications (1998) *The School Health and Safety Management Pack*, Cirencester, Merlin.

National Numeracy Project (1997) *Mathematical Vocabulary*, London, NNP/BEAM (BE A Mathematician).

—— (1997) *Framework for Numeracy Draft November, 1997*, London, NNP.

National Numeracy Project/BEAM /The Hamilton Trust (1997) *Numeracy Lessons*, London, NNP/BEAM.

National Numeracy Project and Hamilton Mathematics Project (1998) *Numeracy in Action*, London, NNP/HMP.

National Society for the Prevention of Cruelty to Children (1989) *Protecting Children: A Guide for Teachers on Child Abuse*, London, NSPCC.

Norwich, B. (1997) *A Trend Towards Inclusion: Statistics on Special School Placements and Pupils with Statements in Ordinary Schools, England 1992–1996*, Bristol, Centre for Studies on Inclusive Education.

Office for Standards in Education (1991) *Well Managed Classes in Primary Schools: Case Studies of Six Teachers*, London, OFSTED.

—— (1994) *Improving Schools*, London, HMSO.

—— (1994) *The OFSTED Handbook: Guidance on the Inspection of Nursery and Primary Schools*, London, OFSTED.

—— (1995) *The OFSTED Handbook: Guidance on the Inspection of Nursery and Primary Schools*, London, HMSO.

—— (1995) *Homework in Primary and Secondary Schools*, HMSO.

—— (1996) *The Teaching of Reading*, London, OFSTED.

—— (1997) *Teachers Count Video*, London, OFSTED.

—— (1997) *Inspection and Re-inspection of Schools from September 1997: New Requirements and Guidance on their Implementation* (August), London, OFSTED.

—— (1997) *Using Subject Specialists to Promote High Standards at Key Stage 2: an Illustrative Survey*, London, OFSTED.

—— (1997) *The Teaching of Number*, London, OFSTED.

Office for Standards in Education/Audit Commission (1996) Keeping Your Balance, London, OFSTED/AC.

Organisation for Economic Co-operation and Development (1997) *Parents as Partners in Schooling*, London, OECD.

Pate-Bain, H., Achilles, C., Boyd-Zaharus, J. and McKenna, B. (1992) 'Class size does make a difference' *Phi Delta Kappa*, Nova 253–55.

Pollard, A. (1997) *Reflective Teaching in the Primary School: a Handbook for the Classroom* (third edition), London, Cassell Education.

Qualifications and Curriculum Authority (1997) *Key Stage 2 Assessment Arrangements 1998*, London, QCA.

—— (1998) *Sharper Focus on Numeracy*, London, QCA.

—— (1998) *Sharper Focus on Literacy*, London, QCA.

Qualifications and Curriculum Authority and Department for Education and Employment (1997) *Key Stage 1 Assessment and Reporting Arrangements 1998*, London, QCA.

Rogers, R. (1994) *How to Write a School Development Plan: Whole School Issues Project*, Oxford, Heinemann.

Sammons, P., Hillman, J. and Mortimore, P. (1995) *Key Characteristics of Effective Schools: a Review of School Effectiveness Research Report, Commissioned by the Office for Standards in Education*, London, Institute of Education and OFSTED.

Sampson, J. and Yeomans, R. (eds) (1994) 'Analysing the role of mentors', *Mentorship in the Primary School*, London, Falmer Press.

School Curriculum and Assessment Authority (1996) *Nursery Education. Desirable Outcomes for Children's Learning on Entering Compulsory Education*, London, SCAA.

—— (1996) *Teaching English as an Additional Language: A Framework for Policy*, London, SCAA.

—— (1996) *Desirable Outcomes for Children's Learning on Entering Compulsory Education*, London, SCAA.

—— (1996) *Baseline Assessment: Draft Proposals September 1996*, London, SCAA.

—— (1996) *Education for Adult Life: the Spiritual and Moral Development of Young People (SCAA Discussion Paper No. 6)*, London, SCAA.

—— (1997) *Target Setting and Benchmarking in Schools – Consultation Paper* (September), London, SCAA.

—— (1997) *The National Framework for Baseline Assessment*, London, SCAA.

—— (1997) *Baseline Assessment Scales*, London, SCAA.

—— (1997) *Baseline Assessment Scales for Children with Special Educational Needs: Teacher's Guide*, London, SCAA.

—— (1997) *Mathematics and the Use of Language: Key Stage 1 and 2*, London, SCAA.

—— (1997) *Baseline Assessment Scales*, London, SCAA.

—— (1997) *Value Added Indicators for Schools Consultative Paper Primary* (June), London, SCAA.

Teacher Training Agency (1996) *Corporate Plan 1996: Promoting Excellence in Teaching*, London, TTA.

—— (1997) *The Graduate and Registered Teacher Programme: Trainers' Handbook 1997–98*, London, TTA.

—— (1997) *Effective Training Through Partnership: a Pack of Working Papers on Primary Partnership from the TTA*, London, TTA.

—— (1998) *National Standards for Special Educational Needs Co-ordinators*, London, TTA.

—— (1998) *National Standards for Subject Leaders Revised Draft July 1997*, London, TTA.

—— (1998) *National Standards for Head Teachers*, London, TTA.

—— (1997) *Career Entry Profile for Newly Qualified Teachers*, London, TTA.

—— (1997) *National Standards for Qualified Teacher Status*, London, TTA.

—— (1998) *Assessing Needs in Mathematics (Diagnostic Feedback/Diagnostic Tasks)*, London, TTA.

—— (annually) *Routes into Teaching* (part of the 'Open Minds Open Doors' series), London, TTA.

Vigotsky, L. S. (1962) *Thought and Language*, Cambridge, Mass.: Massachusetts Institute of Technology.

—— (1978) *Mind in Society: The Development of Higher Psychological Processes*, Cambridge, Mass.: Harvard University Press.

Webb, R. (ed.) (1991) *Practitioner Research in the Primary School*, London, Falmer.

Wragg, E. (1993) *Class Management*, London, Routledge.